King Norodom's Head

King Norodom's Head

Phnom Penh sights beyond
the guidebooks

Steven Boswell

King Norodom's Head:
Phnom Penh Sights Beyond the Guidebooks
by Steven Boswell

Nordic Institute of Asian Studies
NIAS Reference Library, 7

First published in 2016 by NIAS Press
NIAS – Nordic Institute of Asian Studies
Leifsgade 33, 2300 Copenhagen S, Denmark
Tel: +45 3532 9501 • Fax: +45 3532 9549
E-mail: books@nias.ku.dk • Online: www.niaspress.dk

ISBN: 978-87-7694-177-2 (hbk)
ISBN: 978-87-7694-178-9 (pbk)

Typesetting by Donald B. Wagner
Printed in Thailand

Cover: Postcard of the Silver Pagoda and the equestrian statue of King Norodom, mailed from Saigon, Cochinchina, on May 3, 1920. (Courtesy of Kent Davis)

NIAS Press is the autonomous publishing arm of NIAS – Nordic Institute of Asian Studies, a research institute located at the University of Copenhagen. NIAS is partially funded by the governments of Denmark, Finland, Iceland, Norway and Sweden via the Nordic Council of Ministers, and works to encourage and support Asian studies in the Nordic countries. In so doing, NIAS has been publishing books since 1969, with more than two hundred titles produced in the past few years.

UNIVERSITY OF COPENHAGEN

Nordic Council of Ministers

Contents

	Foreword	vii
	Introduction	ix
1.	Anchors Aweigh	1
2.	André Malraux Dined Here	13
3.	The Buddha's Bone	24
4.	An Angkorian Site in Phnom Penh	32
5.	Made for America's Queen	40
6.	The Riverside Shrine and Flag Tower of Preah Ang Dongka	47
7.	Saloth Sar Lived Here	52
8.	The Mysterious Frenchman of Wat Phnom	61
9.	Le Monument aux Morts	67
10.	Thorani, the Earth Goddess	72
11.	Signs of France	78
12.	*Techo* Meas and *Techo* Yort	96
13.	Atop Wat Phnom's Hill	109
14.	The House across from S-21	118
15.	La Taverne, Madame Chum's, and Other Favored Haunts of Days Gone By	122
16.	François Bizot's Gate	139
17.	King Norodom's Head	149
18.	The Streets of Phnom Penh	163
19.	The Assassination of Commissioner de Raymond	183
20.	The US Embassy Was Here	193
21.	The Gold of King Ang Duong	206
22.	Sgt. Charles W. Turberville, and the Last US Dead of the Vietnam War	213
23.	Just beyond the Killing Fields	223
24.	The Graves of Ponhea Leu	227

25. Lest We Forget 238
26. Quan Âm, the Bodhisattva of Compassion 247
27. Ganesha, the God with the Elephant Head 261
28. The Furtive Kouprey 266
29. Lord Vessanda 273
30. The Birthplace of King Norodom Sihanouk 287

    Index 293

Maps

1. Overview xii
2. Northern Phnom Penh xiii
3. Central Phnom Penh xiv
4. Southern Phnom Penh xv

Foreword

It's a pleasure and an honor for me to write a few lines to introduce Steven Boswell's deft, witty and absorbing book.

I'm equipped to do so, I guess, because I've been in and out of Phnom Penh on and off for over fifty years.

In October 1960, as a 27-year-old fledgling US Foreign Service Officer, I arrived in Cambodia for my first overseas posting. I had recently completed thirteen months of Khmer language training in Washington, DC, and I was eager to discover the small, exotic country that a cousin who had worked in Bangkok told me was in some ways "more authentic" than Thailand.

I've written elsewhere that, as the DC-3 from Hong Kong drifted in for a landing at Pochentong,

> The sight of cows being chased off the runway by determined women with sticks foreshadowed some of the rackety charm and "otherness" of Cambodia that has nourished my affection for the country and its people ever since.

For the next 25 months I worked happily in a competently managed embassy, performing a range of tasks, including that of language officer. In my free time I travelled all over the country, but I quickly fell in love with Phnom Penh, which was then perhaps the prettiest city in Southeast Asia. To quote myself again, describing the parts of the capital that I knew best:

> Phnom Penh in those days was a somnolent, handsome city, with mustard colored or whitewashed villas and government buildings, and with wide, almost empty boulevards bordered with flame trees and bougainvillea. It had a sun struck, provincial elegance that reminded some visitors of southern France and others of Celesteville, the African city

ruled compassionately, in a famous children's book written in France in the l930s, by Babar, King of the Elephants.

A great deal has changed since those far-off years. The city in 2015 has at least five times as many inhabitants as it had when I lived there. It boasts some egregious skyscrapers and several air-conditioned shopping malls. Traffic has gone from nearly non-existent to an unmanageable gridlock. English rather than French is now the Western language that local people speak. More importantly of course the city has been buffeted by civil war, the murderous Khmer Rouge regime, a decade of Vietnamese protection and over twenty years of globalized, free market capitalism. No one foresaw any of this when I was soaking up the genteel, Francophone ambience of Cambodia's so-called golden age.

In these closely packed, totally accessible pages Steve Boswell, who has lived in Phnom Penh for many years, takes his readers to nooks and crannies of the city and the countryside around it. One of the sites he discusses dates back thousands of years, before the Angkorian Empire. Another records a brutal massacre that took place as recently as 1997. My favorite chapters deal with traces of the colonial period (1863–1953) when the city assumed more or less its present form. Other readers will have their own favorites. The whole book is masterfully written, and its marvelous illustrations bring the many sites into focus.

For people living in the city and for people who are passing through, *King Norodom's Head* (a title shared with a particularly fine chapter) is bound to enrich their encounter with this fascinating city. Steve Boswell's book is a reader's feast.

David Chandler
April 2015

Introduction

Following my arrival in Phnom Penh in September 2000, it did not take long to tick off the sites in my guidebooks: Wat Phnom, Royal Palace, National Museum, S-21, the killing fields at Chœung Ek, several pagodas. Looking farther afield, I began strolling the city's streets, lanes, and back alleys, copies of detailed city maps dating back to the 1920s ever in hand, searching for what had once been there, what remained, and what was new. I continued doing so over the following years.

These pages come from the results of my wanderings beyond the guidebooks and from the research that followed. The chapters are in no order other than generally that in which I wrote them, with some changes to fit the typesetting. Each centers on a site that can be visited, someplace or something that can be seen and often touched. The hope is that these chapters will give the reader an appreciation of a number of the more obscure places in our city (and some not so obscure but generally little reported) and of the stories associated with them.

But things change. The US Navy's anchor (Chapter 1, *Anchors Aweigh*) was removed from its central location at an annex of the city's port authority near Wat Phnom in October 2010 and now lies in the weeds of an out-of-the-way depot for shipping containers. However, port officials tell me that the anchor will eventually be prominently displayed at the port's new facilities in Kien Svay. With that hope in mind, as well as the fact that it was the first chapter I wrote, I have kept *Anchors Aweigh* in its initial position. In addition, the statue of Georgi Dimitrov vanished during the construction of the prime minister's new offices and, although the street that the Peace Palace is on still retains the name of the former Bulgarian prime minister, I have had to eliminate the chapter about his memorial, though you can see a photograph of it in Chapter 18.

I fear other sites may also soon disappear, in particular the wooden house that was once the boyhood home of Pol Pot (Chapter 7) and the three graves of Ponhea Leu (Chapter 24), which are at risk from the widening of National Road 5.

My principal sources are given at the end of most chapters. In *Signs of France* and *The Streets of Phnom Penh*, the sources are too numerous to mention.

My thanks to Dr. Henri Locard for reading and commenting on the entire typescript. I am also grateful to Dr. Locard for his perceptive depiction of the French protectorate era and the following twenty years, given in his series of lectures sponsored by the Center for Khmer Studies in 2013–14; I have drawn on a number of Dr. Locard's insights in the chapters touching on those periods. As well as answering my queries, Dr. David Chandler, Dr. Christopher Goscha, and Dr. Milton Osborne read and commented on several chapters, for which they have my gratitude. I am particularly indebted to Dr. Chandler for writing the foreword to this book. For their interest and assistance in this project, I would also like to thank François Bizot, Roger Brattin, Margaret Bywater, Hem Chanty, Philip Coggan, Kent Davis, Jean-François de Raymond, Ouk Divan, François Doré, Jean-Michel Filippi, Jack Hicks, Jean-Marc Khao, Neil Manton, Greg Muller, Leo Phiv, Phon Kaseka, Jean-Michel Rocard, Van Vy, Mark Wertheimer, Artis Wick, Y Dara, and my brother Peter Boswell.

I am grateful to Chan Vitharong for allowing me to replicate his photographs of the Vessanda murals from his book, *Wat Phnom, Guide to Art and Architecture*. My thanks also to Roland Neveu for generously permitting me to reproduce his photograph of Monsieur Migot at the gate of the French Embassy. For their first rate photographs, many thanks to Barbara Bickford and Roger Spooner, and to Al Rockoff for his photo of Landing Zone Hotel. Despite our best efforts, we failed to find accurate attributions for a few photographs. If one of these is yours, please contact NIAS Press in order that you may receive the attribution you deserve in the next edition of this book.

I would like to thank Gerald Jackson and the Nordic Institute of Asian Studies for publishing my work, and Chris Goscha for his help in seeing the book into print. Great thanks too to David Stuligross, my editor, whose suggestions and corrections led to significant improvements to this volume. Any shortcomings and inaccuracies are of course my responsibility.

Finally, I would like to dedicate this book to Dany, my wife, and Harry, our son.

The author and son Harry at Angkor; photo by Steve's wife Dany

About the author

Steve Boswell is from Washington, DC. In 1968 he joined the Peace Corps and was sent to teach at a Saharan oasis in northern Chad. He subsequently taught in Laos, the US, Kuwait, Burundi, Palestine, China, Turkey, Vietnam, Tibet, and finally Cambodia, where for nine years he was a lecturer at The Royal University of Phnom Penh. He currently resides in Phnom Penh.

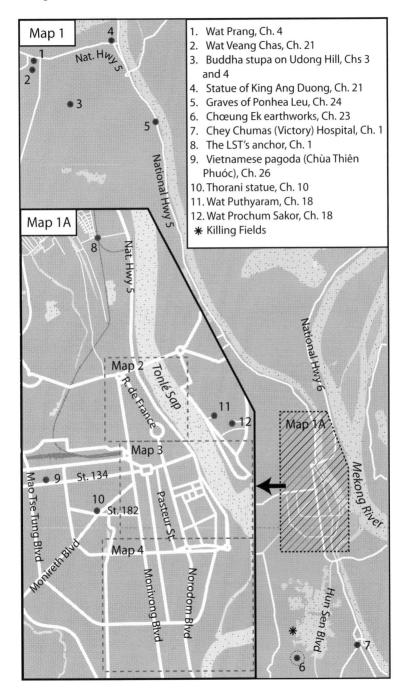

Map 1

Map 1A

1. Wat Prang, Ch. 4
2. Wat Veang Chas, Ch. 21
3. Buddha stupa on Udong Hill, Chs 3 and 4
4. Statue of King Ang Duong, Ch. 21
5. Graves of Ponhea Leu, Ch. 24
6. Chœung Ek earthworks, Ch. 23
7. Chey Chumas (Victory) Hospital, Ch. 1
8. The LST's anchor, Ch. 1
9. Vietnamese pagoda (Chùa Thiên Phuóc), Ch. 26
10. Thorani statue, Ch. 10
11. Wat Puthyaram, Ch. 18
12. Wat Prochum Sakor, Ch. 18
✴ Killing Fields

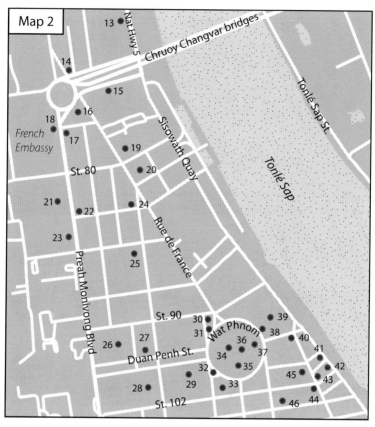

13. Site of Preah Meada church, Ch. 24
14. Lon Non's house, Ch. 7
15. Former French cemetery, Ch. 16
16. Site of Monument aux Morts (now Léopold Sédar Senghor Garden), Ch. 9
17. Khmer Rouge Military Security Committee (now Mekong Bank), Ch. 16
18. Francois Bizot's gate, Ch. 16
19. Wat Phorta Pi Rangsei, Ch. 10
20. Wat Put Kosacha, Ch. 10
21. Hôpital Calmette, Ch. 11
22. École française d'Extrême Orient (now Heng Pich Guesthouse), Ch. 16
23. Institut Pasteur du Cambodge, Ch. 11
24. US Embassy, 1952–54, Ch. 20
25. Wat Srah Chak, Chs 3 and 10
26. Hôtel Le Royal, Chs 5, 11 and 20
27. Bibliothèque, Archives Chs 8 and 11
28. Lycée Français René Descartes, Ch. 11
29. Present US Embassy and Mayaguez memorial, Chs 20 and 22

30. UNTAC memorial and dove statue, Ch. 28
31. Kouprey statue, Ch. 28
32. Royal terrapin statue, Ch. 28
33. Lady Penh statue, Ch. 13
34. Ponhea Yat's stupa, Ch. 13
35. Lost provinces monument, Ch. 11
36. Vessanda murals, Ch. 29
37. Fourcros' grave, Ch. 8
38. de Raymond's stupa, Ch. 19
39. Résidence Supérieure, then Hôtel du Commissariat; now CDC. Chs 1 and 19
40. Cadastral office, Ch. 1
41. Grand Hotel Manolis (now KFC), Ch. 2
42. Bar Jean, Ch. 15
43. La Taverne and Hôtel de la Poste, Ch. 15
44. Banque de l'Indochine (now Van's) Ch. 11
45. Main post office, Ch. 11
46. Hôtel de Ville (Town Hall; now Cambodia Securities Exchange), Ch. 11

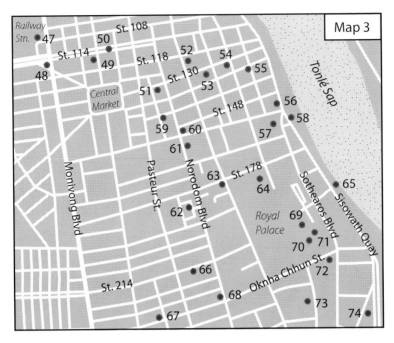

47. Buddha stupa at railway station, Ch. 3
48. Ganesha statue, Ch. 27
49. Café de Paris, Ch. 15
50. Street 114's mahogany trees, Ch. 15
51. Clinique Docteur Bessière, Ch. 11
52. École Miche (now Norton University), Ch. 7
53. Le Nouveau Tricotin (now Sharky), Ch. 15
54. Formerly Hôtel International, Ch. 11
55. Librairie Sy-Cai (now Mr. Butterfly), Ch. 11
56. Site of Hôtel Guerin, Ch. 2
57. Wat Unnalom, Ch. 4
58. Techo Meas and Techo Yort, Ch. 12
59. US Embassy, 1954–65, Ch. 20
60. Ciné Lux, Ch. 11
61. Sirik Matak's second villa, Ch. 7
62. Lycée Sisowath, Ch. 7
63. Penn Nouth's residence, Ch. 11
64. Monument aux Morts remnants, Ch. 9
65. Preah Ang Dongka shrine, Ch. 6
66. La Résidence, Ch. 11
67. US Embassy, 1992–2006, Ch. 20
68. Monument Books, Ch. 16
69. Napoleon Pavilion, Ch. 11
70. Silver Pagoda, Ch. 3
71. King Norodom's Statue, Ch. 17
72. Martyrs of 30 March 1997, Ch. 25
73. Wat Botum, Chs 3 and 7
74. Kram Ngoy Statue, Ch. 27

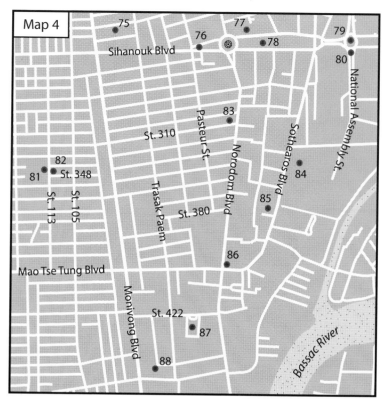

75. Pol Pot's childhood home, Ch. 7
76. Chea Vichea statue, Ch. 25
77. King Sihanouk's birthplace, Ch. 30
78. Norodom Sihanouk Memorial, Ch. 30
79. Chuon Nath statue, Ch. 4
80. Penn Nouth memorial, Ch. 27
81. S-21, Ch. 14
82. The Boddhi Tree, Ch. 14

83. Madame Chum's opium den, Ch. 15
84. Site of Landing Zone Hotel (now the Russian embassy), Chs 20 and 22
85. US embassy, 1969–70, Ch. 20
86. US embassy, 1970–75, Ch. 20
87. Former Chamkar Mon Palace, Ch. 7
88. Sirik Matak's residence, Ch. 7

◎ Independence Monument

1. Anchors Aweigh

Lying among the weeds just inside the Russei Keo container storage depot of the Phnom Penh Autonomous Port is a large cast iron anchor. "1942 US Navy" read the unexpected words embossed on the anchor's right fluke. "Powell P85" can be deciphered on the left fluke, and there are more letters and numbers on both flukes and shaft, though their worn condition attests to a long stretch of time under water.

I first came across the anchor several years ago when it was prominently displayed outside a French protectorate era building with a small square tower on short Street 94, which runs from Sisowath Quay to Wat Phnom. When France ruled, the building was the cadastral office (Map 2, #40), where lands and properties were registered. The edifice was later taken over by the Phnom Penh Port Authority. When the port was recently moved about thirty kilometers downstream to its new facilities in Kien Svay, the

The anchor at its present location just inside the entrance to the container depot in Russei Keo, to the right

building was ceded to other purposes, and the anchor from the American ship was taken to the container depot in Russei Keo, a few hundred meters down a road which branches west off of National Road 5 just beyond Sokimex's petrol storage tanks.

Curious to find the story of this American military remembrance, my inquiries at the USN Naval Museum in Washington DC led to the following: The anchor was manufactured for the US Navy in 1942 by a foundry named Powell, with P85 likely being the reference number for casting. On the shaft is B4659, B referring to Bureau of Ships, while 4659 is the drawing number, the foundry index number for the mold.

The 8117 on the right fluke is a standard stock list number, meaning the anchor was originally purchased by the Navy for use as needed, and it may have spent time in storage. The number also indicates that the anchor is 73 inches long and weighs 5,000 pounds. The Naval Museum could not enlighten me as to how the anchor ended up in Phnom Penh, nor could it shed light on the manufacturer, Powell. My numerous Internet searches for this foundry have been similarly fruitless. I did learn, however, that an anchor of this size would have been used on a ship with the dimensions

The old cadastral office, and the anchor when it was on display there

Right fluke with "1942 US NAVY" and
below, barely visible, "8117"

of an LST (Landing Ship, Tank; a craft designed to plow its bow
onto the shore so that its cargo of battle tanks could roll off) or a
destroyer escort. An LST, of which 1,142 were ordered from November 1941 to the end of World War II, had a length of 327 feet;
a destroyer escort had roughly the same length. I doubt that any
destroyer escort ever sailed up the Mekong or the Bassac, though
one was captured by the North Vietnamese and subsequently used
for training purposes.

As the colonial building behind the anchor then served as an
annex of the Phnom Penh Autonomous Port, I visited their head
office, where I was amicably received by Deputy Director General
Eang Veng Sun and his assistant Koan Chuon. "The anchor was
bought in 1995 from an *et chay* – a scrap dealer – for display as a
symbol of the port," they told me. They were not sure where the
anchor originated, though Mr. Eang Veng Sun speculated it may
have come from a ship which was sunk in the river during the Lon
Nol era, the ship later being salvaged for scrap.

The port authorities later told me that the anchor would eventually be moved to the new port at Kien Svay. Until then, however,
curious readers will have to proceed to the container depot in
Russei Keo (Map 1, #8), where they will be able to gaze upon

3

SS *Columbia Eagle*

the anchor and contemplate the strange saga of Clyde McKay and Alvin Glatkowski.

ON MARCH 14, 1970, four days before Prime Minister Lon Nol and his deputy Prince Sisowath Sirik Matak overthrew Prince Norodom Sihanouk, Cambodia's head of state, an American freighter, the SS *Columbia Eagle*, passed off Cambodian shores with a cargo of napalm bombs intended for US warplanes based in Thailand. Aboard were two young American sailors, Clyde McKay, 26, who had once bribed his way to a medical discharge from the French Foreign Legion, and Alvin Glatkowski, 20. The two were staunch opponents of US involvement in Vietnam, and they shared left-wing political views. Both had feelings of guilt for having worked on ships delivering ammunition to fight what they considered an illegal and immoral war. Both believed they were morally obligated to do something to impede America's bombing of innocent civilians. Though Glatkowski was deeply apprehensive about possible repercussions of their actions on his pregnant wife and their forthcoming child, the two seamen concocted a daring hijacking of the *Columbia Eagle*. They would then steer the ship to Sihanoukville, where they expected to be warmly received by Prince Sihanouk, who was equally opposed to the American role in Vietnam.

Alvin Glatkowski   Clyde McKay

At about one o'clock in the afternoon of March 14, McKay and Glatkowski, armed with pistols and claiming that they had planted a bomb aboard, overpowered the officer on the bridge and sounded the abandon ship alarm. Twenty-four of the thirty-seven crewmen did just that and were later picked up by an American freighter in the vicinity, a ship with its own load of napalm destined to be dumped on the Ho Chi Minh Trail.

McKay, the instigator and leader of the takeover, and Glatkowski took amphetamines to stay awake during the three-day ordeal, but they were not the pill-popping hippie adventurers that much of the media of the time portrayed them to be. As planned, the two steamed the *Columbia Eagle* to Sihanoukville, where they declared their anti-war sentiments and turned the ship and its deadly cargo over to the government.

Prince Sihanouk, however, was out of the country. Lon Nol and Sirik Matak were preoccupied with their conspiracy. The Sihanoukville naval authorities dithered. In the end, they imprisoned the remaining crew on the *Columbia Eagle* and flew the two mutineers to Phnom Penh. The *Columbia Eagle* and the crew on board were released on April 8. The ship then sailed to Subic Bay in the Philippines, where the napalm bombs were unloaded and eventually sent on to Thailand. As for McKay and Glatkowski, when they arrived in Phnom Penh they were given political asylum. Wined and dined, they were put up in a vacant barracks at the Chruoy Changvar naval base on the Mekong River outside Phnom Penh. The two hoped to

LST prison ship anchored at the Chruoy Changvar naval base.
Andrew Antippas, a US Embassy official who was involved in
the McKay-Glatkowski drama, took this photo. Judging from the
height of the Mekong River, the photo may well have been taken
in August, when the two mutineers were still on board.

eventually be granted political refuge in a communist country, notably Cuba or the Soviet Union, or perhaps in Sweden.

Then came Sirik Matak and Lon Nol's right-wing coup.* The
two pro-communist mutineers were now confined to the naval
base. Some weeks later, they were taken to a *landing ship, tank* –
thus the connection with our anchor – either anchored or stuck in
Mekong mud at the Chruoy Changvar base. The rusting hulk had
been turned into a prison. Its cells had metal walls and a roof of
corrugated tin sheets. The two Americans' twelve or so fellow
inmates were political prisoners, including Oum Manorine, half-
brother of Prince Sihanouk's wife Monineath and once head of the
national police and secretary of state for national defense who,

---

* Technically, it was not a coup, as the National Assembly had "unanimously" voted to
withdraw confidence in Sihanouk and replace him as head of state (the actual vote was
89–3, but was later changed to unanimity). Nonetheless, Sihanouk's ousting is often
regarded as a coup. Sihanouk himself considered his overthrowing to be illegal as the
constitution of the time contained nothing which allowed the National Assembly to
depose the chief of state. Throughout his life, Sihanouk was convinced that the US was
behind the coup, though to date no evidence has come out proving as much.

fearing the worst after being questioned about corruption by the National Assembly, had unsuccessfully attempted a counter-coup against Lon Nol. Another prisoner was Larry Humphrey, an anti-war US Army corporal who had deserted in Thailand and come to Cambodia seeking political asylum.

April and May are among the hottest months of the year, and prisoners McKay and Glatkowski must have sweltered in their metal inferno. Strings of dead Vietnamese civilians floated by, victims of Lon Nol's racial pogrom. These were most likely among the 800 men who were shepherded onto a landing craft on the Mekong River by Lon Nol's troops, tied up in groups of ten, and at rifle point shoved into the river. The soldiers then opened fire with automatic weapons. Those who were not killed outright soon drowned.

Both McKay and Glatkowski tried to renounce their American citizenship. The US chargé d'affaires tried to visit them, but McKay refused to be interviewed. They did talk to journalists. "I am a Marxist," McKay told AP reporter T. Jeff Williams in July. "I believe in the Marxist way of life." He said that the hijacking was the initial shot in a revolution which would overthrow President Nixon and set the US on the path to socialism. "I feel like an American revolutionary, not a criminal," Glatkowski added. "Morally I believe I was 100 per cent right. I would do it a hundred times again."

They told the American reporter that they used some of the $2,000 they had brought with them to buy a small television and invited their guards to watch Armed Forces Television programs beamed from Vietnam. "The guards are friendly, and we are allowed to send out for things we want," such as scotch and wine, but they were unable to obtain English language books, hard to get in Cambodia at that time.

Seated under trees on the riverbank during an August interview with a UPI reporter, the two said they were well treated and well fed. They reiterated that they had no regrets over their actions. "We are Marxist revolutionaries without an American revolution. But it's building up." US Air Force Phantom jets would "go out of their way to buzz" the prison ship. "They love to harass us. We go out on deck and give them the peace sign."

Things went downhill for Glatkowski. He was disheartened by the news that the *Columbia Eagle* and its load of napalm had been released, thereby nullifying the goal of the mutiny. He worried whether he would ever see his baby, born after the *Columbia Eagle* had set sail. His wife started divorce proceedings. He became depressed and increasingly unstable. To ease his despair, he began taking opium, purchased from his guards. He tried to escape by jumping overboard but was soon caught and placed in solitary confinement. When he took to eating his feces and drinking his urine, he was sent to the Son Mam Psychiatric Hospital in Takhmau (today the Chey Chunmeas "Victory" Hospital, see Map 1, #7; in Khmer Rouge days it was the first location of what was to become S-21, the KR's infamous detention/torture center).

Glatkowski eventually turned himself in to the American Embassy and was extradited to the US on a military plane. He was put on trial in California, the only person in US history to be indicted for mutiny on the high seas. Although Glatkowski believed he was innocent, his lawyer convinced him to plead guilty to mutiny and assault, for which he received a sentence of ten years in prison. He served seven. In later years, he never expressed any remorse for the mutiny; he only wished he and McKay had sabotaged the ship and sunk its deadly cargo.

On October 31, McKay and Humphrey, who had become an annoyance to the Cambodian administration, were moved to a government guesthouse in Phnom Penh. That guesthouse, incidentally, presently houses the Council for the Development of Cambodia, on the northeast side of Wat Phnom's hill (Map 2, #39). Built in the 1930s, it previously was the French protectorate's *Résidence Supérieure*, the abode of France's highest official in Cambodia, and became a state guesthouse following independence in 1953 and the departure of the French administration.

Shortly after McKay and Humphrey were moved to the guesthouse, they managed to evade their guards while eating at a downtown restaurant and fled on a stolen motorcycle. There is speculation that the Cambodian government abetted the getaway in order to rid themselves of this embarrassment. "The Cambodian authorities were really kind of fed up with these guys ... They didn't want them," reported the US Embassy's political officer in an interview many years later. McKay and Humphrey crossed the Japanese Friendship Bridge and headed northeast to Kompong Cham province, where they sought out the Khmer Rouge; not a wise move.

McKay and Humphrey were declared missing in November 1970. One report had them killed by the Khmer Rouge in February 1971, perhaps because Prince Sihanouk had said the *Columbia Eagle* mutiny was a CIA plan to deliver weapons to Lon Nol, which would not have endeared McKay to the Khmer Rouge. Another report put them in a Khmer Rouge detention camp in 1973, guarded by North Vietnamese soldiers, and a third and most unlikely story had them married to local women and farming in Ratanakkiri province. However, based on later accounts by former Khmer Rouge who had been in close contact with McKay and Humphrey during their confinement, the two were executed in May 1971 in Bei Met village in Kompong Cham province after they had the audacity to question the Khmer Rouge's authority to detain them, fellow revolutionaries.

In 1991, fragments of three teeth and a filling were unearthed in Bei Met village. They were believed to be those of Sean Flynn (son of actor Errol Flynn) or Dana Stone, two journalists who were captured in Cambodia and later executed by the Khmer Rouge (see box). In 2003, however, DNA testing by the Pentagon's Central Identification Laboratory in Hawaii proved that the teeth were those of McKay. Clyde McKay's scanty remains were later returned to his family.

I am not aware of Humphrey's remains having been found, and I have not seen his name on the Department of Defense's prisoner of war and missing in action lists, though soldiers who had gone AWOL from a country such as Thailand were apparently not included on such registers. (As of April 2014, fifty-three Americans from the Vietnam War were unaccounted for in Cambodia, while

Sean Flynn was captured by the Viet Cong along with fellow photojournalist **Dana Stone** on National Road 1 near the Vietnamese border on April 6, 1970. There is some speculation that Flynn, who was on commission for *Time* magazine, was hoping to contact the Viet Cong in order to film the war from the other side. The two were handed over to the Khmer Rouge toward the end of the year and kept in captivity in Kompong Cham province, frequently moved from one village to another. Flynn and Stone, 28 and 31 years old at the time, were apparently executed by the Khmer Rouge some months later. Despite extensive searches following the war by Flynn's good friend and fellow war photographer Tim Page, during which he was able to interview a number of Cambodians who had contact with Flynn and Stone in the course of their imprisonment, no traces of their bodies have ever been found.

Flynn and Stone are among the thirty-seven Cambodian and foreign media personnel who died or went missing during the civil war here between 1970 and 1975. Their names are etched on a memorial honoring those correspondents, photographers, and cameramen, which was erected in May 2012 in the gardens across the street from Le Royal Hotel (Map 2, #26), where many of the journalists stayed before Phnom Penh fell to the Khmer Rouge in April 1975.

thirty-seven bodies had been recovered here. The search for MIAs continues.)

Prince Sihanouk's brother-in-law Oum Manorine survived his ordeal on the prison ship, from which he was released in June 1973. The following November he accompanied Queen Kossamak to Beijing to join her exiled son Sihanouk. In 1993 Oum Manorine became Cambodia's ambassador to the People's Republic of Korea, and he was later appointed to the Senate by King Sihamoni, where in 2012 at the age of 88 he was that body's oldest member.

As for that LST-turned-prison ship, following the wars it must have been sawed up and sold for scrap. A 327-foot long ruin would have earned an *et chay* a few bucks. The LST's anchor must have been 73 inches long and weighed 5,000 pounds. Surely it is the anchor which until recently was on display outside the old protectorate cadastral office on Street 94. And even if by chance it isn't, the bizarre story of Clyde McKay and Alvin Glatkowski is nonetheless worthy of a footnote to Cambodia's recent history.

Let me add in finishing that, in addition to the LST prison ship, the Cambodian Navy at that time had two other landing craft, including the US Army's LCU 1577, detained in July 1968 after inadvertently entering Cambodian territory (see Chapter 15). LCU 1577 was 119 feet in length, considerably shorter than an LST's 327 feet, so our anchor could not have come from that vessel. However, I am not sure of the specifications of the third landing craft.

Those two craft were used in April and May 1970 during Lon Nol's continuing racial killings to transport up to three thousand Vietnamese men and boys who had been rounded up mainly on the Chruoy Changvar peninsula to a place called Con Trong, some distance upstream from Neak Luong, where cars traveling on National Road 1 now cross the Mekong on a new bridge. Once there, the landing craft lowered their fronts, and the Vietnamese civilians, hands tied behind their backs, were led off to be shot dead by Cambodian soldiers. There were only about twenty soldiers, so it took a long time to finish their cowardly slaughter. Twenty-eight

Vietnamese survived by feigning death, and they eventually found their way back to their villages. About two weeks later, Cambodian authorities took them and the Vietnamese women and children of Chruoy Changvar to a schoolhouse where they were kept for six weeks, having to find their own food and water, before being evacuated to Saigon by boat.

Sources

T. Jeff Williams, "Ship Hijackers Now Are Jailed in Cambodia," *The Day*, New London, Connecticut, Friday July 3, 1970.

John Hanna, "Mystery of the SS Columbia Eagle Hijacking," *VIETNAM*, February 2001.

Kurt Volkert and T. Jeff Williams, *A Cambodian Odyssey*, iUniverse publications, 2001.

Richard Linnett and Roberto Loiederman, *The Eagle Mutiny*, Naval Institute Press, 2001. (A well-researched, fascinating account of the mutiny, particularly revealing of the personalities and motivations of McKay and Glatkowski.)

Andrew F. Antippas interviewed by Charles Stuart Kennedy, July 19, 1994, Foreign Affairs Oral History Project, The Association for Diplomatic Studies and Training, 1998.

Julio Jeldres (ed.), *Shadow over Angkor: Memoirs of His Majesty King Norodom Sihanouk of Cambodia*, Monument Books, 2005.

Denis Warner, *Not Always on Horseback*, Allen & Unwin, 1997.

David P. Chandler, *The Tragedy of Cambodian History*, Silkworm Books, 1993 [Yale, 1991].

2. André Malraux Dined Here

KFC on Sisowath Quay, once the Grand Hôtel Manolis

He did indeed, here (Map 2, #41) where KFC has one of its several Phnom Penh outlets, though it's doubtful Malraux feasted on Col. Sanders' fried fowl or a Zinger Burger. The future World War II resistance hero, acclaimed writer, and de Gaulle's minister of culture was confined with his wife Clara for several months in 1923–24 to the hotel which once occupied this building following their arrest for the theft of sculptures from Banteay Srey temple twenty-five kilometers northeast of Angkor.

They had been married only ten months when André lost virtually all of Clara's dowry and inheritance betting on the stock market, notably on a Mexican silver mining company. To replenish their empty bank accounts, André devised the idea of looting Cambodian temples of Buddhas and Shivas and selling them to American collectors. In a Paris library they came across an article on the wonders of the Banteay Srey ruins, which had only been "found" in 1914 and had since been neglected. André was even able to get documentation from the Colonial Office, saying he was on an official archaeological mission.

Together with Louis Chevasson, André's pal since school days, the Malraux sailed from Marseille in October 1923 aboard the steamship *Angkor*, appropriately enough. Following visits to Saigon and Hanoi, where they learned that all antiquities from both dis- covered and undiscovered temples in Siem Reap had to be left *in situ*, the trio arrived in Phnom Penh in December. The men were suitably decked out in white linen suits, black string ties, and cork pith helmets. Shortly thereafter they embarked on a riverboat for Siem Reap with a servant named Xa and wooden chests labeled "Chemical products" to carry home the loot.

In Siem Reap, the trio hired oxcarts and, trying to remain incon- spicuous while slashing through vegetation, made their way to the pink sandstone temple of Banteay Srey. Using crowbars, chisels, and wedges, they pried loose seven slabs of stone carved with bas-reliefs of *apsara* and *devata* (female celestial beings), then lowered them with winches into the chests and onto the carts. The chests were then taken back to Siem Reap and loaded onto a boat for the trip downriver.

But their expedition had not gone unnoticed. In Phnom Penh, George Groslier, director of the Albert Sarraut Museum (today the National Museum) had become suspicious of the trio's motivations. Groslier reported that Malraux seemed to have an antiquarian's interest in Khmer art, notably in the heads of Angkor era statues of mysterious provenance on sale at a Paris antique dealer at fabu- lous prices. In Siem Reap, a French functionary named Crémazy welcomed the Malraux and Chevasson and even took them on a tour of Angkor Wat. But Crémazy had been alerted – perhaps by Groslier – to the Malraux's dubious claims of being nothing more than archaeological scholars exploring the region and studying the relationship between ancient Khmer and Siamese art. Rather than warning them, Crémazy had them shadowed and he subsequently informed his superiors in Phnom Penh of the results.

When the riverboat reached Kompong Chhnang, the police and Groslier were waiting. After prying open the chests, they charged

André on his Asian adventures in 1923

the three with possession of stolen antiquities. Under police escort, the Malraux and Chevasson proceeded downriver to Phnom Penh. They arrived in the city on Christmas Eve and were allowed to spend the rest of the night in their cabins. "What am I going to tell *Maman*?" Clara asked herself.

The next morning the three thieves were placed under house arrest at the Grand Hôtel, just across the street from the landing stage, where today one can dine on Kentucky fried wings and thighs. They were allowed to come and go during the day but had to remain within the confines of the city.

The Grand Hôtel at that time was owned and run by a Greek named Nicolas Manolis, and in fact it was commonly referred to as the Hôtel Manolis. The Grand was an establishment of limited comfort, but nonetheless in 1923 it was the city's best hostelry. As Clara wrote in her memoirs, "Our room with whitewashed walls was large, furnished with an expansive bed enveloped in its mosquito net and with a round table of dirty wood; it was one of the better rooms in the best hotel of Phnom Penh: we were to spend four months there."

The Grand Hôtel c. 1913

For New Year's Eve the next week, a military band played while colonial administrators, military officers, settlers, and their spouses danced and sipped champagne. Clara in a black dress and André in a white tuxedo made a fashionable entrance exactly at midnight, just as the band was launching into *Auld Lang Syne*. The colonials seemed to keep a certain distance from them, doubtless aware of their reputation as adventurers *cum* looters.

They passed the days reading books from the city's library and newspapers from their hotel. Clara came down with dengue fever. Her mother wrote urging her to divorce André. The Malraux soon ran out of funds, and they owed the hotel three months' room rent. They had to give up pastries and cigarettes, and André had to do without alcohol (Clara didn't drink). It was clear that one of them needed to return to France to raise money for their defense.

Clara devised a secret plan. She feigned suicide from an overdose of sleeping pills, dissolving the tablets in a washbasin. André, unaware, entered the room and saw his collapsed spouse and the empty tubes of pills. He shouted for help. A stretcher arrived, and two light-footed bearers carried Clara to the hospital. As it was a charity hospital, André was able to move into his wife's ward free of charge. But the fake suicide attempt did not result in her release from Phnom Penh. Still at the hospital, Clara now went on a hunger strike, surviving only on orange juice. Her weight fell to a skeletal thirty-six kilos.

Either due to her condition or the presumption that Clara was just a faithful wife following her husband, the judge dropped the charges against her. They had spent over three months at the Grand and another three at the hospital. Clara would now return to France to sell their Picasso and raise further funding for her husband's defense. Her father-in-law sent money for a return boat ticket as well as some pocket money, which she gave to her "companion," as she continually refers to André in her memoirs, though whether he used it to pay his bill at the Grand is uncertain.

Clara was en route home when the two-day trial began. Still claiming to be a scholar of antiquities, André pleaded innocent, his rationale being that Banteay Srey had not yet officially been listed as a historic site. The prosecution accused Malraux of being an enemy of France (their secret dossier on him labeled André as a Bolshevik sympathizer and his wife as a Jew of German extraction). On July 21, Judge Jodin sentenced André, as leader of the "official mission," to three years in prison, Chevasson to eighteen months. France would keep the stolen sculptures. The case now went to the appellate court in Saigon. Malraux and Chevasson left Phnom Penh and the Grand Hôtel for that city.

In France, Clara received the backing of illustrious literary and artistic figures, including the writers André Gide and André Maurois, who wrote articles and signed petitions in support of Malraux. In October, the appellate court levied a one-year sentence for André and three months for Chevasson, but the judge then suspended the punishments, thereby sparing the two even one day in jail. Perhaps the judge was swayed by the defense lawyer's claim that the pair's theft of antiquities was no different from what governors and other officials had been doing since the early days of the protectorate (not to mention the scholars and artists who carted off statuary on a much greater scale and which can be seen today, for example, in the Musée Guimet in Paris). Nonetheless, André was incensed by the verdict, still proclaiming his innocence, and he filed an additional appeal. Malraux and Chevasson soon departed for France. As for the appeal, it was never addressed in court. The Supreme Court of

Appeal in Paris voided the verdict on a technicality and sent the case back to the Saigon court, where it seems to have just faded away.

However, from their stay at the charity hospital, from their walks in the "native" parts of the city, and from their perception of the bias of the protectorate's judiciary, the Malraux had discovered the misery of the common people and the "cruel injustice" of France's colonial system. This would lead André and Clara to return to Saigon and write for a local newspaper, supporting the rights of the Vietnamese and publicizing colonial abuse.

In 1930 André published *The Royal Way*, a fictional rendition loosely based on his Cambodian adventures, though *sans* a Clara character. André Malraux went on to great literary and political fame, but he never apologized for the thievery he had committed in Cambodia, and to this day he remains Cambodia's most illustrious looter.

THE GRAND HÔTEL DATES to the late 1890s, though it was not the city's first such establishment. In 1881, a barber and small-time trader named Jean Guérin and his wife Marie Laty added two lodging rooms to the bar they had opened the previous year, dubbing their expanded enterprise Hôtel Guérin (Map 3, #56). This so-called hotel (they later rather grandly renamed it Hôtel Phnom Penh) was in all probability located on the Grand' Rue, as today's Sisowath Quay was then known, in the vicinity of the present streets 148 and 154. There are also references to a hotel named Laval, whose proprietors, Monsieur and Madame Laval, arrived in Cambodia in 1890. In fact, as Jean Guérin died in 1888 and his wife Marie Laty in 1892, the Hôtel Laval may have been the Hôtel Guérin renamed.

Describing the daily life of protectorate officials in the early 1890s, M. J. Agostini wrote that "office work occupies them until 10 a.m. at which time they install themselves under the *pankas* [arm or leg-powered ceiling fans] of the Laval and Féraud [Monsieur Féraud came to the city in 1887] cafés to enjoy an aperitif. At 11:00 one is seated for lunch – which may last for three hours – before retiring for a siesta." At the Hôtel Laval, guests dined on the "far from execrable" dishes of a Chinese chef named Balthazar.

As for the lodgings, they do not seem to have lived up to Balthazar's cuisine. The Laval was most likely the hotel described by Le Comte Barthélemy, a visitor to Phnom Penh in 1894: ". . . as for a hotel in this city there was but a poor café which had a couple of rooms with dilapidated furniture." And Paul de Neufville, who visited the following year, wrote: "It was difficult to find lodgings for the five of us, as the two inns in Pnom-Penh [*sic*] were small and dirty." Clearly, better lodgings for the city's guests were a necessity.

The Grand Hôtel was the inspiration of *Résident Supérieur* Huyn de Vernéville, France's highest representative in Cambodia, who negotiated with a merchant named Borelly to create a hotel-restaurant "of European standards" which would be subsidized by the protectorate in return for the permanent reservation of seven rooms for official guests of the French government. The Grand was one of the first places in Phnom Penh to make ice, no doubt highly appreciated by guests and residents alike.

Ice notwithstanding, the Grand may not have risen to de Vernéville's expectations. In the late 1890s, one of the hotel's first guests, Eugéne Lagrillière-Beauclerc, described his accommodation as "a vast chamber, a sort of cage for mosquitoes in which I played, in spite of myself, the role of nurturing father." Two Belgian travelers, Mr. and Mrs. Émile Jottrand, he a legal adviser to the government of Siam, arrived in Phnom Penh by ship from Saigon in October 1900. Though they had a room with a view of the river, the couple's impressions of the Grand were less than flattering, as reported in their journal entry of October 18:

> We stay at the Grand Hotel of Phnom Penh, believing that we
> will enjoy a little more comfort than on the ship. The rooms
> they have reserved for us are spacious and have been built on
> a grand scale but they have not been well maintained. The
> ceiling is devoid of plaster and shows the woodworks, all of it
> reflects a dubious cleanliness. The shower, an indispensable

The Grand with W. Somerset Maugham's "terrace"

luxury in a hot climate, does not work. Nobody bothers with the guests; let them sort it out themselves! Our astonishment, first great, has instantly disappeared when we learned that the hotel is largely subsidized: 10,000 francs per year, just that amount! Well then, they even subsidize hotels here? What providence, what a mother this government is!

"The hotel is large, dirty, and pretentious," sniffed the writer W. Somerset Maugham about his stopover at the Grand in 1922, four years after Nicolas Manolis purchased the hotel, "and there is a terrace outside it where merchants and innumerable functionaries may take an 'apéritif' and for a moment forget that they are not in France."

After Monsieur Manolis, a Greek from Rhodes who had originally come to Cambodia to construct the Phnom Penh-Battambang-Sisophon railway, took over proprietorship of the hotel in 1918, it was referred to interchangeably as the Grand or the Manolis, or by the two names joined together in Grand Hôtel Manolis. Here is the impression of Henry Franck, a writer who stayed at the hotel a year after the Malraux:

> The Grand Hotel, N. Manolis, Propriétaire, might like all the others in Indo-China, have been in Paris – except for the heat – tourist prices and all. Here again were the same

"Tourists concerned with comfort and
good food stay at the Grand Hotel"

marble-topped tables, the same zinc *comptoir* presided
over by a sharp-eyed and caustic-minded matron, the same
flimsy newspapers in awkward holders, the same letter-
paper headed by an advertisement of the Maison Dubonnet.

The 1939 edition of *The Madrolle Guides* gives the following information about the Grand: de la Grandière Quay, opposite the
landing-stage. 40 rooms with running water, from 0.5 piasters to 5
piasters. Breakfast 1.5 piasters, lunch 2 piasters, dinner 2.5 piasters.

KFC today occupies the original building, whose architecture
can be better seen from its sides on streets 98 and 100 than from
its garish fast-food front. By the 1940s, the hotel had expanded
from its main entrance on today's Sisowath Quay all the way to the
post office plaza on Street 13, though the building there is clearly
a separate one from KFC's. The plaza building was once the city's

The Grand viewed from St. 100 (left)
and from the corner of 98 and 13

chamber of commerce and, after liberation in 1979, post office employees were lodged there.

The Grand Hôtel Manolis was replaced as Phnom Penh's hotel of choice in 1929 with the opening of the far more well-appointed Hôtel Le Royal. The Grand continued to serve visitors for many more years, apparently under the direction of Nicolas Manolis'

The Grand Hôtel Manolis, center right, with the
post office behind, in the late 1920s

son, André. Although the hotel is clearly marked on my 1966 map, it is not listed in my 1971 guidebook. The historian David Chandler told me it was indeed closed when he visited the city in 1971. By the 1990s the Grand had been divided into small private lodgings and, today, numerous families inhabit many of the former hotel's rooms. In the early 2000s the riverside portion of the Grand became a *suki soup* restaurant, but it seems present day Phnom Penh palates favor more western fare.

There remains, however, a hint of what the Grand may have been like in the old days: drop in for an *apéro* at Chez Rina, a delightful cocktail bar which occupies a part of the former hotel on Street 98. Closed Sundays.

Sources

Axel Madsen, *Silk Roads,* Taurus, 1990.

Jean Lacouture, *Malraux, une vie dans le siècle,* Versaille, 1976.

Clara Malreaux, *Le Bruit de Nos Pas II: Nos Vingt Ans,* Grasset, 1966.

Kent Davis, "Le Khmérophile: the Art and Life of George Groslier," in George Groslier, *Cambodian Dancers, Ancient and Modern,* DatAsia, 2011.

Gregor Muller, *Colonial Cambodia's 'Bad Frenchmen,'* Routledge, 2006.

M. J. Agostini, "Phnom Penh," in *Le Tour du Monde,* #25, June 18, 1898.

Le Comte Barthélemy, *En Indochine 1894–95,* Plon, Nourrit, 1899.

Paul de Neufville, *Un Voyage en Indo-Chine et à Java,* Kessinger, 1896.

Phnom Penh, développement urbain et patrimonie, Ministère de la Culture, 1997.

Eugéne Lagrillière-Beauclerc, *Au Cambodge et Annam: Voyage Pittoresque,* Albin Michel, 1900.

Captain Georges Chaudoir and Mr. and Mrs. Émile Jottrand, *Belgian Tourists in Burma, Siam, Vietnam and Cambodia,* White Lotus, 2011 [1889].

Henry Franck, *East of Siam: Ramblings in the Five Divisions of French Indo-China,* Century, 1926.

Somerset Maugham, *The Gentleman in the Parlor,* Orchid, 1930.

3. The Buddha's Bone

On January 16, 1957, in the city of Kandy, Ceylon, Prince Norodom Sihanouk received a tiny piece of a bone of the Buddha, a gift from the Ceylonese people to mark the 2,500th anniversary of the Buddha's birth. On the day of the anniversary, May 12, at a grand ceremony in the plaza in front of Phnom Penh's railway station attended by King Suramarit and Queen Kossamak as well as monks from Ceylon and India, Prince Sihanouk placed the relic in the specially constructed sky blue stupa, which still stands

Buddha Stupa, with the railway station behind

24

there (Map 3, #47), though recently it has been resplendently repainted in gold.

The stupa was the first monument built in Phnom Penh following independence in 1953. The reliquary that carried the Buddha's bone from Ceylon to Phnom Penh is now in the Silver Pagoda of the Royal Palace (Map 3, #70). That reliquary, a miniature silver and gold stupa, is inside a glass case in front of the pagoda's main altar and to the left of the gold, diamond encrusted statue of the Buddha Maitreya, Buddha of the Future.

Before the Buddha's extinction and passage into nirvana, he had instructed his disciples to cremate his body and then distribute the relics among groups of his followers. The relics were to be placed in stupas, specially built hemispherical shrines whose origins can be traced to pre-Buddhist burial mounds (on their journey to Cambodia, stupas became conical). Ten sets of relics were distributed, eight from bits of his remains that survived the burning, one from the bucket used to carry them, and one from the ashes. He then said that the sites where his relics would be enshrined should be places of pilgrimage.

Murals depicting the distribution of the Buddha's relics are common in Cambodia's pagodas. Crowds of the faithful are sometimes pictured trampling one another in their rush to receive a portion. Some in the crowd are dressed in foreign garb, even modern western suits and military uniforms, symbolizing the wide distribution of the vestiges.

King Asoka of the Mauryan dynasty, responsible for the spreading of Buddhism over almost the entire Indian subcontinent in the 3rd century BC, divided the relics into parts (84,000 according to tradition) and ordered the construction of stupas, to which his emissaries brought the relics.

Some of these relics eventually found their way to Southeast Asia, including one to Shwedagon Pagoda in Yangon, and another, following its lengthy stay in Kandy, to our stupa in Phnom Penh. To the faithful, these stupas were not mere reliquaries but were considered to contain the Buddha himself, so seeing the stupa

The distribution of relics, Wat Srah Chak, Oknha Hing Peng Street (St. 61, see Map 2, #25). Notice the various western and Asian costumes and the man on the left who has fallen in the rush to collect a relic.

was almost to see the Buddha, and the stupas thus became sites of pilgrimage, as the Buddha had instructed.

Facing the sunrise, the golden stupa by the railway station is decorated with reliefs of four episodes from the Buddha's life: his first footsteps, immediately after his birth; his defeat of Mara, king of devils and symbol of our desires and sins; his first sermon following his enlightenment; and his entrance into nirvana.

The first panel illustrates the Buddha's birth, which took place in Kapilavastu, in present day Nepal. When the future Buddha was about to be born, his mother Maya stood up and raised her right arm to grab the branch of a tree. The Buddha emerged from under the arm. He then took seven steps, and a lotus flower blossomed from each one. Pointing to the heavens with his right index finger and to the ground with the left, he proclaimed that between heaven and earth he was foremost among all beings, and that this life would be his last. He was given the name Siddhartha Gautama. Siddhartha in Sanskrit translates as "he who achieves his aim," while Gautama was his family name. The Buddha is frequently referred to by his

The Buddha's birth and first footsteps

clan name, Sakyamuni, "the sage of the Sakya clan." In Khmer he is usually called Preah Put, "Lord Buddha."

The next of the stupa's panels represents Mara's defeat. On the left, the six-armed Evil One is seated atop an elephant, brandishing a bow and leading an unsuccessful attack of his army of devils against the Sakyamuni Buddha, seeking to disrupt his meditation. In the center, Sakyamuni sits in quiet contemplation under a boddhi tree, apparently oblivious to any attack. The fingers of his right hand touch the ground, calling upon Earth to bear witness to the firmness of his purpose and his resulting victory over evil. Below Sakyamuni, the Earth is represented by Thorani, Goddess of the Land and the Seas, who responds to his call. Thorani loosens her hair and unleashes from it a flood of water and hungry crocodiles. On the right, the army of monsters is drowned by Thorani's waters or devoured by her reptiles, while above them Mara acknowledges defeat. Four of his hands now hold lotus buds, symbols of peace, and his other two hands *sompeah* respectfully to the Buddha. Even Mara's elephant has abandoned the sword held in its trunk in favor of a bouquet of lotus buds. Sakyamuni now continued his meditation, and by dawn he had achieved enlightenment. (For more on the Buddha's victory over Mara, see Chapter 10.)

The future Buddha spent the remainder of his life teaching the way to enlightenment. His first sermon was delivered at a deer park in Sarnath to five ascetics with whom he had once stayed, as is depicted in the next panel. Along with meditation, these five ascetics had encouraged Sakyamuni to lead a life of fasting and deprivation. After following this path of physical punishment for six years, however, Sakyamuni realized it was not the way to enlightenment. He then began to propagate the "middle way," a system of thinking and living which included the avoidance of extremes. Disgusted by this discarding of deprivation, the five ascetics deserted him. When they later encountered him in the deer park at Sarnath, however, they realized that he had changed. To them Sakyamuni now preached his first and most important sermon, one in which he revealed that the way to enlightenment and breaking the cycle of birth and rebirth was to be found in the Four Noble Truths: life is suffering, suffering has causes which can be traced back to their origin, one's goal should be the elimination of suffering, and suffering can be ended by following the path to nirvana. This path essentially involves three aspects: ethics or avoiding nonvirtuous actions; meditation, which comes from extensive practice; and wisdom, which is the result of meditation and is hard to achieve. This was not a new path, Sakyamuni said, but one which had been taught before but had been forgotten over the many years since the disappearance of the last buddha. His teachings too would eventually be forgotten, only to appear again in the distant future with the coming of the next buddha, Maitreya.

The final representation is the Buddha's death at the age of 80 and his passage into nirvana. He lies on his right side, his right hand propped under his head on a pillow. Around him are his weeping disciples and lay followers. The dying Buddha here is about to achieve the Buddhist goal of entering nirvana, or "blowing out," the cessation of suffering, now and forever.

The Buddha Stupa, however, no longer contains its Buddha relic. Because of the increase in traffic and noise along Monivong

Boulevard, as well as the disorder caused by the arrival and departure of trains, the site was no longer conducive to reflection. King Sihanouk and Queen Monineath proposed that the relic be moved to a quiet spot on the royal hill at Udong, some forty kilometers north of Phnom Penh. A tall white stupa was raised on the north slope of the hill, built with contributions of the faithful, including the king and queen. Escorted by a long procession of believers, the tiny bone fragment was brought from Phnom Penh on December 19, 2002, and placed in the Buddha Stupa on Udong's hill (Map 1, #3).

Buddha Stupa on the royal hill at Udong

Yet that stupa, too, may no longer contain the Buddha's bone. During the night of December 10, 2013, the relic in its golden urn and several Buddha statues were stolen from inside the stupa, which normally is accessible only to members of the royal family. Among the five men detained were the head of security at the stupa and three of his guards. The following February, however, police arrested a 24-year-old farmer and petty thief in Takeo province when they found the golden urn hidden under his bed, as well as most of the missing statues. A Royal Palace minister and the deputy chief monk of the Mahanikay order verified the authenticity of the relic and the urn. The relic and its urn are presently being kept at the Royal Palace. They are scheduled to be returned to the Buddha Stupa (where an alarm system and other security measures have been put in place) in May 2016 during the Visak Bochea holiday, which celebrates the Buddha's birth, enlightenment, and passage into nirvana.

It should be noted that the Buddha relic mentioned here is not the only one in Phnom Penh and its environs. Another possible one is in an ancient stupa at Wat Unnalom, but that relic too might be in the Buddha Stupa at Udong, as you can read in Chapter 4. Relics of the Buddha are also kept at Wat Botum (Map 3, #73), one of the city's oldest wats, in a stupa which was built in 1909.

Outside Wat Botum's compound are three boddhi trees that were given to the pagoda as saplings in 1886 to commemorate its reconstruction. The saplings were cuttings from a boddhi tree in Anuradhapura, Ceylon, which itself was a cutting from the boddhi tree in Bodhgaya, India, beneath which the Buddha was meditating when he achieved enlightenment. In honor of the 1886 occasion, King Norodom himself presided over a grand festival, which included the young plants being transported in procession through the city's streets followed by thousands of monks, each one carrying a lotus flower.

Sources

Donald S. Lopez, Jr., *The Story of Buddhism*, Harper Collins, 2001.

Ray Zepp, *A Field Guide to Cambodian Pagodas*, Bert's Books, 1997.

Cristian Violatti, "Siddhartha Gautama," *L'Écho du Cambodge*, #172, April 2015.

Buddha Relics Stupa at Wat Botum

Inscription:
This stupa enshrine[s] sacred relics of the Buddha. [It] was built in the year
of [the] cock, first saka, B.E.2452/A.D.1909, restored in B.E.2546/A.D.2002
The upper-floor enshrines sacred relics of the Buddha and relics of an
Arhant. The lower-floor enshrines ashes of three former sangharajas
[Buddhist Supreme Patriarchs] of the Kingdom of Cambodia . . .

4. An Angkorian Site in Phnom Penh

O ne might be excused for thinking the oldest site in our city is Wat Phnom and its manmade hill. In fact, a visit to Phnom Penh's most venerable traces requires a walk to Wat Unnalom, located just off the riverside where Sothearos Avenue splits away from Sisowath Quay (Map 3, #57).

Behind the pagoda's *vihara*, the main sanctuary or prayer hall, is the *Preah Chedi Thom*, or Great Stupa. This rather elaborate stupa faces east and five small cells are attached to its sides. A careful look at the junction of the western cell and the stupa reveals sandstone blocks, each about fifty centimeters in height, that form the walls of an Angkor era tower. Similarly cut stones are evident inside the stupa's chamber, where plaster has been chipped away to reveal the ancient structure. As the sandstone quarries went silent at the end

The Great Stupa   Blocks of the ancient stupa's wall

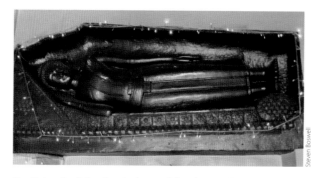

Steven Boswell

Reclining Buddha lintel: the Buddha dies and enters nirvana

of the 12th century or the beginning of the next, the tower most likely dates from that time.

Inside, the reclining Buddha lintels in the cells and the seated Buddha statue at the rear of the main chamber postdate the tower. Outside the stupa's northern cell and next to the loo are several cut laterite stones, perhaps remains of the original enclosing wall. More such stones are hidden under two upturned tables to the right of the enclosure's western entrance.

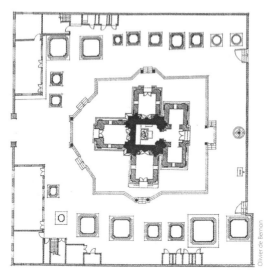

Olivier de Bernon

Wat Unnalom's Great Stupa, the
Angkorian tower highlighted in black

The Angkorian tower was not originally a stupa but more likely a *prasat*: a sanctuary in the form of a tower, inside which may have been a stone *linga*, a phallus shaped symbol of the Hindu god Shiva in his role as creator. However, the tower was turned into a stupa, most likely by Buddhist monks in order to house a relic of the Buddha. The relic is a hair, or *loma* in Pali, from a small tuft, or *unna*, that grew between the Buddha's eyebrows (a circle of hair between the eyebrows is one of the thirty-two marks of a buddha). Hence the pagoda's name.

The most common version of the relic's story is that it was brought here by the Venerable Assaji, one of the five ascetics to whom the Buddha preached his first sermon following his enlightenment. Another account is that the *unnalom* is from Assaji himself, for he also gained enlightenment and became a buddha. To add to the uncertainty, an oral tradition dates the arrival of the relic to the first years of Buddhism in Cambodia, long after the lifetimes of the Buddha and Assaji.

Stupa cross section: the central core of sandstone
blocks is the Angkorian tower

34

The Buddha in meditation, Angkorian wall
behind; his hair is perhaps concealed below

Who the hair is from and when it was brought to Wat Unnalom thus remains a bit of a mystery, but it was placed in the stupa before King Ponhea Yat moved the capital to Phnom Penh in the 1430s or 1440s, as indeed the stupa bore the name Unnalom before Ponhea Yat's arrival. Whether the hair is still *in situ* is also a matter of debate. According to historian George Cœdès, writing in 1918, the solitary hair was transferred to Wat Prang in Udong (Map 1, #1) in 1909. However, the present caretaker of the Great Stupa says the *unnalom*, the Buddha's hair, is indeed right here at Wat Unnalom, buried under the stone statue of the meditating Buddha in the central chamber.

At Wat Prang in Udong, the monks tell a different story. The *unnalom* was moved here "one hundred years ago" and placed in a specially made stupa outside the pagoda's *vihara*, which is consistent with Cœdès' assertion. Then, they say, when the Buddha relic from

35

the stupa in front of Phnom Penh's railway station was moved to the new Buddha Stupa on Udong hill in 2003 (Map 1, #3; see also Chapter 3), the *unnalom* was also placed there. A couple of years later, the monks say, the old stupa at Wat Prang was completely rebuilt, thanks mainly to donations from the Lim family, including relatives in New Zealand. This new pyramid, magnificent though it is, contains no relics of the Buddha.

The present Wat Unnalom was founded by King Ponhea Yat well over a century after the erection of the Angkorian tower. Though the exact year of Wat Unnalom's construction is not known, one document states it was inaugurated in 1442. Ponhea Yat, after enlarging Wat Phnom's hill, restoring its pagoda, and raising the stupa behind, ordered the building of several pagodas, including in addition to Wat Unnalom, Wat Botum, Wat Puth Khoussa, Wat Lanka, and Wat Koh, all of which still stand. The first three are in their original location. Wat Lanka and Wat Koh were just to the east of the *phnom*, the first where the Council for the Development of Cambodia currently resides and the latter on the present emplacement of Électricité du Cambodge's head office. Wat Unnalom's *vihara* has been rebuilt many times, most recently in 1957 in honor of the 2,500th anniversary of the Buddha's birth.

Renovated stupa at Wat Prang, Udong

Chuon Nath at Wat Unnalom

Chuon Nath at Samdech
Hun Sen Circle

As at all Cambodian pagodas, scattered around the compound of Wat Unnalom are a number of stupas of varying styles and sizes, resting places for the ashes of the departed. The most notable one, located in the northeast corner of the pagoda's compound, is the tall, gray stupa of the Venerable Chuon Nath (1883–1969), highly respected supreme patriarch of the Mahanikay sect of Theravada Buddhism. A modernizer who at times clashed with traditionalist members of the clergy, Chuon Nath translated Buddhist texts into Khmer from their original Pali, a language of northern India closely related to Magadhan, the language the Buddha himself may have spoken. Chuon Nath then had the texts published, thus making them available to a much wider audience of young monks and lay Buddhists. For similar reasons, Chuon Nath advocated preaching not only in Pali but also in Khmer. He was also the principal composer of the *Khmer Dictionary*, a major work of scholarship, and, incidentally, the author of a booklet on the Unnalom stupa itself. A statue of Chuon Nath stands in Samdech Hun Sen Circle (Map 4, #79), near the Buddhist Institute.

Wat Unnalom houses less imposing stupas as well. Just to the southwest of the Great Stupa is a much smaller, whitewashed one bearing a bronze plaque whose message in Khmer and French includes these sad lines:

Here lies Monsieur Duong Sung

Born in 1908 at Chea Sman, Siem Reap Province, died in 1973 in Phnom Penh

Rice merchant, doctor of traditional medicine, and master of ceremonies of Phrom Chan Pagoda at Damdek, Siem Reap.

His wife Chheng Suor, his two children Duong Sung San and Duong Roeun, and his grandchildren Phrom Chayya and Aline were victims of the Khmer Rouge and have no tomb.

May their souls rest in peace.

Restored in 2007 by his grandchildren Isabelle Charya, Sahavanna Nathalie, Nimithida Carole, Patricia Kantabopha

One final note about Wat Unnalom: Towards the end of World War II, the pagoda was attacked by US B-29 warplanes following reports that Japanese troops were hiding there. Perhaps the reports were based on the fact that many Japanese soldiers shaved their heads, as do monks. In any event, there were no Japanese in the pagoda, but about twenty monks and many civilians died during the air strike, which caused significant destruction all the way from the river to the railroad station.

Sources

If you read French, you can learn more about the Great Stupa from Olivier de Bernon's article listed below, from which much of my information was taken, as were the two diagrams. The *École française d'Extrême-Orient* has an office and a library – where you can find de Bernon's article – in Wat Unnalom's compound, just inside the wall running along Sothearos Boulevard. The article is available online through www.efeo.Fr/base. php?code=97 (click on "portai Persée"), as are the 1901–2003 issues of the *Bulletin*.

Olivier de Bernon, "Le plus ancien édifice subsistant de Phnom Penh: une tour angkorienne sise dans l'enceint du Vatt Unnâlom," *Bulletin de l'École française d'Extrême-Orient* #88, 2001.

George Cœdès, "Articles sur le pays Khmer," *Bulletin de l'École française d'Extrême-Orient*, 1913.

Bruno Bruguier and Juliette Lacroix, *Phnom Penh et les Provinces Méridionales*, Reyum, 2009.

Penny Edwards, *Cambodge: The Cultivation of a Nation, 1860–1945*, Hawaii, 2007.

5. Made for America's Queen

As you walk down the corridor from the main doors of Hôtel Le Royal (newcomers to the city often call the hotel the Raffles, but we pedantic old Francophiles prefer to use its inaugural name; see Map 2, #26) to the Elephant Bar for its splendid happy hour (4:00 to 8:00 every day, half price on all drinks but wine, with a complimentary basket of taro chips and salsa, and Roel Manalo at the piano), stop a moment at the glass case on your right and admire the display of long-stemmed cocktail glasses, some embellished

One of the 108 glasses made for Jackie

40

with Le Royal's crest and insignia, others with a royal headdress, all specially made for the visit in 1967 of Jacqueline Kennedy, widow of President John F. Kennedy. The notice in the display case reads:

> **Femme Fatale Glass**
>
> In 1967, Jacqueline Kennedy visited Cambodia, fulfilling a "lifelong dream of seeing Angkor Wat."
>
> During her stay in Phnom Penh a banquet in her honor was held where Prince Sihanouk played his own compositions, [and] a champagne cocktail as red as her lips was served.
>
> For this event, a special glass was made . . .
>
> Years later during renovation, the glasses were found in our cellar.

Jackie may indeed have had a "lifelong dream of seeing Angkor Wat," but her so-called private trip was also a carefully planned diplomatic undertaking aimed at improving the strained relations between the US and Cambodia, a stratagem devised by Secretary of Defense Robert McNamara. Prince Norodom Sihanouk, Cambodia's head of state, had been alienated from the US for some time, largely over America's involvement in Vietnam and his belief that the US supported the Khmer Serei (Free Khmer), a dissident Cambodian group; in fact, the prince himself had cut diplomatic ties in May 1965. It was hoped that Jackie's huge international popularity would temper any anti-American feelings held in Cambodia due to US activity in Vietnam. Her legendary charm had, after all, captivated de Gaulle, another leader with disagreements with the US' Vietnam policies, and perhaps it would do the same with Prince Sihanouk and Cambodians more generally. It was also hoped that Jackie or a member of her entourage would be able to appeal to Prince Sihanouk to use his influence with North Vietnam to get information on American prisoners in Vietnam, both civilian and military.

On the trip Jackie would be accompanied by Lord Harlech (David Ormsby-Gore), former British ambassador to Washington, Kennedy family friend, and widower. Denials notwithstanding, romantic rumors about the two had been bruited about since she saw him on a trip to Ireland and he subsequently visited her in the US. So when Jackie announced her trip with an entourage including Lord Harlech, the tabloid press had a field day. "Premarital honeymoon," they crowed, and even "Cambodian wedding." It seemed a fine cover, if not a perfect one, and few in the accompanying press were aware of the sensitive mission behind the visit.

On her arrival in November, Jackie was met at Pochentong Airport by Prince Sihanouk himself. Her motorcade was greeted by wildly cheering crowds lining her route down USSR Boulevard and on to her suite at the Royal Palace. Dressed in a wardrobe designed by Valentino, her favorite couturier, Jackie chatted with Queen Kossamak, Sihanouk's mother, fed bananas to the sacred white elephants and, at Le Royal, listened to Prince Sihanouk's jazz compositions "November Breeze" and "The Evening I Met You" while

Jackie welcomed by Prince Sihanouk upon her arrival at Pochentong Airport, red carpet strewn with rose petals.

sipping champagne cocktails from one of those 108 specially made long-stemmed glasses. Jackie called Phnom Penh "one of the nicest cities I have seen and the cleanest of all."

Prince Sihanouk was enchanted. In his toast at a formal dinner at Chamkar Mon Palace (Jackie wore a Grecian turquoise gown) he praised President Kennedy, whom he had once called "the great boss of aggressors" for the US' Vietnam policy. He presented Jackie with an elaborately filigreed silver tray, finger bowls, and plates. She offered him a leather-bound copy of JFK's The Strategy of Peace, among other gifts. They went to Sihanoukville, where the prince named a four-kilometer street Avenue J. F. Kennedy, with Jackie unveiling the commemorative plaque before a throng of spectators. Later, when asked why he had named a street after Kennedy in Sihanoukville rather than one in Phnom Penh, the prince answered, "Sihanoukville is very important. It is named after me. Anyway, I have run out of streets in Phnom Penh." (The street's name was changed in the 1980s and it is now 2 December Street, which runs along Independence Beach.)

But Prince Sihanouk did not change his opposition to US involvement in Vietnam and he insisted as much to the press.

Prince Sihanouk and Jackie at the unveiling in Sihanoukville

Concerning the American civilian prisoners in Vietnam, the Prince refused to intercede on their behalf. He put it this way in a statement delivered on November 8, "Why have pity on these civilians while the Americans and South Vietnamese martyr so many innocent Vietnamese civilians?" And as for US pilots shot down over North Vietnam, he said, "That beats everything. Intervene for those who murder with their bombs more civilians, more children than soldiers." However, Sihanouk added in the same statement, "A single exception will be made in respect of Mr. Ramsey [see box], in whose fate Mrs. Kennedy asked me to interest myself in order to get information for her and the prisoner's family."

In his memoirs *Souvenirs doux et amers*, Prince Sihanouk insisted that Jackie's trip had no political agenda. "Contrary to what many thought at the time, Jackie Kennedy gave to me no message, either verbal or otherwise, from the American authorities. She did not say

The **Mr. Ramsey** to whom Prince Sihanouk referred was Douglas K. Ramsey, a US Foreign Service Officer who was captured in a Viet Cong ambush on January 17, 1966, while transporting food and medical supplies to "refugees and evacuees" at a camp northwest of Saigon. Ramsey spent the next seven years as a prisoner of war in the forests of South Vietnam and Cambodia. He was freed on February 12, 1973, as part of Operation Homecoming, during which 591 American prisoners of war were released by North Vietnam following negotiations with the US. Ramsey later wrote: "I consider myself extremely fortunate to have survived the occasional wanton neglect and sadism of a few of my captors (most were fairly decent most of the time); the anger and hatred of both the local population and the VC/PAVN troops; several B-52 strikes; outright starvation during the Cambodian operation; 136 attacks of malaria, mostly falciparum (killer); the numerous infections and swellings produced by scurvy and beriberi; and my own foolishness at times." Ramsey added that he wanted to express his appreciation "for the efforts of . . . individuals to gain information from the VC as to my status, notably Jacqueline (Kennedy) Onassis and Prince Norodom Sihanouk."

La Femme Fatale, "as red as her lips"

one word about the state of relations between the United States and Cambodia. She was sincere when she affirmed *urbi et orbi**despite general disbelief, that she only wanted to visit Angkor!"

Whatever the case, Jackie's mission led to a more substantive one the following January by Chester Bowles, the US ambassador to India, during which the Cambodian prime minister let it be known that Prince Sihanouk desired to normalize diplomatic relations, which finally happened in 1969.

As to Lord Harlech, after admiring the wonders of Angkor with Jackie for three days, he returned to England, while she flew on

---

* *Uurbi et orbi*: "to the city and to the world," an expression used by the pope when giving a blessing.

to Thailand in an American military plane. The next year Jackie married Aristotle Onassis.

So, with Jackie and happy hour in mind, you should now leave the display case with the unearthed glasses and move on to the Elephant Bar, where you can order *La Femme Fatale*, the cocktail of champagne, cognac, and *créme de fraise sauvage* that was created in her honor. Don't forget to have it served in one of Jackie's green-stemmed glasses (one of which retains traces of her lipstick, or so the hotel likes to say). And if you really want to treat yourself, spend a night at Le Royal's Jacqueline Kennedy Suite for a cool $390. Remember, however, that she never slept in that bed.

Sources

C. David Heymann, *A Woman Named Jackie,* Signet, 1989.

Neil Manton, *Strange Flowers on the Diplomatic Vine*, Manton, 2007.

Norodom Sihanouk, *Souvenirs doux et amers*, Hachette, 1981.

Life, November 20, 1967.

Newsweek, November 20, 1967.

60 Years of Diplomatic Relations: United States-Cambodia 1950–2010, Public Affairs Section, US Embassy, Phnom Penh, 2010.

On Douglas Ramsey, www.pownetwork.org/bios/r/r600.htm.

6. The Riverside Shrine and Flag Tower of Preah Ang Dongka

S troll along the riverside and when you reach the gardens in front of the Royal Palace you will come across a large pavilion from which the king watches the Water Festival boat races every November. The pavilion stands between two small shrines with glazed orange- and green-tiled roofs typical of Cambodian places of worship. Religious faithful visit the southernmost shrine, the one near a tall metal flag tower flying the royal insignia, when they wish to appeal to Preah Ang Dongka (Map 3, #65).

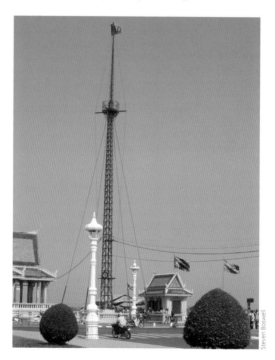

The flag tower and, on the right, the small shrine of Preah Ang Dongka

Preah Ang Dongka

On the altar inside the shrine is an Angkorian-style six-armed statue. A small image of the meditating Amitabha Buddha on the front of the headdress identifies the statue as representing the Bodhisattva Avalokiteshvara, "Lord Who Looks Down from Above," also known as Lokeshvara, "Lord of the Worlds." Here, Avalokiteshvara, the Bodhisattva of Compassion, holds in his three

Avalokiteshvara, like other bodhisattvas, is revered in Mahayana Buddhism. This is the tradition which was followed by the great Angkorian king Jayavarman VII (reigned 1181–c.1219), during whose time the cult of Avalokiteshvara reached unprecedented popularity, and to whose time the original Preah Ang Dongka statue may well have dated. Avalokiteshvara is still popular today in the form of the Bodhisattva Quan Âm in Vietnam, who is known as Kuan Yin in China and Kannon in Japan (see Chapter 26 for more on bodhisattvas). In the Theravada Buddhism of Cambodia and other Southeast Asian countries, bodhisattvas play a much lesser role.

right hands a string of prayer beads, a baton, and a lotus bud, while his three left ones clasp a palm leaf manuscript on which is written a sacred text, a short sword, and a flask of the nectar of immortality. The figure is painted black and clothed in a saffron colored robe, and a garland of flowers often hangs round his neck. The statue was brought from Udong to Phnom Penh when King Norodom moved the capital here in 1866 (see box above).

This is perhaps the most popular shrine in the city and, on the days that mark the four quarters of the moon's monthly cycle (roughly one day per week, the eighth and fifteenth days of the waxing and waning moon, to be precise), the area around the shrine is crowded with worshippers. Floral offerings are on sale. For a small fee, a caged sparrow can be bought and then released, thereby bringing its redeemer a touch of merit towards a higher rebirth in the next life.

The worshipping faithful revere the statue not as Avalokiteshvara but as the embodiment of a powerful *neak ta*, or tutelary spirit, who resides in the statue and protects the city. This divinity is Preah Ang Dongka, one of the most potent spirits of the kingdom, who is also known as Macha Bong Chaktomuk, the "deity of the four faces" of the Mekong River, the four countenances consisting twice of the Mekong, which makes a sharp bend here, together with its Tonle Sap tributary and its Bassac distributary.

In return for Preah Ang Dongka's help, the devoted make pledges to the spirit, and, if their pleas are heard, offerings will be made in fulfillment of the vow. Those who want to swear that something is true often do so at the shrine, with Preah Ang Dongka as witness. The divinity is also frequently beseeched for good health. When my wife suffered complications during her pregnancy, she went to Preah Ang Dongka's shrine and implored the spirit to keep our baby healthy. She promised a pig's head and two chickens if he would do so. Two months later, Preah Ang Dongka received his meal.

As the flag tower with its royal standard is also associated with Preah Ang Dongka (*dongka* in fact means "flagpole"), it has unusual powers as well. At this site in the past, mediums in trances communicated Preah Ang Dongka's predictions to assembled followers. In 1929, a medium standing beside the flagpole predicted the terrible drought that followed and, in 1941, another foretold the impending death of King Monivong.

In February 1970, a poor peasant from Kompong Speu province arrived at Preah Ang Dongka's shrine in a deep trance. Scaling the flag tower, he sat himself in the lotus position of meditation on the small platform two-thirds of the way up the pylon, twenty meters above the ground. From the palace, Queen Kossamak, mother of Prince Sihanouk, forbade the police to intervene. She ordered monks to pray to the most powerful spirits for the peaceful departure of the meditating peasant.

King Norodom with his son
Prince Chantaleka in 1900

The next morning, the farmer, still in his trance, announced that he had an important message for Prince Chantalekha, 80 years old and the last surviving son of King Norodom. The message was from the long-deceased rebel prince Sivutha, Norodom's half-brother and rival. What is known of the content of the communication is that it presaged the imminent fall of Prince Sihanouk and a period of great misfortune for the country. The next month, Sirik Matak and Lon Nol engineered Prince Sihanouk's overthrow, thereby setting the stage for the coming of the Khmer Rouge.

When Pol Pot came to power in 1975, the Khmer Rouge destroyed Preah Ang Dongka's pavilion and his statue as well. The present image, therefore, is not the one that followed King Norodom when he moved his capital to Phnom Penh in 1866, a statue which reputedly dated from the time of Angkor. Nonetheless, pre-Khmer Rouge photographs show that today's statue is a faithful copy, down to the myriad small Buddhas carved in relief on its torso, though it is painted black while the desecrated sculpture was gilded, at least it was at the time of its demolition.

Sources

Charles Meyer, *Derrière le sourire khmer*, Plon, 1971.

François Bizot, "La Consécration des statues et le culte de la mort," in *Recherches nouvelles sur le Cambodge*, École française d'Extrême-Orient, 1994. Bizot's article includes a photograph of Preah Ang Dongka taken in February 1975, prior to its destruction by the Khmer Rouge.

7. Saloth Sar Lived Here

This unpretentious traditional wooden house at #44 Street 242 (Oknha Peich Street) once belonged to Saloth Suong, older brother of Saloth Sar, who is better known to history by his *nom de guerre* Pol Pot. Their grandfather Phem had been a staunch royalist during the anti-French rebellion of 1885–86, and in return for his loyalty Phem's daughter Cheng – Saloth Suong and Saloth Sar's aunt – was given a position in the Royal Palace during King Norodom's reign. In the mid-1920s, Cheng's daughter Meak became a concubine to the future king Sisowath Monivong and bore him a son, Kusarak. (Prince Kusarak was thus a half-brother to Queen Sisowath Kossamak, the mother of King Norodom Sihanouk.) Meak later brought to the palace her sixteen-year-old cousin, Roeung, sister of Saloth Suong and Saloth Sar, and she too became a favorite of Monivong, one of the king's sixty-odd concubines. Thanks to his cousin Meak, Saloth Suong became an

Pol Pot's childhood home

52

official in the palace's protocol office. Sometime around 1930 he built his residence on Street 242, number 44 (Map 4, #75).

In 1934, nine-year-old Saloth Sar came to Phnom Penh from his native village in Kompong Thom province, and after a year studying at Wat Botum Vaddei, one of the city's oldest pagodas, he moved into his brother Suong's house on Street 242 and remained there until 1943. (Note that there are disagreements about dates related to Pol Pot's birth and childhood; some believe he was born in 1923 or 1924, rather than 1925, and some think he spent several years at Wat Botum, not just one.) Saloth Sar made frequent visits to his older sister Roeung and his cousin Meak in the Royal Palace, and being but a boy he was permitted entry into the compound of the king's concubines. There he learned the royal vocabulary. In fact, King Sihanouk would later recall that of all the Khmer Rouge only Saloth Sar could speak to him politely in the refined language of the palace.

The young Saloth Sar's footprints in Phnom Penh can also be traced to the present Norton University at #152 Street 118 (Map 3, #52), which in Sar's day was École Miche, a private Catholic primary school run by the Christian Brothers of Jean-Baptiste de la Salle. There he followed lessons in French, studied catechism, and learned about his Gallic ancestors. An unexceptional student, Sar took eight years to finish primary school, having failed twice along the way. (Many of the students at École Miche were Vietnamese, which may have been a source of Pol Pot's anti-Vietnamese attitude when he led the Khmer Rouge.) Later, when Saloth Sar became Pol Pot, he never publicly spoke of his days as a novice at Wat Botum, of his Catholic education at École Miche, or of his connections with the Royal Palace, passing himself off as a child of the paddy fields.

Incidentally, École Miche, which opened in 1911, was named in honor of Monsignor Jean-Claude Miche (1804–1873), the Vatican's first apostolic vicar of Cambodia. A staunch advocate of French intervention in both Vietnam and Cambodia, believing this would lead to increased conversions, this scholar-priest advised King Ang Duong to seek French protection from Siamese and Vietnamese encroachment in the 1850s, and he was instrumental in the establishment of the French protectorate in 1863. More than one hundred years later, in March 1970, after Prime Minister Lon Nol and Prince Sirik Matak ousted Prince Sihanouk, Cambodia's head of state, École Miche was closed by the new government, as were other non-Khmer language schools, notably Chinese schools, part of Lon Nol's racist policies. As the war against the Khmer Rouge progressed and refugees filled Phnom Penh, the former École Miche was used as a refugee camp. The school's Catholic church, Church of the Sacred Heart, was destroyed by Pol Pot's Khmer Rouge when they controlled Phnom Penh.

Saloth Sar left Phnom Penh in 1943 for a four-year stint at a new middle school, the Collège Norodom Sihanouk,* in Kompong Cham, where he continued his studies in French and enthusiastically practiced the violin. One of his schoolmates was Khieu Samphan, who would later be Democratic Kampuchea's head of state and who in 2014 was sentenced to life in prison for crimes against humanity by the Khmer Rouge tribunal (formally known as the Extraordinary Chambers in the Courts of Cambodia). Saloth Sar then returned to his brother's house in Phnom Penh for the 1947–1948 school year. Cambodia's first secondary school, inaugurated in 1935, was Lycée Sisowath on Norodom Avenue, still today a fine example of colonial architecture (Map 3, #62). Ever the mediocre student, Sar had failed the school's entrance exam in 1943 – hence his transfer to Kompong Cham – but was successful in 1947. He studied at Lycée Sisowath for that school year, all the while again staying with his brother Suong on Street 242.

At Lycée Sisowath, Sar befriended Ieng Sary, who would later be the Khmer Rouge's foreign minister and who died in March 2013 while, like Khieu Samphan, on trial for genocide and crimes against humanity. Sar was joined at Lycée Sisowath by Lon Non, one of his best buddies from their schooldays in Kompong Cham. Lon

---

* Shortly after his coronation, the French government gave Sihanouk 50,000 piasters to build a new residence at the resort on Bokor Mountain. Instead, Sihanouk chose to use the funds to construct the *collège* in Kompong Cham; it was a replacement for the school in Battambang which was lost when that province was ceded to Thailand by the French Vichy government – under Japanese pressure – in 1941.

Non would later become head of security in the government of his brother Lon Nol, who overthrew Prince Sihanouk and was president of Cambodia from 1970 to 1975. Lon Non himself was executed by his high school chum's Khmer Rouge shortly after they entered Phnom Penh in April 1975. (One report says that the Khmer Rouge chopped up Lon Non and Sirik Matak into small pieces which were then used as fertilizer for newly planted coconut palms around the Central Market. The palms allegedly never bore fruit.)

Saloth Sar endured more academic failures at Lyceé Sisowath, so in 1948 he moved on to the much less prestigious Phnom Penh Technical School. (When I started writing this book, those buildings still stood in the city's northern suburbs, on the left hand side of National Road 5 beyond Sokimex's petrol storage tanks, but they have recently been demolished and replaced by four-story apartments with shops on the ground floor, nondescript contemporary versions of the old Chinese shophouses.) The school was founded by the French in 1903 as the École Pratique and was renamed the Phnom Penh Technical School in 1942. While boarding at the school Sar studied carpentry, which was regarded as the easiest subject, though apparently he was more interested in reading novels than working with wood. Nonetheless, he did well enough that upon graduation in 1949 he received a highly coveted Cambodian government two-year scholarship to study radio technology in Paris, though this achievement may have been helped by his links to the palace and his support for the Democratic Party, which then led Cambodia, to the extent the French allowed them.

Saloth Sar's scholarship to France was revoked after he failed his exams for the second consecutive year, his priorities being geared more to radical political meetings than to his studies. When he returned to Phnom Penh in January 1953 after more than three years abroad, he stayed at his brother Suong's house for a month before leaving to join the underground resistance. Let me note here that had Saloth Sar not had those family connections with the Royal Palace, he would most likely not have come to Phnom Penh, obtained that scholarship to France, and become Pol Pot.

Saloth Sar's childhood home in Phnom Penh also served to hide another older brother, Saloth Chhay (who had also lived at the house during his school days), for a short time in June 1955. Chhay was the editor of an opposition newspaper, *Sammaki* ("Solidarity"), which ten days before had been banned by the Sihanouk government on the pretext of having opposed a Cambodian agreement with the US for military aid. Fearing arrest, Chhay escaped to his brother Suong's home, which the police were not allowed to enter since Suong was a palace official. The police kept close watch on Chhay from just outside the house until King Suramarit ordered his incarceration. Saloth Chhay was released from jail the following year.

Today the blue-washed house at #44 Street 242 is the only remaining wooden house in the area. Originally set high on wooden posts, the once-empty space below has been transformed into apartments. Three families live downstairs and one upstairs. One of the residents, a doctor, told me that all the families had come in 1979 following the Khmer Rouge's flight from the city. He did not know when the house was built or who had resided there previously. Indeed, he was surprised to hear that his house had once belonged to Pol Pot's older brother and that as a schoolboy Saloth Sar had lived there. I'm not sure whether he believed me.

As to that older brother who built the house, Saloth Suong survived the Khmer Rouge, all the while not knowing that his younger brother Sar headed it. After that dark age was over, Suong's wife, Chea Sami, who had once been a dancer at the palace, was instrumental in revitalizing the royal ballet troupe that her brother-in-law had demolished. Saloth Suong died in 1997, a year before his infamous brother. Suong's cousin Meak, who had brought him to Phnom Penh, died during the Khmer Rouge period. Prince Kusarak, Meak's son with King Monivong, became an officer in the Royal Cambodian Army; he died in 1975 under the Khmer Rouge. Saloth Suong and Saloth Sar's sister Roeung, who according to King Sihanouk himself and contrary to common accounts was not at King Monivong's side when he died in 1941, survived the Pol Pot era and returned to a life in the countryside of Kompong

Thom, marrying a local policeman. In a 1997 interview she told Seth Mydans of *The New York Times* that her "grandchildren refer to their great-uncle dismissively as 'a-Pot,' which means 'despicable Pot.' " Saloth Roeung died in 2005. And as for Pol Pot's brother Saloth Chhay, who in the early 1970s became an orderly for one of Lon Nol's generals, the warlord Prince Chantaraingsey, and also edited a newspaper owned by Lon Non, he collapsed and died while trudging north following the evacuation of Phnom Penh in April 1975, a forced departure ordered by his younger brother Pol Pot.

MENTION HAS BEEN MADE above of Sirik Matak and Lon Non, the latter Pol Pot's schooldays chum and brother of Lon Nol, Sirik Matak's co-conspirator in the overthrow of Prince Sihanouk in March 1970. Like Pol Pot's childhood home, the Phnom Penh houses of Sirik Matak and Lon Non (often disdainfully referred to as "Little Brother") still stand though they are of more recent dates and of very different styles.

Prince Sisowath Sirik Matak, minister of foreign affairs and of defense in the 1950s, was the main instigator of the March 18 coup against his cousin Sihanouk. ("He had hated me from childhood days because he thought his uncle, Prince Sisowath Monireth, should have been placed on the throne instead of me," wrote Prince Sihanouk in his memoirs, though for years Sirik Matak had been the prince's trusted ally, as had Lon Nol, whom Sihanouk often called *mon bras droit*, my right arm.) In fact, according to the historian David Chandler, on the day of the coup Sirik Matak had to force the prevaricating Lon Nol at gunpoint to sign a decree approving Sihanouk's ouster.

Sirik Matak once lived in the villa pictured below at #24 Street 462 (Map 3, #88; his family owned two other houses in the neighborhood), not far from Prince Sihanouk's Chamkar Mon Palace where, following the 1970 coup, Lon Nol would take up residence after fitting it out with an air raid shelter (Map 4, #87). Sirik Matak's villa today houses the renowned law firm Sciaroni & Associates. "Sirik Matak was a refined and haughty man who received visitors in his silk peignoir and lived in a princely residence filled with sumptuous

Sirik Matak's residence

furniture and marble statues," according to Sihanouk's biographer Jean-Marie Cambacérès. It may well have been in this house that a high-ranking meeting took place on the night of March 16 to final-ize the coup against Sihanouk. "We have gone too far now to turn back," one of the plotters reportedly said, which might lead one to believe some were having second thoughts. Two years later, in 1972, partly through the influence of his younger brother Lon Non, Lon Nol turned against Sirik Matak, who resigned from the government. The following year, Lon Non had Sirik Matak's house surrounded by heavily armed troops, ostensibly for the prince's protection but in fact to isolate Sirik Matak in a form of house arrest. American pres-sure on Lon Nol led to Sirik Matak's release.

Sirik Matak also owned a villa at #50 Norodom Boulevard (Map 3, #61). This house, which has seen significant architectural changes, was originally designed by the French architect Henri Chatel, who worked in Cambodia from 1949 to 1961 and also designed the National Bank of Cambodia on Norodom Boulevard, two apartment buildings for the bank's personnel (see Chapter 20), and the Ministry of Defense on Russian Federation Boulevard. Chatel also supervised the construction of Phnom Penh's Notre Dame Cathedral, which was later dynamited by the Khmer Rouge.

Sirik Matak's house at #50 Norodom Boulevard

As for Lon Non, interior minister in his brother Lon Nol's government, responsible for carrying out his brother's brutal, spineless massacre of Vietnamese civilians in Phnom Penh, involved in heroin trafficking and in selling Cambodian military weaponry to his communist enemies (from which he reportedly raised $90 million), and one of seven on the Khmer Rouge's list of "arch-traitors" destined for hasty execution, he lived at #1 Col de Monteiro Street

"Little Brother's" House at #1 Col de Monteiro Street

(St. 72, see Map 2, #14). The house is at the street's end on the corner of Street 91, near Chruoy Changvar Circle with its knotted gun statue. The villa, pictured above, was designed in 1970 by Chhim Sun Fong, who also worked on the Chenla Theater and who died during the Khmer Rouge period. Lon Non, however, might not have passed many nights in his new house as he reportedly stayed most of the time with his brother Lon Nol at Chamkar Mon Palace. In March 1973 the palace was bombed by Captain So Photra, an air force pilot and husband of Sihanouk's daughter Princess Botum Bopha, who had been imprisoned by the Lon Nol regime following the 1970 coup. Forty-seven people were killed in the blast, but Lon Nol and Lon Non were unharmed. So Photra eventually escaped to China, where he was reunited with his wife when she was exiled there in November 1973. At Sihanouk's suggestion, they returned to Cambodia with their four children in 1975. All died under the Khmer Rouge, for which Sihanouk would never forgive himself.

Sources

Philip Short, *Pol Pot: The History of a Nightmare*, Holt, 2004.

David Chandler, *Brother Number One*, Westview, 1999.

David Chandler, *The Tragedy of Cambodian History*, Silkworm Books, 1993 [Yale, 1991].

Ben Kiernan, *How Pol Pot Came to Power*, Yale, 2004.

Julio A. Jeldres, *The Royal House of Cambodia*, Monument Books, 2003.

Seth Mydan's article appeared in the August 6, 1997, issue of the *The New York Times*.

Helen Grant Ross and Darryl Collins, *Building Cambodia: New Khmer Architecture*, Key, 2006.

Norodom Sihanouk, *Shadow Over Angkor*, Volume One of the *Memoirs of His Majesty King Norodom Sihanouk of Cambodia*, from the original transcript of *The Cup of Dregs*, edited, introduced and with new material by Ambassador Julio A. Jeldres, Monument Books, 2005.

Jean-Marie Cambacérès, *Sihanouk, le roi insubmersible*, Le Cherche Midi, 2013.

8. The Mysterious Frenchman of Wat Phnom

Any guidebook will tell you that the tall stupa atop the hill of Wat Phnom (Map 2, #34) contains the remains of King Ponhea Yat (c. 1402–1471), considered to be the monarch who brought Cambodia's capital to Phnom Penh in the 1430s or 1440s. Scattered about the top and the eastern half of the hill are a number of other stupas of varying size, memorials to forgotten members of the kingdom's royalty.

However, unknown to tourists, guidebook writers, and, surprisingly, the numerous authors who have recorded their impressions of the site since the early days of the French protectorate is that among these entombed royals is a solitary Frenchman. His remains lie just to the left of the main stairway leading up the hill's eastern slope to the pagoda above, in a masonry tomb that, at least the part which emerges from ground and vegetation, has received a rather incongruous baby blue paint job (Map 2, #37). The site is hidden by newly placed flowering plants, but parting the foliage in front of the tomb reveals a marble slab which reads, in French, "J. Fourcros, Principal Agent of the Farm, died the 4th of November 1882 at the age of 37 years."

J. Fourcros' tombstone

Who was Monsieur Fourcros and how did he receive the honor of being interred among princes? The brief references to Fourcros that I came across in Gregor Muller's deliciously researched description of the early years of the French protectorate, *Colonial Cambodia's "Bad Frenchmen,"* mention him as being an impoverished Frenchman who arrived in Cambodia in 1876. The following year he was given work by a notorious French adventurer – and failed merchant, manufacturer, teacher, and planter – Frédéric Thomas-Caraman, in his recently established brickworks. Once Fourcros was employed, he repeatedly handed Caraman scraps of paper asking him "to please have the goodness to give [me] one piaster so that I can eat, I have nothing to buy food."

During his frequent absences from the capital, Caraman put Fourcros to other use, asking him to watch over his infant son while ensuring "that the mother eat in the European manner." Perhaps Fourcros received a few of his requested piasters in exchange for instructing Caraman's nameless Cambodian concubine proper knife and fork etiquette.

Or perhaps not. Letters now in French archives show that Fourcros repeatedly claimed Caraman owed him money, while for his part Caraman blamed his brickworks' problems on his assistant's incompetence. In fact, Caraman's brick factory did not last long and it was deserted by the following spring, the machinery invaded by vegetation and Fourcros and the other workers gone.

Our marginal friend reappears in the archival records in 1881 in connection with the French merchant house Vandelet, Dussutour, and Faraut, which in July of that year had gained from King Norodom the kingdom's opium concession, outbidding by three times the Chinese who had previously held the monopoly. Octave Vandelet then hired Fourcros and other "destitute local whites" to sniff around the city and ensure no one was cooking up or smoking opium other than theirs, regularly beating and blackmailing anyone they caught doing so. Fourcros' work with Vandelet permitted the title on his gravestone, Principal Agent of the Farm, the last word referring to Vandelet's contract for the opium concession.

J. Foucros' tombstone prior to the 2013 landscaping

A visit to the National Archives (located behind the National Library, it was largely spared damage during the Khmer Rouge era, though the ground floor where newspapers were kept was used as a piggery; see Map 2, #27) revealed the next of Fourcros' exploits, this one with Auguste Patou, another opium agent. On August 12, 1882, the two wrote to *Monsieur le Représentant du Protectorat* asking him to forward their request for the free of charge acquisition of ninety hectares of unused land in Prey Krebas province for the raising of livestock. (Prey Krebas is now in northeastern Takeo province.) The process was impressively speedy, and on September 20 Fourcros and Patou were in possession of a letter from the royal cabinet granting them the ninety hectares for twenty-five years, "His Majesty the king of Cambodia desirous of encouraging in his kingdom the raising and commerce of livestock." What happened to that venture I do not know (though when Patou died in 1894 his estate included land rights, all of which he willed to Nou, his Cambodian concubine), but six weeks after receiving the land Fourcros was dead and buried in that fine grave on the slope of Grandmother Penh's hill.

For many months I wondered what Fourcros had suddenly died of at the age of 37, and how his remains merited the singular distinction of being interred on our city's iconic hill rather than in a local Catholic graveyard or the French cemetery in Saigon. Then I was fortunate enough to be put in contact with Gregor Muller, who had written the book about those "bad Frenchmen."

Dr. Muller promptly responded to my queries, saying that it gave him pleasure "to see that there are others out there interested in some of these obscure characters of the early colonial period." His database of the Overseas Archives in Aix-en-Provence, France, includes an entry dated November 4, 1882, when Vandelet went to meet Representative of the Protectorate Augustin Fourès and inform him that Jules Fourcros, ". . . agent of the Opium Farm, residing in Phnom Penh, of an unknown father and Victoire, residing in Toulouse, has died in Phnom Penh on the 4th of November 1882, at one o'clock in the afternoon . . ."

The question of Fourcros' cause of death and unusual burial spot was answered in another document from the Aix-en-Provence archives, a letter from Fourès to his boss, Governor of Cochinchina Le Myre de Vilers. Fourès was reporting on a number of deaths from cholera in Phnom Penh that week, including that of Fourcros. Fourcros was already in a weakened state of health, suffering from severe anemia and chronic dysentery. Thus, when the cholera struck at 4 a.m. that November 4, the unfortunate Fourcros survived for only a few hours, expiring at one o'clock that afternoon.

Before dying, Fourcros asked to be buried at the foot of Wat Phnom's hill. Fourès granted him his request, and to justify this decision to the governor he explained that the protectorate's cemetery in Phnom Penh was still under preparation. Moreover, Fourès added somewhat defensively, he wanted to avoid the calumnies of any spiteful individuals who may have seen in his refusal a reproach on the dying man. Fourès thus approved an "out of view" burial site at the foot of the hill, and he allowed the inhumation to proceed, though he refused Vandelet's request that he deliver a funerary speech, suggesting that Vandelet give the encomium himself. At the time, Wat Phnom was a thatched structure in disrepair and the hillside was overgrown, so Fourcros' grave may indeed have been at least partially hidden from view. In any event, the issue was decided

Fourcros' tomb is behind the stupa on the left, a man standing in front. Considerably more of the tomb can be seen in this early photo than today. Though undated, the photo was clearly taken after the pagoda's 1894 restoration.

in a matter of hours, and Jules Fourcros, a marginal colonial at best, was interred among royalty at six o'clock that same evening.

The mystery of the Frenchman of Wat Phnom had now been solved, though a gruesome murder or despondent suicide might have made for a better story than a sad death from a virulent disease.

Let us leave Monsieur Fourcros and his grave with this footnote: On August 1, 2006, a skeleton was dug up a short distance to the right of Fourcros' tomb during reconstruction of the pagoda's main stairway. When I queried the keeper of Sambo, the elephant who until recently was in daily attendance at the foot of the *phnom* for tourists desirous of a leisurely ride round the hill (sadly, 51-year-old Sambo had to be retired in January 2012 due to a serious foot injury), he told me the skeleton was found about three meters deep under the present second and third steps of that stairway, on the left side near the balustrade's naga (snake) heads. Wary about disturbing the bones – or more precisely their spirit – the workers reburied them at the same spot, and a ceremony was held, attended by the city's governor, or so I was told.

My friend the elephant keeper speculated that the skeleton was that of someone, perhaps a prisoner or criminal, who was killed

Fourcros' tomb at center left, behind the stupa. The skeleton was found under the second and third steps, to the right of the sign. Flowering plants now obscure the view of the tomb.

and buried at the foot of the hill in order to protect the pagoda atop. This was something of a custom in the old days, he said. (This brought to memory the rumors that spread through the city a few years ago that during the construction of the new Monivong Bridge men in a black car with tinted windows kidnapped two garment workers as they were leaving their factory, tossed the poor women alive into the bridge's foundations, then covered them forever with poured cement, protection for the span and all who pass over it.)

You may wonder whether the skeleton found at the foot of Wat Phnom could be that of Monsieur Fourcros, but the fifteen or so meters between his tomb and the stairway seems too great a distance for gravity or erosion to have moved his bones there.

Source

Gregor Muller, ed (2006), *Colonial Cambodia's "Bad Frenchmen": The rise of French rule and the life of Thomas Caraman, 1840–87*, Routledge, 2006.

9. Le Monument aux Morts

Visitors walking through the forecourt of the National Museum (Map 3, #64) will notice on either side of the museum's main doors a bronze elephant head with tusks painted white, the one on the left still holding in its trunk a lotus bud, symbol of peace. These caparisoned elephant heads once graced the massive war memorial France built to commemorate soldiers who died on the battlefields of World War I.

Two more elephant crania rest in the garden on the north side of the museum, and opposite the second are other pieces of the monument. The memorial was blown up by the Khmer Rouge, presumably out of objection to things colonial rather than for the sculpture's metal content.

Roger Spooner

The memorial had three sections, first a tall square stone base with an elephant at each corner and a seven-headed hooded naga above each elephant. On the base behind the elephants and nagas (one of which is on display in the National Museum) and rising above them was the bell shaped body of the monument, of which we only have those pieces in the museum garden.

These pieces, about half of the original middle section, depict a Cambodian scene of offering. When moving counterclockwise from the left, a sarong wrapped woman holds a child in her left arm, sugar palms in the background. The mother has the cropped hair of married women of the time, while her child has a shaved head but for a forelock tuft and a long tress above his ear. The woman's right arm reaches out to touch a three-layered parasol of the sort used to shade noble pates from the tropical sun (Figure 1). The parasol is one of two, each held by a mustachioed bearer wrapped in a sarong. Paddy rice grows behind them (Figure 2).

The parasols protected a now departed nobleman who had been standing and offering a plate of fruit. Kneeling in front of him is an acephalic woman whose now severed arms once stretched high with an offering of lotus blossoms. In the background a river, perhaps the mighty Mekong, flows through a forest. Next comes a kneeling woman bowing low, hands pressed together in *sompeah*, her silver bowl carrying an offering of fruit. Above her bended back another baby is held out by the hands of its now gone mother (Figure 3).

These worshippers are giving thanks to the two soldiers of the third and topmost section of the memorial, which did not survive the Khmer Rouge's desecration. The two warriors stood tall atop the monument, a Frenchman in his greatcoat and a Cambodian holding olive branches in his raised hands.

Engraved on the eastern and western sides of the now gone base of the monument were the names of 33 French government officials and other colonials who perished during the war, while inscribed on the northern and southern sides were the names of 155 Cambodian soldiers who had made the ultimate sacrifice, including one of royal blood, Prince Sisowath Leng, who died in the waning days of

Figure 1   Figure 2

Figure 3

the conflict. King Sisowath, the prince's father, had indeed encouraged his subjects to volunteer for service in the war effort, either as soldiers or workers. Fewer than 2,000 followed their king's request, considerably fewer than the French had hoped for. Among them was Sisowath's son and successor, Prince Monivong, though he was not allowed near the front lines. Reports tell that the soldiers fought bravely on the western front and in the Balkans.

The monument was designed by the French sculptor Paul Ducuing (1867–1949), who also cast the gold-plated copper statues

Monument aux Morts at about the
time of its inauguration in 1925

of King Sisowath and King Monivong that stand beside the king's
seat in the Throne Hall of the Royal Palace.

The war memorial's inaugural festivities, which lasted three
days from February 27, 1925, opened with a banquet and ball in
honor of the veterans. At the monument's unveiling on March 1,
King Sisowath gave a five-minute speech. He was followed by *Résident Supérieur* François-Marius Baudoin, France's highest official
in Cambodia, who pronounced that the war to end all wars had
"sealed in blood" the bond between Gaul and Khmer.

Then came the march past: French legionnaires and marines,
colonial infantry, sailors from the fleet, Cambodian and Vietnamese
sharpshooters, native guards, royal guards, bemedalled veterans of
the Great War, and armored cars and tanks, while a squadron of
military planes passed overhead. They were followed by the civilian
element of the parade: school children first then ethnic minorities
including "Annamites," Chinese, twenty Burmese from Battambang,
twenty-five "Malays" from Kompong Cham, twenty-five Lao and as
many Phnongs from Kratié, twenty Kouys from Kompong Thom,

and twenty Khas from Steung Treng. Last was a squad of "Malay" cyclists followed by scores of caparisoned elephants.

That evening the people of Phnom Penh were treated to dances, theater performances, and an open-air film, while the ruling elite savored a gala dinner at the *Résidence Supérieure*, with royal dancers providing cultural entertainment.

The monument stood not far from the present French Embassy, in the small park bordered by Monivong Boulevard, Chruoy Changvar Circle (with its knotted gun monument), Rue de France (St. 47), and Oknha Dekchoey Street (St. 76). Today, the original site of the Monument aux Morts is a garden (Map 2, #16) dedicated to Léopold Sédar Senghor, the first president of Senegal, in recognition of his work in establishing the Association of Francophone Cities, of which Phnom Penh is one. Or perhaps it used to be one: a 2004 study by the International Francophone Organization concluded that only 0.3 percent of Cambodia's population could speak French, though no doubt the figure for Phnom Penh would be higher.

The memorial in the distance as seen from a biplane in 1929; the French cemetery was among the trees in front, and the grandiose De Vernéville Bridge – commonly referred to at the time as the "Dollars Bridge" because of its substantial construction costs – crossed the canal. Like the monument and the cemetery, the bridge and the canal are now gone.

10. Thorani, the Earth Goddess

At the rather complicated intersection of Charles de Gaulle Boulevard, Street 182, Monireth Boulevard, and Czechoslovakia Boulevard (Map 1, #10), stands a statue of an inspiringly clad woman, her hands wringing a fountain of water from her ankle-length hair. At her side is a crocodile, mouth open wide. She is Thorani, the Earth Goddess, responsible for the planet's fertility, and also known to Cambodians as Neang Kong Hing.

While Sakyamuni, the future Buddha, was meditating under a boddhi tree (*ficus religiosa*, also known as bo, pipal, and sacred fig) on the eve of his enlightenment, determined to find a state

Thorani and her crocodile at the end
of Charles de Gaulle Street

beyond the cycle of birth, death, and rebirth, Mara, the evil god of desire and king of devils, devised several ploys to interrupt the future Buddha's reflection, afraid that enlightenment would free Sakyamuni – and potentially all humans – not only from desire and passion but also from Mara's control.

First, Mara unleashed nine storms, of wind, rain, rocks, weapons, live coals, burning ashes, sand, mud, and darkness. Mucalinda, the king of snakes, then rose and spread his seven-headed hood over the meditating Sakyamuni, protecting him from the downpours. Next, Mara sent his three beautiful daughters, Lust, Pleasure, and Discontent, to dance sensuously before Sakyamuni and seduce him out of his pensive state, but Sakyamuni paid them no heed. Finally, Mara in despair ordered his army of devils and monsters to assault Sakyamuni. Sakyamuni, still seated in the lotus position under the boddhi tree, touched the ground with the fingers of his right hand thus calling on the Earth to bear witness to the firmness of his resolve, to his steadfastness in resisting Mara's temptations, and to his consequent victory over evil. The Earth responded in the form of the beautiful Thorani (whose name in fact means "earth" in Pali and Sanskrit). She rose from below, let down her long tresses, and then wrung from them a flood of water replete with crocodiles, sharks, and swordfish. Thorani's waters and aquatic forces swallowed up Mara's monsters, and the king of devils had to admit defeat. The Earth trembled, thus showing recognition of Sakyamuni's victory, and Mara withdrew. Sakyamuni was now free to continue his meditation, which he did throughout the night, and at dawn he awoke from ignorance. He had achieved enlightenment. At the age of 35, he had attained buddhahood. The Buddha would continue to preach for many years, but he had destroyed *samsara*, the cycle of birth, death, and rebirth, and at his death he reached nirvana.

In Cambodia, Mara, his nine storms, his three daughters, and his army of demons symbolize our dark side and the evil actions done in present and previous lives. The *Maravijaya*, the Buddha's Victory over Mara, represents victory over earthly desires and attachments, thus breaking the cycle of birth and rebirth and leading the way to nirvana.

Maravijaya, or the Victory over Mara.
On the left, Mara on his elephant leads the attack of his forces of evil against the meditating Buddha, seated under the boddhi tree. Below him, Thorani rises from the earth and from her tresses wrings a flood of water and crocodiles which drown and devour Mara's army of demons. Above them, on the right, Mara himself salutes the Buddha and admits defeat. Wat Put Kosacha, Rue de France (St. 47, see Map 2, #20)

Thorani is thus the main protector of the Buddha and she consequently is frequently represented in Khmer art, though not always as scantily dressed as on her aforementioned statue. She is sometimes depicted on *sima* or boundary stones, eight of which

Thorani wrings her hair on a *sima* stone at Wat Phorta Pi Rangsei. (Map 2, #19)

She does the same on the exterior of the back wall of Wat Srah Chak. (Map 2, #25)

and in the *vihara* of Wat Phnom. (Map 2, #36)

are placed around the most sacred area of the temple, usually the *vihara*, the main prayer hall, thereby offering her protection. The image of Thorani loosening her hair and drowning Mara's monsters is frequently portrayed in pagodas, often in murals on the rear wall of the *vihara*, behind the main altar. Although a female earth deity

Thorani on a Lon Nol era anti-North Vietnamese poster. The caption
calls for the destruction of all "thmil," a Buddhist term meaning
nonbelievers which Lon Nol used to refer to his communist enemies.

appeared in Buddhist iconography in India long ago, today Thorani
and her story appear to be particular to Theravada Buddhism in
Southeast Asia.

Posters from Lon Nol times recreated the *Maravijaya*, with
Mara on a tank rather than an elephant and his army of demons
replaced by monstrous North Vietnamese and Viet Cong soldiers
in conical hats emblazed with the communist red star. The soldiers
charge the meditating Sakyamuni from the left while, below,
Thorani produces that flood from her hair and, on the right, her
waters engulf the enemy and her crocodiles prepare to feast on any
surviving VC, some of whom now *somphea* to Sakyamuni.

Thorani's statue at that Phnom Penh intersection was erected in the early 1960s on orders of the city's mayor at the time that nearby Olympic Stadium was being built. Thorani is associated with female mediums, who keep figures of her on their altars. In January 1972 one of these mediums, a woman named Kaye, climbed upon Thorani while possessed. On the statue, she sang, danced, and sent messages from beyond to the mass of people who came to see her. So many came, in fact, that eventually the police arrived and escorted her away.

I wonder if the descendants of those mediums have found another place for their encounters. I recently spent most of a morning watching Thorani and the traffic before her, but not one faithful approached to burn incense, place a flower, or mouth a prayer.

Sources

Elizabeth Guthrie, "Outside the Sima," *UDAYA, Journal of Khmer Studies,* Number 2, 2001, pp. 7–18.

Donald S. Lopez, Jr., *The Story of Buddhism,* Harper, 2001.

An appropriate symbol

11. Signs of France

*B*aguettes notwithstanding, remembrances of the days of the French in Phnom Penh seem to disappear year by year. Though some buildings of those days remain, notably around the post office plaza, others, like the *École Professionelle* on Street 82, have recently met the wrecking ball and still others, such as the *Hôtel Renakse*, are at serious risk of following suit. Then there is the former *Grand Hôtel Manolis* on the riverside, once the city's finest hostelry, which has been subjected to an appalling makeover; Kentucky Fried Chicken should be ashamed of itself (see Chapter 2).

There also remain written remembrances of French times though they too are becoming less common, French being replaced by Khmer and English. *Rue*, for example, has given way to "Street" on most of Phnom Penh's new street signs, though with some notable exceptions, such as this one:

Nonetheless, when walking the city streets, look closely at the buildings on either side and you might see fading signs which reflect that bygone era. Sometimes you will see a name, sometimes a bit of advertising. Emblems on wrought iron gates or on escutcheons above a window betray the identity of those who once lived there or the original function of the building. And some later French wording illustrates the language's continued influence in the years following Cambodia's independence.

The oldest bit of French calligraphy on public display is no doubt the letter *N* on the glass door panels of the all-metal Napoleon Pavilion (Map 3, #69), complete with cupola and clock, inside the Royal Palace. The letter stood for Emperor Napoleon III, who had the prefabricated building constructed for the comfort of his wife, Empress Eugénie, during her visit to Ismailia, Egypt, for the inauguration of the Suez Canal in 1869. There is some question as to how the "Iron House" wound up in King Norodom's palace. Some say that having served its purpose, the pavilion was given to the king by Emperor Napoleon himself, though there apparently is no documented proof of such. Paul Doumer, the governor-general of Indochina from 1897 to 1902, wrote in his memoirs that King Norodom purchased the structure. A more common view is that the building was a present of the Third Republic, the government that followed the overthrowing of Napoleon III, which wanted to get rid of the encumbrance. The gift allegedly dates to 1876 (which would write off the notion of Napoleon III being the source of the gift, as he died in 1873), though that too is a matter of question. In any event, there was no need for King Norodom to change Emperor Napoleon's royal *N* on what was said to be the king's favorite building in the palace.

Glass door panels of the palace's Napoleon Pavilion, with the emperor's *N* also used for Norodom

Also inside the Royal Palace, the inscription on the base of King Norodom's statue in front of the Silver Pagoda should be mentioned; translated, it reads "To Norodom I King of Cambodia, His grateful mandarins and people, 1860." That date, however, is clearly an error, as you can discover in Chapter 17. On the statue itself are the names of the French artist and caster. Still dating to the 19th century is the inscription on the tombstone of Jules Fourcros, described in Chapter 8. There are also the inscriptions on the seven gravestones kept in the compound of the French Embassy, the oldest of which dates to 1889, all that remains from the now destroyed French era cemetery, as is reported in Chapter 16.

In 1907, due to French pressure, Siam returned to Cambodia the three provinces of Siem Reap, Sisophon, and Battambang, which the Siamese had annexed in 1795. The event was commemorated in a monument erected two years later on the southern flank of Wat Phnom's hill (Map 2, #35). Designed and completed in France by Théodore Rivière, here a regally gilded King Sisowath presides. To His Majesty's right, three Angkorian *apsara*, or celestial divinities, representing the three returned provinces, bow in homage and present offerings to their king. To his left, a Cambodian soldier holds a billowing *tricolore*, symbolizing France's protection, above a stele on which is noted the historic event; at the end of the flag are the letters *RF*, for *République Française*. Below the inscription, hidden when the grasses have not been trimmed, is Durosau de Gulsand, French consul at Battambang, who died there in 1903. To the left, a stone stele inscribed in French commemorates the treaty,

The monument on Wat Phnom's hill recognizing the treaty with Siam, in which the provinces of Siem Reap, Sisophon, and Battambang were returned to Cambodia

while another to the right does the same in Khmer. The present statue of King Sisowath, it should be noted, is of concrete and dates to the 1990s; Rivière's original bronze statue was removed to the National Museum following the Sirik Matak-Lon Nol coup of 1970, which perhaps saved the monument from Khmer Rouge desecration.

Also from the days of the protectorate, the *PT* above the windows of the city's main post office (Map 2, #45), built in the 1890s, stands for *Postes et Télégraphe*.

PT, above a post office window

Nearby, both the gates to Van's Restaurant and the floor of the main dining hall carry the monogram of the *Banque de l'Indochine*, which the building once housed (Map 2, #44). The bank was established in Cambodia in 1890 mainly to serve Chinese merchants and the French, and the present edifice was built in the early 1900s to replace the original one. Inside, you can still see the three vaults. Their reinforced steel doors were made by the Parisian firm *Fichet*, and should you be in the market for one such portal, the company's address is given: *43, Rue de Richelieu, Paris.*

The National Museum of Cambodia opened in 1920 largely due to the efforts of George Groslier, who designed the building and was the museum's director until 1942. Three of the building's

BIC, for *Banque de l'Indochine*, still on the gates and the main floor of what is now Van's Restaurant, on the corner of streets 102 and 13

On the reinforced steel doors of the bank's vaults,
now the restaurant's administrative office

original roll-up metal shutters remain, two on the west or back wall and one on the south, but only one on the back wall retains the label of the makers, the French company *Peyrichou et Malan*, which still exists near the city of *Pau*.

Roul Mieu, or "rolls better," on the metal shutter
of a National Museum window

Recently resurrected from the museum's storerooms, no doubt to mark the 100th anniversary of the outbreak of World War I, and placed on its front terrace is a bronze memorial which consists of two entwined wreaths of oak and olive leaves surrounding the following words delivered by France's Marshal Joseph Joffre on September 6, 1914, to rally French troops retreating from invading German forces in the early weeks of the war:

> At this moment when a battle for the preservation of the nation is taking place, it is imperative for all to remember that this is not the time to look back; all efforts must be devoted to attacking and repulsing the enemy. An army that can no longer advance must, cost what may, hold the conquered land and die rather than retreat. In the present circumstances, no weakness can be tolerated.

Inspired by Joffre's stirring lines, the French army stopped the German advance at the battle of the Marne (September 5–12), forcing the invaders to abandon their march on Paris and leading to four years of slaughterous trench warfare on the western front. Joffre (1852–1931), retired from the army in 1919. In 1921 he embarked on an official mission to several southeast and east

Asian nations to express France's thanks for their contributions to the allies' victory. The memorial was originally placed at Phnom Penh's *Hôtel de Ville*, or town hall (on Street 106 between streets 13 and 19, the building still exists and is the Cambodia Securities Exchange; see Map 2, #46), and commemorated a visit to the city by Marshal Joffre, as the inscription on the reverse side explains: "During a mission to the Far East, Marshal Joffre, the glorious victor of the Marne, stayed at this town hall on the 13th, 14th, and 18th of December 1921." The memorial was designed by the French sculptor Paul Ducuing (1867–1949), whose other works in the city include the monument to the dead of World War I and the statues of King Sisowath and King Monivong in the Throne Hall of the Royal Palace (see Chapter 9).

The National Library on Daun Penh Street (St. 92, see Map 2, #27) was inaugurated in 1925 and still maintains its French designation, *Bibliothèque*. On the right hand wall of the library's entrance porch, a sign above the door reads "Force binds for a time, ideas join forever," words attributed to François Baudoin, France's *résident supérieur* in Cambodia from 1914 to 1927.

Behind the *Bibliothèque*, the ground floor of the *Archives Nationales* (Map 2, #27), where newspapers were kept, was used as a pig sty by the Khmer Rouge, but almost all the documents on the floors above survived that sad era.

The National Library, which dates to 1925

"Force binds for a time, ideas join forever"

The National Archives

The *Hôtel Le Royal* (Map 2, #26), also on Daun Penh Street, was built in 1929 and renovated in the 1990s.

The Khmer Rouge in 1976 destroyed Phnom Penh's Roman Catholic Notre Dame Cathedral both to recover building materials (the iron reinforcing rods were taken to the city's small smelting

works where they were turned into nails and agricultural implements) and to thumb their nose at Vietnam, as the great majority of the church's flock was Vietnamese. Among the thousands of workers involved in the cathedral's demolition were idealistic students who had been pursuing their education in France and had returned to Cambodia to help advance the revolution. Few of them survived those miserable years. All that remains of the cathedral, which was located on Monivong Boulevard where Telecom Cambodia now resides, at the west end of the esplanade that begins at Wat Phnom's hill, are a couple of bells, now displayed on the front terrace of the National Museum, just in front of the aforementioned memorial to Marshal Joffre. The inscription on the bell dubbed *Angeline* says that it was blessed in 1954 by Monsignor Chabalier, the bishop of Cambodia at that time. The cathedral itself was inaugurated in 1955. The bishop's house next door is now the seat of the Phnom Penh Municipal Government, but the wall in front retains its crosses.

In the museum's interior courtyard there is another bell, a much older one, with reliefs of Jesus on the cross and the Virgin Mary, and

Angeline, cast at the Paccard foundry in Annecy,
now on display at the National Museum

an inscription naming its manufacturer: *Eugène Baudoun, fondeur á Marseille, 1883*. Photography prohibited.

PN is inscribed on the front gate of a colonial era residence on the corner of streets 178 and 19 (Map 3, #63). These initials announce that Penn Nouth (1906–1985), veteran Cambodian statesman and seven times prime minister, once resided in this house, where today you can degust South American fare at The Latin Quarter Bar and Restaurant.

The former *Hôtel International* on the corner of streets 130 and 13 (Map 3, #54) was previously *Au Petit Paris*, a Cambodian version of the great French department stores. Before World War I, the store was owned by a German who had to leave Cambodia following the outbreak of hostilities between Germany and France.

Penh Nouth's residence, on the
corner of streets 178 and 19

Formerly the *Hôtel International,* on the corner of streets 130 and 13

Bijouterie (jeweler) and *Horlogerie* (watchmaker)
inside the lobby of the old *Hôtel International*

It was later owned by a gentleman of Indian descent who was the father-in-law of Son Sann, for many years a leading politician.

Inside the *Hôtel International*'s lobby were a *Bijouterie* (jeweler) and an *Horlogerie* (watchmaker), as one can still read today, while between them a shop sold *Nouveautés Français* (novelties from France), though these last words are now hidden by a sign. In 1971 a night in one of the hotel's twenty-two air conditioned rooms went for between $4.55 and $6.50, while the twelve fan-cooled rooms cost $3.30. The building is now divided into private dwellings and ground floor shops.

One can barely make out *Citroën* on what used to be that company's assembly plant on Street 82, in what was the predominantly French part of the city.

Former *Citroën* assembly plant, now divided into private residences

Still supported by the French government and staffed largely by French teachers, the *Lycée Français René Descartes* was established in 1951 and is the oldest international school in Phnom Penh (Map 2, #28), though it has lost much of its grounds to the adjacent National University of Management. One morning in 1974, as the Khmer Rouge were tightening the noose around Phnom Penh, KR artillery shells struck the school's compound, killing ten children. Following their takeover of the city, the KR used part of the *lycée* to lodge the army's troupe of dancers, singers, and musicians. More notoriously, the KR used it as a base for their security police, *santebal*, giving it the code name K-33. The KR planted a forest of banana trees in the *lycée*'s courtyard, where they also raised pigs and chickens.

Hôpital Calmette at #3 Monivong Boulevard was opened in 1959 as a state-of-the-art private research hospital, subsidized and managed by France (Map 2, #21). The hospital is named after the French bacteriologist and immunologist Albert Calmette (1863–1933), who founded the Pasteur Institute in Saigon in 1891 and later developed a vaccine against tuberculosis. During the Pol Pot period, *Hôpital Calmette* was rechristened Hospital P1 and catered to the children of the Khmer Rouge elite. They were cared for with modern techniques, equipment, and antibiotics. The hospital's director was the daughter of Ieng Sary, the Khmer Rouge's foreign minister who died in detention in March 2013 while awaiting trial for crimes committed by that regime, and Ieng Thirith, the KR's minister of social affairs, released in 2012 from the same due to dementia. Keep in mind that during those dark days the Cambodian peasants in whose name the Khmer Rouge had undertaken their revolution had but the most rudimentary medical services. Since many trained medical personnel of the old regime had been eliminated, "doctors" were often poorly educated soldiers appointed to their positions with virtually no training, and the "nurses" of the revolution were often illiterate teenage girls, which resulted in the preventable deaths of thousands. In addition, "hospitals" in rural areas had little medicine or equipment. The water from green coconuts was used as intravenous serum. Proper medicine could only be obtained on the black market in exchange for valuables such as gold links from a hidden necklace or bracelet. After the Khmer Rouge were ousted from the city, *Hôpital Calmette* became Revolutionary Hospital and was reserved exclusively for high level government officials of the communist regime and their Vietnamese associates. Today, it is considered to be Cambodia's finest government owned hospital.

Next to *Hôpital Calmette* and dating to 1953, *Institut Pasteur du Cambodge* (Map 2, #23) was first located on the Chruoy Changvar peninsula on the site of a veterinary station. The institute there was destroyed by the Khmer Rouge. Many of its personnel were killed. It was reopened at the Monivong Boulevard site in 1986. The original *Institut Pasteur* was founded in France in 1887 by the

Hôpital Calmette

chemist and microbiologist Louis Pasteur (1822–1895), noted for his work in pasteurization and vaccines. *Institut Pasteur* is dedicated to research in biology, diseases, and vaccines.

Still *en français*, but things are changing, as can be seen
by the sign on the right, "Laboratory – Vaccination"

The 1960s and early '70s were the heyday of Cambodian cinema. Over 350 films were shot, many with such superstars as Kong Sam Oeun, Chea Yuthorn, Som Van Soudany, and Vichara Dany. The city at that time boasted at least thirty-one cinemas, but the only one still functioning as a movie theater today is the *Ciné Lux*, which dates to the 1950s (Map 3, #60). The first public showing of Prince Sihanouk's film *Apsara* took place here in May 1966.

The *Ciné Lux,* on the corner of Monivong
Boulevard and Street 154

Look up when you walk along Street 130 between Norodom
Boulevard and Street 51 (Map 3, #51). On the left there was once a
private clinic, *Clinique Docteur Bessière,* which dates, I believe, to
the 1950s.

Clinique Docteur Bessière, now private
apartments and businesses, Street 130

Keep looking up, and on the other side of St. 130 from the
former clinic, on the corner of street 51, you will see several metal
advertising signs, including ones for *Melia* and *Bastos* cigarettes,
and another for *CKT,* though I can but guess as to what those three
letters signify.

Melia cigarettes   *Bastos* cigarettes   *CKT*

To see the signs above you need to look up, but elsewhere you need to look down:

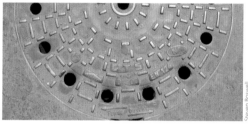

City drains: 'turn counterclockwise to open'   "Water"

On the corner of streets 5 and 136, the *Librairie Sy-Cai*, a bookstore, is now Mr. Butterfly, a bar-restaurant (Map 3, #55).

A number of government departments and universities continue to indicate their presence first in Khmer then *en français*:

The electricity company   University of Health Sciences

Pharmacies also tend to keep their signs in French, perhaps because the study of French language is encouraged at the government's *Université des sciences de la santé*.

The well-known Station Pharmacy, on Monivong Boulevard

Police stations are often identified in French, as on Street 174:

94

Needless to say, there are newer establishments with a French name, such as *La Résidence* (Map 3, #66), a sophisticated – and pricey – restaurant located in the villa of Princess Marie, ex-wife of Prince Norodom Rannarith, who himself is a son of King Sihanouk and was First Prime Minister from 1993 until he was ousted by Second Prime Minister Hun Sen in 1997.

Princess Marie's restaurant
at #22/24 Street 214

Lastly, of course, we have this:

12. Techo Meas and Techo Yort

G randly positioned along the riverside opposite Wat Unnalom, the equestrian statues of *Techo* Meas and *Techo* Yort were inaugurated with much fanfare on September 1, 2012 (Map 3, #58). The event was reported in *The Cambodia Daily* and on a number of Cambodian government websites, but although the accounts included descriptions of the statues' size (3.06 meters high and weighing two tons, all atop a thirty-ton pedestal of Kompong Thom sandstone) and their casting (the lost wax method, which took six months to complete), virtually nothing was said about the exploits of these two heroes, only that during the time of King Serey Soriyopor in the 17th century Meas and Yort were military leaders who led the fight against Siamese invaders.

Curious as to why the two were honored with statues placed in such a prominent place, I asked Cambodian friends about the pair. Although they had heard of them, they knew little more than

The heroic *Techo* Meas, on the right, and
his young protégé *Techo* Yort

the few words in the previous paragraph. I then queried a close relative. "It's because of their title, *techo*, which is only conferred on valiant leaders who have protected the country. The title has also been given to our prime minister, and he can therefore bask in the reflected glory of Meas and Yort," she opined. *"Techo* Meas was the teacher," she added, "and *Techo* Yort was his student." Shortly thereafter I came across a May 2012 speech by Prime Minister *Samdech Techo* Hun Sen in which he said that in 1630 Meas and Yort were the first to be awarded the title *techo* to honor them for their victory over the invading Thais in Kompong Thom province, thereby forcing the enemy to withdraw and leave the country. In the term *techo*, incidentally, the *"t"* is pronounced as *"d"* and the *"ch"* is pronounced as in "tea*ch*er" rather than as in "te*ch*nology."

So who exactly were these mysterious heroes? I could find no reference to them in my English language history books, notably those by Chandler, Tully, and Vickery, but in his *Histoire du Cambodge*, based largely on the Cambodian Royal Chronicles as well as European sources of the time, Mak Phœun reports on a certain *Ukaña Tejo Brah Ang "Mas,"* who it turns out is none other than *Techo* Meas. And then my wife recalled a Khmer language book she had once read, *Techo Meas and Techo Yort*, written by Kong Bun Chhoeun, who, my wife added, wrote a number of songs for Sin Sisamouth and Ros Sereysothea. It should be remembered that the Royal Chronicles contain a certain amount of fiction, and Kong Bun Chhoeun's book "seems like fifty percent history and fifty percent legend," according to one of my nephews who summarized it for me.

Although Kong Bun Chhoeun doesn't give his sources, much of the legendary part seems to come from the Royal Chronicles, notably one drawn up or copied in 1941 by a monk named Has Souk from Dik Vil monastery in Saang, Kandal province. Has Souk followed another rendition of the chronicles dating to at least 1901. Mak Phœun translated into French portions of Has Souk's account – my main source for much of the apparently legendary parts of this chapter – as well as several other versions of the chronicles in

Chroniques Royales du Cambodge (de 1594 à 1677), in which Meas is mentioned under no less than thirty-eight different names and titles. The existing Royal Chronicles, it should be noted, were written by palace officials or by Buddhist monks based on older versions – the oldest extant one, or at least its remaining fragment, dating to 1792 – and on oral traditions.

MEAS WAS BORN DURING the time of King Sattha (reigned 1576–1594). His father was the chief of a village in Kompong Svay, a large province which at the time stretched from the Mekong and Tonle Sap rivers to the Dangrek Mountains in the north. Just like all village children of his age, young Meas tended the family water buffaloes. A born leader, he organized the village children into groups to catch insects and small animals to supplement their meals. His father later entrusted him to the care of a monk named Sin, the abbot of Treal pagoda in nearby Baray. Sin soon recognized Meas' natural abilities, so in addition to reading, writing, and Buddhism, the monk taught him the secrets of magic. When Meas had completed his studies, Sin sent him to the court of King Chau Ponhea Nhom (r. 1600–1602), warning the monarch that in later years there would be serious troubles in the country brought on by a powerful magician whom only Meas would be able to defeat. The king paid little heed to Sin's advice; indeed, he paid little attention to governing and consequently was forced to abdicate after only two years. Frustrated by the king's lack of interest, Meas decided not to pursue a career in administration but to take to the road and see what fortune would bring him.

One night when Meas was sleeping at a pagoda in Samrong Tong province west of the Tonle Sap river, a small snake tightly encircled his neck. The pagoda's abbott saw the snake and immediately recognized it as an auspicious omen. He threw a bucket of water on Meas, and the snake slithered away to the southeast. "You will become a great warrior and defeat enemies coming from all directions," the monk told Meas. "Follow the direction the snake took and you will find a precious object." (Incidentally, the snake had left red scars on Meas neck, explaining his popular sobriquet *Techo Krahom Kou*, "*techo* of the red neck," though the wounds seem to have been overlooked by the sculptor of the Sisowath Quay statue.)

Meas obediently followed a path to the southeast. That night he had a dream in which a buffalo-headed spirit told him where to dig to find a magic treatise, one that would tell him how to achieve success. The next day, Meas dug at the designated site and unearthed a bronze box that contained a copy of the Golden Treatise, a divination manuscript written on palm leaves.

Meas now engaged in commerce, notably the trade of elephant tusks, animal hides, and exotic woods. Thanks to the magic treatise, whatever he bought he was able to sell for five times more. While searching for tusks near the Dangrek Mountains, he purchased a youth named Yort, a member of the Phnong ethnic minority, as a slave. Yort was orphaned as a boy after his parents were trampled by a rampaging elephant. The young man was well-built and long-haired, and he had dragons tattooed on either shoulder. He was known by all in the area as being extremely brave. Meas soon recognized Yort's potential, and he became the youth's mentor. Meas now taught his protégé the skills he had learned from Sin the monk.

Meas' business acumen and hard work soon bore fruit and he became a wealthy man, but success did not go to his head. He helped all in need, regardless of whether they were rich or poor, and by so doing won the people's respect and trust. When the governor of Samrong Tong died, it was therefore not surprising that the people decided Meas should take his place. Moreover, they enjoined Meas to marry the deceased governor's widow, the beautiful and wise Sraen, who was to play an influential role in his life. Meas' sound leadership soon won the respect of the people of Samrong Tong.

Cambodia's new King, Serey Soriyopor (r. 1602–1619), the uncle of the ex-king Chau Ponhea Nhom, had established his capital at Koh Slaket (an island that has since disappeared; it had been opposite Phnom Penh just off the point of land where the Bassac separates from the Mekong). Meas went to greet the new king with five elephants and fifteen horses. When the king learned of Meas' abilities, he not only confirmed Meas as governor of Samrong Tong, but also appointed him military commander and gave him a sword with a golden hilt sheathed in a golden scabbard. This sword itself was the insignia of royal military power, which gave Meas the right to put to death anyone who dared to defy him, fellow Cambodians included. The king then ordered Meas to reestablish control over all of Cambodia, which had been divided into a number of essentially independent fiefdoms following the fall of the royal capital at Longvek during the Siamese invasion of 1593–94.

Meas, seconded by Yort and with his magical powers – he defeated one enemy by making himself invisible – proceeded to do just as ordered, first pacifying the restive provinces east of the Mekong as far as Prey Nokor (Saigon) and then taking Phnom Penh and other southern provinces, killing in the process a number of rebel governors and self-appointed kings, including the abdicant king Chau Ponhea Nhom, who had risen in revolt. Meas then subjugated the seditious provinces to the west as far as Siam, followed by those to the north all the way to the lands of the Lao. The families of the rebellious kings and their adherents were sold into slavery. Cambodia had now recovered its lost lands and was once again unified and at peace, thanks in large measure to the military leadership of Meas.

SINCE ITS DEFEAT IN 1594, Cambodia had been under the suzerainty of Siam, paying an annual tribute and sending the king's sons to Ayutthaya as hostages. Serey Soriyopor himself had been captured at Longvek during the 1593–1594 war and spent eight years in the Siamese capital before being allowed to return to Cambodia. The Siamese released Serey Soriyopor's own sons three years after he became king. Once his sons were safely home in Cambodia, Serey Soriyopor stopped sending tribute and, toward the end of his rule, he entirely renounced Siamese suzerainty.

In a somewhat delayed response in 1622, the Siamese king Song Tham invaded, leading an army of 60,000 warriors, 300 elephants, and 500 horses (the accuracy of these numbers is questionable) through Battambang toward the new Cambodian capital at Udong. Another army went by sea to Cambodia's southern coast. King Serey Soriyopor was now dead; his son and successor Chey Chetha II (r. 1619–1627) advanced to confront the Siamese with Meas leading an even larger force: 66,000 troops, 700 elephants, and 1,000 horses.

The armies met in Pursat province, at which point Meas managed to get behind the Siamese troops and then attacked from three sides. The result was a stunning – and bloody – Cambodian victory. Over 10,000 Siamese soldiers were killed and 30,000 captured. King Song Tham fled to the hills with Meas in chase. To slow his pursuers, the Siamese king had his men throw everything of value in the Cambodians' path, including his diamond-encrusted royal headdress. The ploy worked. Meas' soldiers paused to collect the loot, and Song Tham managed to escape back to his capital at Ayutthaya.

As for the Siamese forces coming by sea, whether they even landed is unclear. It is possible that they were scared away by a flotilla sent by the Vietnamese lord Sai Vuong, Chey Chetha's father-in-law, whose daughter Chey Chetha had married in 1617, two years before he became king. However, a tradition says the Siamese attacked Cambodia's southern provinces and occupied Kompot. The wily Cambodians then managed to poison a substantial number of enemy soldiers, and they followed this up with an assault that routed the invaders. (Prime Minister Hun Sen mentioned the event in his speech, saying the enemy suffered food poisoning from eating the fruit of the *krasaing* tree, *Feroniella lucida*. A bit of this tough-skinned fruit is often added to soup to give a sour taste.)

THE COUNTRY WAS NOW at peace with Siam, but once more there were internal troubles. In Kompong Chhnang province, a certain Somrei proclaimed himself king of the Somrey, a people who lived in the vicinity of the Tonle Sap lake (only about 300 still remain today, still living near the lake's western shore), and rose in revolt. Meas gathered 200 men and went off to suppress the uprising. Somrei, however, was also versed in magic; among other things, he could summon the rain to water his peasants' crops. From his citadel at Svay Rumpear (on the left bank of the Tonle Sap river, across from the city of Kompong Chhnang), he chanted magic formulas and, from his opened mouth, emitted a torrent of bees, hornets, and tigers that stung, bit, and clawed Meas' men, forcing them to retreat. Meas now called on the king to send soldiers to join him, and together they attacked Somrei. As they closed in on the rebel king, however, not only did he again open his jaws with the same results as before, but he brought to life dummies made of straw and had them surround the royal troops, who uselessly spent all their bullets and arrows shooting at them.

Enter Meas' wife Sraen, who devised a plot to put an end to Somrei. She shared her plan only with her husband, his beautiful and devoted maidservant Neang Mai, and his protégé Yort. Putting the plan into action, Sraen feigned quarreling with Meas, openly and volubly, and soon they separated. Taking with her one cartful of tasty dried fish and another of finely crafted swords and other metal weaponry, Sraen left for a town today called Kompong Leng, just across the Tonle Sap river from Kompong Chhnang city, which bordered the lands controlled by Somrei and those of King Chey Chetha. Here Sraen opened two shops, each manned by her servants, one shop selling the fish and the other the swords. She ordered her shopkeepers to sell their goods at a low price to the soldiers of Somrei who frequented the town, and at a high price to those of Meas.

Word soon reached Somrei not only of the bargains that could be found at Sraen's two shops, but also of her unsurpassable beauty and intelligence. Somrei already knew about Sraen and her separation from Meas; now that he learned that Sraen was nearby, he let it be known that he was desirous to meet her. For her part, Sraen arranged a marriage between her own maidservant and one of her shopkeepers, and she invited Somrei to the wedding feast. There, Somrei's soldiers were plied with alcohol while Sraen entertained Somrei in a luxurious tent, coaxing him to down glass after glass of fiery spirits. When all were suitably inebriated, Meas, Yort, and their men bounded forward, disarmed the drunkards, and dragged Somrei off to get his just deserts.

When the king learned of this great victory, Meas and Yort were showered with praise and given the highest honors. Kompong Leng officials and their family members were exempted from paying taxes for three years. Statues of *Techo* Meas, Sraen, and *Techo* Yort were raised on nearby Tuk Meas mountain at a place still called *Neak Ta Krahom Kou*, "spirit with the red neck."

MEAS AND SRAEN HAD no children of their own, so Sraen decided to persuade her husband to take his beautiful and loyal maidservant, Neang Mai, as a minor wife. Meas at first refused, preferring Neang Mai to marry Yort, whom he regarded as his son, but in the end he followed his wife's counsel.

One day not long after their wedding, Neang Mai was sitting on their bed sewing when Meas playfully put his leg across hers, as a newlywed might be wont to do. Neang Mai turned to him and pretending to be cross held up her sewing needle menacingly in front of his face, at which he instinctively recoiled, throwing his hands up for protection.

"You are a great general," teased Neang Mai. "You have faced hails of bullets as close as the falling rain, swords as cutting as diamonds, yet you were never fearful, you never recoiled, but now you are afraid just because of me."

Meas was taken aback by these words which called his courage into question. "I have never been defeated by anyone," he said to himself, "not by their abilities, their words, or their intelligence. Now, because passion made me err, I have been beaten by the words of this woman."

Meas convened Sraen, Yort, and his closest followers. "The noble Buddhist belief that passion is the enemy of man is true. I must now take leave of you." Meas brought all his magical treatise and formulas, all his books on military strategy and tactics, and gave them to Yort. He wrote a message to the king telling him he had been in royal service for many years, and the time of his leaving was now at hand. He then asked the king to appoint Yort to replace him as commander of the army.

Before the king could reply, Meas took his best sword and ordered his men to fill a cast iron forge with wood. When the fire was in full flame, he climbed onto the iron forge and sat down. His women and followers tearfully begged him to come down, but Meas refused. No one dared to try to pull him from the flames as he was holding his powerful sword in his hands.

After three days, the fire had still not consumed Meas. He therefore took a cup of tea and uttered magic formulas to suppress his supernatural powers. As soon as he had drunk the tea, his powers faded, the flames seared him, and he died.

The king was deeply shocked by his general's death. After providing for a grand funeral for Meas, he ordered that Neang Mai and her family be enslaved for seven generations, and he named Yort to take the place of the departed Meas.

When King Chey Chetha II appointed Yort to replace Meas as governor of Kompong Svay, he also gave Yort a sword with a golden hilt and golden sheath similar to the one King Serey Soriyopor had bestowed on Meas. Such a sword, as will be recalled, gave its possessor the right to slay all who dared opposed him, including fellow Cambodians.

The 30,000 Siamese prisoners from the 1622 war were distributed among the provinces and given lands to till. However, many of them revolted soon thereafter, perhaps at the instigation of Siamese king Song Tham, and they gathered in Pursat province. King Chey Chetha ordered two of his generals to assemble an army and suppress the revolt, but at first they were unable to do so. (Though the king had royal guards, he had no standing army at that time. When needed, the king would call on the country's princes, high officials, and provincial governors to levy troops from among the people.) The king then appointed Yort to raise the needed troops and lead them into battle. However, perhaps because Yort was from the

Phnong minority and had once been a slave, Meun Chai Chongra, brother of Nu, one of the king's wives, refused to follow Yort's orders, including raising troops to fight the enemy, and he persuaded others to do the same. In response, Yort had Meun Chai Chongra arrested, shackled with chains, and paraded about in public for three days before executing him.

Nu, Meun Chai Chongra's sister, pleaded his case to her husband the king, saying that Yort was but a Phnong and if he were allowed to kill Khmers of higher birth, then the Khmers would revolt and turn to Siam for assistance. King Chey Chetha was convinced, and he called Yort to appear before the court. Demanding to see his accuser, Yort confronted Nu, the royal consort: "Is it you who raised yourself above the laws of military authority? We have the royal mandate to fight the kingdom's enemies. Yet certain members who reside in the palace refused to raise troops to fight the Siamese. We were invested with royal military authority. Your brother disobeyed this royal authority, and swayed others to do the same. By taking his side and going against royal authority, you show that you despise our country, and your actions favor the enemy. Do you want our kingdom to fall to Siam?" Then, brandishing his sword, Yort slit Nu's throat. The royal consort died on the spot. Yort mounted his horse and led his men off to fight the rebellious Siamese.

When King Chey Chetha learned of this, he ordered that from that day on no wife or concubine be permitted to speak to the king about any government official. He would listen only to his ministers.

Yort now had no trouble making himself obeyed, and he went on to rout the rebellious Siamese prisoners and execute their leaders. He then proceeded to the royal palace, shackled himself in irons, and offered himself up for the king's judgment, ready to die if the king so ruled.

"Yort has a strong heart," the king told his court. "He has knowledge and intelligence, just as *Techo* Meas told me. Reward our victorious soldiers, and give Yort his freedom. Tell him to return to his province. There is no need for him to come and make obeisance to me."

FOLLOWING HIS VICTORY, YORT returned home. He had a statue of Meas erected so he could show his respect to his mentor. One day as Yort was praying before the image, the statue said to him, "You are old, yet you are not married. Do you not have anything in your heart?"

"I love Sraen," replied Yort, "but I dare not express my feelings to her because she is Meas' widow. Moreover, she is Khmer while I am not, only a man from the far hills."

Though Yort was too timid to tell Sraen of his affection for her, he did mention it to those close to him, and it wasn't long before word of Yort's love reached Sraen's ears. The faithful Sraen, however, would have nothing to do with him. Moreover, Yort, it will be recalled, had once been her husband's slave.

Yort and those close to him now hatched a plot. He had one of his servants steal some wood from the steps of Sraen's house. With the wood, they carved a statue of the Buddha as well as another of Meas. When the work was finished, Yort invited all to a ceremony to consecrate the Buddha statue and to pay their respects to *Techo* Meas.

Sraen was pleased when she heard of the ceremony, and she arrived in high spirits. She prostrated herself before the Buddha statue and then did the same before the image of her husband. Seeing this, Yort demanded, "Why do you bow before these statues which were made from the wood of your steps, upon which people place their feet? As for me, it is true that I was once your slave, but the king has made me governor of our province. You must therefore show me respect, just as you showed respect to these wooden statues."

Deeply upset, Sraen said nothing. Instead, she fled to the king and recounted what Yort had done. "You should not be offended," the king told her. "Yort is only trying to gain your affection. He is indeed a great general and governor. You should not refuse him."

Loyal to her king as well as her husband, Sraen did as she was advised and accepted Yort's proposal. After their marriage, they returned to their province where they raised statues of *Techo* Meas at a number of propitious places.

In 1630, CHEY CHETHA II's son and successor, Ponhea To (r. 1627–1632), took advantage of dynastic discord in Siam to attack that country, revenge for the Siamese invasions against his father. Under Yort's command, the Cambodian army moved north from Siem Reap, crossed into Siamese territory, and won decisively at Nokor Reach Sima, (today's Khorat). The army then halted its attack and returned to Cambodia with much booty and many captured Siamese.

The reason for the abrupt termination of the campaign was most likely internal problems in Cambodia, though the most colorful explanation is that prior to the battle Yort made an offering to a statue of *Techo* Meas. Meas' spirit, awakened by the offering, entered a high court official and, through him, proclaimed that the army would achieve certain victory, but great troubles would soon erupt in the kingdom and even *Techo* Yort would not be able to protect the king. Hence, King Ponhea To quickly recalled the royal army, though the move failed to save the king from his uncle, who killed him two years later.

So end the exploits of *Techo* Meas and *Techo* Yort. From that time till the end of the century, the state of tension and hostility between Siam and Cambodia remained, though, ironically, the only major battles, in 1680, saw the two kingdoms on the same side, when Siam sent troops to help the Cambodian king defeat an attack by a rebel prince supported by Chinese mercenaries.

THERE IS SOME QUESTION as to when Meas received the title *techo*, though it should be noted that dates often vary from one chronicle to another. Prime Minister Hun Sen in his speech mentioned the year 1630, but one of the annals says it happened when Meas was appointed governor of Samrong Tong – which would have been before most of his military exploits – and that the title was originally reserved for governors of that province. Indeed, one of the chronicles mentions an *Okna Techo*, probably a governor of Samrong Tong, who had led a Cambodian military expedition against the Cham and was later killed by the Spanish soldier/

adventurer Blas Ruiz in 1597 during the period of internal troubles which followed the Siamese invasion of 1593–1594. The title *techo* was later attributed to the governors of Kompong Svay province, Meas' native land.

Sources

Mak Phœun, *Chroniques Royales du Cambodge (de 1594 à 1677)*, École française d'Extrême-Orient, 1981.

Mak Phœun, *Histoire du Cambodge*, École française d'Extrême-Orient, 1995.

Kong Bun Chhoeun, *Techo Meas and Techo Yort*, 2002.

Svay Muoy, "Histoire de Keo Preah Phleung," *Bulletin de la Société des Études Indochinoise*, Volume XLVII, 1972.

13. Atop Wat Phnom's Hill

In the season of high waters many years ago (1372, according to tradition), Grandmother Penh saw a *koki* tree trapped in an eddy after it had floated down the Mekong all the way from Laos. As the wood of a *koki* is valued in construction, she had her fellow villagers pull the tree ashore. Inside a hollow in the trunk they found four bronze Buddha statues and a stone figure of a four-armed divinity. The villagers all rejoiced at such a find, and Grandmother Penh had no difficulty persuading them to heighten the low mound in front of her house and use the *koki* wood to build a small sanctuary atop the knoll to shelter the statues and thus protect them from future floods.

So goes the well-known story of the origins of Phnom Penh's hill (*phnom*, in Khmer), a story one can follow on the concrete bas-reliefs around the base of the recently placed statue of Lady Penh

Not atop the hill, but Grandmother Penh's monument is on the site of her home

Grandmother Penh in her shrine just behind the pagoda's *vihara* on the terrace southwest of her hill (Map 2, #33), just where her cottage once stood. She also has a small but well-frequented shrine of her own on the hill, right behind Wat Phnom's *vihara*, or main prayer hall. Here, a simple likeness of Lady Penh anachronistically sports spectacles, while a multi-colored halo glows behind her and joss sticks smolder in front.

One wonders whether Grandmother Penh was aware that by building the hill she was following the Angkorian royal tradition of raising a hill, sometimes a symbolic one, and constructing a sanctuary on top, a practice that originated from Hindu beliefs in ancient India. The main tower of an Angkorian temple represented Mount Meru, the abode of the gods. At these temples the kings of Angkor prayed for prosperity. To continue this communication between heaven and earth, Hindu-influenced cities of Southeast Asia had as their center a hill with a shrine atop, as can be seen today in Vientiane, Luang Prabang, Yangon (Rangoon), and of course Phnom Penh, though the sanctuaries themselves are Buddhist.

When King Ponhea Yat brought the Khmer capital to Phnom Penh in the 1430s or 1440s, he named the city Krong Chaktomuk, "City of the Four Faces," referring to the meeting of the Tonle Sap, the Bassac, and the two parts of the Mekong, here where the river makes a great turn to the southeast. In deference to Grandmother Penh he added her name and her hill, the city thus becoming Krong Chaktomuk Phnom Daun ("Lady") Penh, eventually shortened to simply Phnom Penh. Ponhea Yat enlarged the hill and raised its height, and he also reconstructed Grandmother Penh's by then decrepit pagoda on top.

Behind Wat Phnom's *vihara*, the great stupa, which has been rebuilt many times, was erected by Ponhea Yat to house the four bronze Buddha statues that Grandmother Penh had found in that *koki* tree long before, as well as other sacred statues the king had brought from Angkor. Following Ponhea Yat's death in 1467, his son and successor, Noreay Reachea, had the king's ashes placed in the stupa.

A stupa such as this is a representation of the Buddhist view of the three different levels of beings. The square, bottommost

Roger Spooner

King Ponhea Yat's stupa atop the *phnom*

section of the stupa represents the netherworld, the realm of hell beings and ghosts, some of which inhabit the human world. The central, bell-shaped part is the middle world, the terrestrial world of human beings and animals, though animals are considered to be far below humans; the sacred relics are kept in a chamber in this part of the stupa. The top section and the spire comprise the upper world, the celestial abodes of gods and divinities, some of whom, such as Indra, who rules the lowest heaven, were subsumed from Hinduism. The Buddhist belief in reincarnation or, more correctly, transmigration of the soul (*samsara*, or "wandering" in Sanskrit, the language of Hinduism in ancient India), means that all living beings, even gods, can after death move within one world

111

The *phnom* with its stupa and thatch-roofed wat c. 1870

or from one world to another, higher or lower, depending on the law of karma, according to which virtuous deeds in previous lifetimes bring happiness in future ones and nonvirtuous deeds cause suffering. Beyond the stupa, above the three worlds and higher even than the realm of gods, is the other world or nirvana, where buddhas achieve extinction, freedom from countless lives of desires and suffering.

Charles-Émile Bouillevaux, a French missionary who lived in Cambodia from 1848 to 1856, reported that Wat Phnom was well frequented but exceedingly dilapidated. Around the hill were Chinese and "Cochinchinese" (i.e. Vietnamese) graves, and here Cambodians cremated their dead.

During the 1885–86 rebellion against the increasing encroachment of the French protectorate on the rule of King Norodom, the *phnom* was cleared of trees and the stupa became a watchtower with a walkway around its top, reached by a bamboo ladder, that allowed the occupying soldiers a clear view of potential danger coming from land or water. On May 5, 1885, the troopers on the stupa's walkway would have watched with increasing alarm as 500 fighters of the rebel Prince Sivutha, armed with spears, swords, and primitive rifles that shot stone balls, advanced on the capital from

King Ponhea Yat's stupa in 1885,
when it served as a watchtower, with
thatch-roofed Wat Phnom in front

three sides, even reaching the city center before being repulsed after fierce fighting.

The French often referred to Ponhea Yat's stupa as a *pyramide*. In 1894, Huyn de Vernéville, Phnom Penh's first *résident supérieur*, France's highest official in Cambodia, had the "pyramid" rebuilt. The pagoda was renovated with masonry walls and a tiled roof, a monumental stairway replete with Angkorian motifs was constructed, and gardens were landscaped round the hill. Many of the other thirty-one stupas (see box) on or about the hill were also restored. Some years later, a small menagerie of local fauna (tigers, panthers, sun bears, monkeys, and snakes) and an aviary for a large

The thirty-one other stupas include seven small ones on the square base of Ponhea Yat's stupa and one across the street on the grounds of the Council for the Development of Cambodia (CDC). Most no doubt contain the remains of royalty, though some may be for members of the nobility or the Buddhist community of monks. For whom most of the stupas were built is a mystery as only four have been identified: one for Ponhea Yat's son and successor, Noreay Reachea, another dated 1930 for the parents and family of the last head monk of Wat Phnom, *Preah Sirei Sangkea Muni* Ros, and the third for the Venerable Ros himself, who died in 1947. Often the remains of several members of a family are kept in the same stupa. Regarding the fourth identified stupa, the one on the grounds of the CDC, see Chapter 19.

variety of Cambodian birds were built on the western side of the hill for the enjoyment of colonial offspring. Perhaps the occasional macaques which today inhabit the *phnom* and promenade around its neighborhood are descendants of those simians. The rest of the animals disappeared long ago and a visitor in the mid-1950s reported that, when walking around the hill, he "came to some cages which used to contain wild animals but now seemed to be occupied by squatters." Although Wat Phnom has no resident monks today, some had lived in small huts at the base of the hill at least until the renovation of the *phnom* in the 1890s, and monks were attached to the pagoda up to the late 1940s.

In 1974, in the waning time of Lon Nol's rule, a lightning bolt felled the top of the stupa, an event which Phnom Penh's people viewed as an omen predicting the demise of the regime, which indeed occurred a few months later with the victory of the Khmer Rouge.

The ousting of the Khmer Rouge from Phnom Penh in 1979 spared both Ponhea Yat's stupa and Wat Phnom from the wrecking ball. Not long before, Pol Pot had ordered their demolition and in their place the construction of an eight-meter tall concrete statue of himself standing majestically above flag-waving farmers, his right hand stretching out toward the sky, his left holding a revolutionary book, perhaps Chairman Mao's little red one. (But perhaps not: Mao's *Little Red Book* was never translated into Khmer, and I doubt Pol Pot would have immortalized himself holding a French version.) The sculpture in its entirety was supposed to symbolize the victory of class struggle, though to some it might seem more like the beginnings of a personality cult *à la* Mao, which, if so, would have indicated a significant change from the Khmer Rouge leader's penchant for secrecy. As he used to say, "If you preserve secrecy, half the battle is won." Perhaps by the time he ordered the statue, he thought he had won not just the battle but the war. A model of the statue was made for Pol Pot's endorsement, but his ousting from Phnom Penh by the Vietnamese put a welcome end to that project, and to many others.

Let me include here a word on the *koki* tree, native of Indochina and the Malay Peninsula whose scientific name is *Hopea odorata* but which is without a common English name. The *koki*, which grows to a height of 20 to 35 meters, is believed to have something almost sacred about it, and in the old days it could only be planted by a monarch or a monk. It is widely sought for the construction of houses

Wat Phnom following French renovations in
1894, looking much as it does today

Koki trees at the base
of the *phnom*

Flying fox, *Pteropus lylei*

and boats, and its bark can be used to treat diarrhea, inflammation of the gums, and incontinence. *Koki* trees, according to some, are also a favorite resting place of ghosts. A number of aging *koki* are around the *phnom* (several new ones have recently been planted), and one on the grounds of the Council for the Development of Cambodia, just east of the hill, is home to a large colony of flying foxes (*Pteropus lylei*), rare in an urban area. These bats are the largest in the world and their wingspan can reach 1.5 meters. During most of the day they hang upside down from the *koki*'s branches, wings furled. Usually one male and a number of females hang from one branch. They feed on fruit, blossoms, nectar, and pollen, but not on insects, unlike other bat species. Different from smaller bats, they do not use echo-location to navigate but rely on their large eyes. When the bats take wing at dusk, it is a most impressive sight.

A final word on our city's *phnom*: in the 1980s, the years after Cambodia's liberation from the Khmer Rouge, various factories –

all government run under the communist regime which supplanted the Khmer Rouge – would take turns holding rowdy parties with much imbibing and dancing, perhaps as much to incur the favor of invited government officials as to let loose following years of deprivation. The preferred drink was *Bayon*, an eighty proof pink-colored mixture of rice wine and selected ingredients "so strong that one shot would make you burn from one end to the other," according to one participant in the revelries. *Bayon*, he reported, was distilled right here on Grandmother Penh's hill.

Sources

George Cœdès, "La fondation de Phnom Péñ au XVe siècle d'après la chronique cambodgienne," in *Bulletin de l'École française d'Extrême-Orient*, 1913.

Charles-Émile Bouillevaux, *l'Annam et le Cambodge, voyages et notices historiques*, Victor Palmé, 1874.

Paul Collard, *Cambodge et Cambodgiens*, Cedoreck, Phnom Penh, 2001 [Société d'Edition, 1925].

Khin Sok, *Chroniques royales du Cambodge (de Bana Yat jusqu'à la prise de Laenvaek: de 1417 à 1595)*, École française d'Extrême-Orient, 1988.

Bernard Dupraz, Jean-Marie Sorya Birsens, and François Ponchaud, *Insights into the Religious Background of the Khmers*, undated.

Vann Nath, *A Cambodian Prison Portrait*, White Lotus, 1998.

Dy Phon Pauline, *Plants Used in Cambodia*, 2000.

U Sam Oeur, *Crossing Three Wildernesses*, Coffee House Press, 2005.

Chan Vitharong, *Wat Phnom, Guide to Art and Architecture*, Chan's Arts, 2013.

14. The House across from S-21

The Boddhi Tree (Map 4, #82) is a popular restaurant and guesthouse located on Street 113 across from the Tuol Sleng Genocide Museum (Map 4, #81). The museum had been a secondary school before the Khmer Rouge turned it into the notorious interrogation and torture center known as S-21. The Boddhi Tree used to be directly opposite the main entrance to S-21, the one through which the victims passed, until a couple of years ago when the museum relocated access to the corner of Street 350, a half block south. Wooden houses such as The Boddhi Tree were typical Phnom Penh residences not long ago but are increasingly being demolished in favor of reinforced concrete and masonry constructions.

Tuol Sleng, which originally was the name of a primary school situated behind the secondary school whose buildings now compose the genocide museum, translates as "hillock of the *sleng* tree." The *sleng* tree, *Strychnos nux-vomica*, has seeds with a significant strychnine content, a high dose of which can be fatal. Thus, the name of the museum can be appropriately rendered as "hillock of the poisonous tree."

At dinner at The Boddhi Tree one evening a few months back, my wife was telling me that acquaintances of hers who live on Street 131 directly behind the museum had described to her the cries of ghosts they frequently heard at night; she added that her friends would make offerings of food and drink to appease those wandering souls. My contribution to the conversation was that her friends' houses were built on the site of the aforementioned primary school. During Khmer Rouge times the S-21 dead were buried there until the space filled up in 1977, at which time the infamous killing fields at Chœung Ek took over as mass burial ground. Hence the hungry cries at night.

Moreover, many of those incarcerated at this secret facility had been interrogated and tortured in the house where we were then dining, as well as in other wooden houses along that block of Street 113, five of which still remain today. "I was taken to a house in front of the S-21 compound for interrogation," reports Bou Meng, one of the handful of prisoners who survived S-21, in *Bou Meng: A Survivor from Khmer Rouge Prison S-21*, by Huy Vannak. From his cell, Bou Meng "heard people crying and sighing around the building. I heard people crying out, 'Mother, help me! Mother, help me!'"

In Chann, a sculptor who was another S-21 survivor, describes his early days in the prison in Rithy Phan's film *Bophana, a Cambodian Tragedy*: "They took us to a cell on the top floor and locked my feet. After ten days, they started to interrogate me. They blindfolded me and took me to a house outside. I don't know which house because I was blindfolded and couldn't see anything. The interrogation started at 7 o'clock in the morning and lasted till 11. Then in the afternoon from 2 until 5. At night from 6 to 11."

One of the most gruesome tortures at S-21 was the total draining of blood from living prisoners. This too was done across the street from the prison, most likely at what today is The Boddhi Tree, as the interrogator Prak Khan revealed to Rithy Phan:

> For the blood-taking, prisoners were brought to the doctors' house, which was across the street from the entrance to S-21. They were handcuffed to iron beds, blindfolded, and gagged. Then a vein in each arm was punctured and tubes inserted that led down to blood bags under the beds. I asked the doctors how many bags of blood they took from each prisoner. Four bags per person, they told me. Once the blood-taking was completed, prisoners were placed on the floor next to the wall and left there. Their breathing sounded like crickets chirruping, and their eyes were rolled up in their heads. And not far away, their graves were being dug.

Let me note that when Prak Khan testified at the trial of Kaing Guek Eav, better known as Duch, the director of S-21, he refused to repeat what he had told Rithy Phan about the bloodletting, citing his right to remain silent. Duch himself testified at his trial that a hundred prisoners died from the blood draining and that the practice ceased only after all those capable of performing the procedure had themselves been purged. The blood was reportedly used in the treatment of wounded Khmer Rouge soldiers.

Most visitors to S-21 come away thinking the inflicting of pain on those prisoners took place in the rooms of buildings A and B in the diagram below. This is correct to an extent, but to keep the interrogations secret from the prisoners in the cell blocks (as well as from the rest of the prison's staff: secrecy was an obsession at S-21) much of the horror was carried out in the wooden buildings

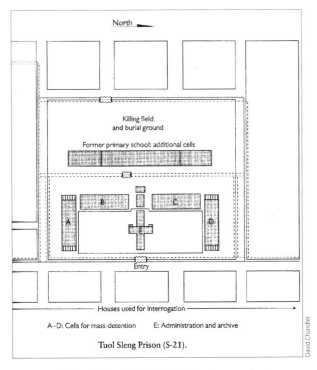

Toul Sleng Prison. The Boddhi Tree is opposite the entry in the diagram, though the entrance to the present museum is now half a block to the south (left) of the one in the diagram, near building A.

120

across the street from the compound. Then, in 1978, the last year of Khmer Rouge control of Phnom Penh, some interrogations were moved from the wooden houses to building B because women questioned in those houses were often raped by their interrogators. By relocating the interrogations to the main prison compound, authorities could more easily control the process. Nonetheless, many of the more than 16,000 prisoners who passed through S-21 suffered torment and even death in these wooden houses.

"Here?" shuddered my wife.

"Yes, right upstairs."

When I asked the manager if they ever heard ghosts, he replied that prior to the opening of the guesthouse monks were invited to perform a ceremony intended to purify the building and exorcise it of any unwanted spirits. Spectral cries, if any, were thus a thing of the past.

Nonetheless, our dinner ended early that evening and my wife won't think about dining there again. She's right, and I should have known better than to suggest eating there in the first place. The wooden house should be part of the museum, revealing to visitors the viciousness and terror of those days, not a place of pleasant dining and repose.

Sources

Huy Vannak, *Bou Meng: A Survivor from Khmer Rouge Prison S-21*, Documentation Center of Cambodia, 2010.

David Chandler, *Voices from S-21: Terror and History in Pol Pot's Secret Prison*. Berkeley: University of California Press, 1999.

Rithy Phan, *The Elimination*, Other Press, 2013.

Rithy Phan, *Bophana, a Cambodian Tragedy*, 1996 (film).

Youk Chhang, "The 'poisonous hill' that was Toul Sleng," *The Phnom Penh Post*, May 1–15, 1997.

Thierry Cruvellier, *The Master of Confessions*, HarperCollins, 2014 [Gallimard/Versilio, 2011].

Dy Phon Pauline, *Plants Used in Cambodia*, 2000.

15. La Taverne, Madame Chum's, and Other Favored Haunts of Days Gone By

Accounts of Phnom Penh in the 1950s, '60s, and '70s up to the victory of the Khmer Rouge in 1975 often feature the names of certain bars and restaurants – and one particular opium den – often in conjunction with the colorful personalities who ran them. Phnom Penh in those years was considered by many foreigners to be Indochina's most attractive city, and the comfortable expatriate lifestyle, at least until 1970, was accentuated by the pleasures offered by these establishments. (I should add that, in addition to expats, the city's elite were among the most prominent customers, as were army officers clearly living beyond their military pay.) While all of these enterprises have now vanished and the locations of some are forgotten or in dispute, they still retain a place in the story of the city.

La Taverne (Map 2, #43), a French restaurant run by Monsieur Mignon, offered its famed *steak au poivre vert*, Bokor asparagus, and smoked ham for many of those years. "*La Taverne* served the best French food in Cambodia at an astonishingly low price," wrote Christopher Pym, who was in the city in the mid-1950s.

> It also reminded its clients of France, which is the highest tribute one can pay to a Phnom Penh eating-house. It became a haven for many of the French settlers, and, as they grew in numbers, the expatriate nationals of the various countries who loaned experts to the Khmer Government. These experts had one thing in common – they complained. If they did not complain about local conditions, they complained that the Khmer Government ignored the advice which they, the experts, offered.

Monsieur Mignon, originally from the Limousin region of France, came to Cambodia in the 1930s, was interned by the Japanese in 1945 (as were many French colonials) and stayed on after independence. Like other former French *colons*, he was apparently "unprepared to sever ties with an *Indochine* that no longer existed," according to the historian Milton Osborne, who as a young diplomat at the Australian Embassy in 1959 became an aficionado of the house's pepper steak.

La Taverne had an open front giving onto the sidewalk, on which several tables, sheltered by an awning, permitted dining *al fresco*. On the upper floor, private dining rooms allowed European and Chinese businessmen to carry out their dealings unobtrusively. Downstairs, the main dining hall had a long counter presided over by a Chinese bartender with an impeccable bow tie. The tables in front of the bar were covered with immaculate white cotton tablecloths. "Table linens," Monsieur Mignon would say with pride, "define the level of the establishment."

Among the restaurant's colorful clientele was a certain Doctor Leuleu who, having fought with the French troops in Indochina, chose to remain behind. According to Samyl Monipong Sisowath, nephew of Queen Kossamak and thus King Norodom Sihanouk's cousin, the doctor was famed for making improbable bets. For a glass of *bière 33*, he would wager that he could swallow alive and in its entirety one of those wall lizards so common in the tropics and, to the horror of the unfortunate bettor, he would proceed to do just that. Dr. Leuleu did more than ingest small reptiles; he also discreetly healed many of the city's poor and destitute without ever asking for anything in return, perhaps his way of thanking the country in which he had chosen to live.

In *Phnom Penh, a Cultural and Literary History*, Dr. Osborne recounts the following about La Taverne's M. Mignon: "Categorizing Australians as *Anglo-Saxons* and so not truly appreciative of the joys of food and wine, he would upbraid me for asking whether the seafood he served had been kept on ice as it journeyed up from the coast during the hottest months of the year. The taste is what matters, he would insist over and over again, not what happens in your stomach afterwards."

The most improbable guests at La Taverne were undoubtedly the eleven American soldiers of a US Army landing craft, LCU 1577, who were invited by the Cambodian government to dine at the restaurant on November 9, 1968, to celebrate the fifteenth anniversary of Cambodia's independence from France. Four months before, on July 17, 1968, LCU 1577 was on its way from the Vietnamese port city of Vung Tau to Can Tho when it took the wrong branch of the Mekong River delta and ended up in Cambodian territory. "They had a few cases of beer. I guess they all got 'bombed out of their minds' somewhat," reported a US diplomat. "General Abrams [Creighton Abrams, commander of US forces in Vietnam] was mad as hell that this had happened." LCU 1577 was soon detained by a Cambodian gunboat and taken to the Chruoy Changvar naval base on the Mekong River outside of Phnom Penh. Cambodia had severed ties with the US in 1965, so negotiations between the two governments were handled by the Australian Embassy. In exchange for the detainees' release, Prince Sihanouk, then head of state, who thought the incursion was deliberate, wanted US apologies for the deaths of Cambodian civilians from American bombings as well as US recognition of Cambodia's borders, a long standing demand. Negotiations dragged on, but the detainees were well treated and in good spirits; according to the same US diplomat, "they were taken to 'floating brothels' for feminine companionship." Then for Independence Day, Prince Sihanouk made a gesture. He sent a tailor to fit out the detainees in white suits and subsequently invited them to the celebrations at Independence Monument, where the prince himself warmly greeted each American. Next it was on to La Taverne for a lunch featuring filet mignon, "the biggest *bombe Alaska* I have ever seen," according to one of the diners, and the soldiers' first beers since their detention on July 17. In the end, Prince Sihanouk, hoping to improve relations with the US, freed the detainees in time for Christmas. Diplomatic ties were restored the next year. As to LCU-1577, it appears to have served in the

Cambodian Navy until sometime in the 1970s when it disappears from the record (see Chapter 1).

At one point in the 1960s, Monsieur Mignon took over the building next door, #18 Street 13 (where the three-story Data Management Center of the Ministry of Posts and Telecommunications has recently been constructed; see Map 2, #43) and opened a hotel there appropriately called Hôtel de la Poste. The fourteen-room hotel would have served lodgers as a replacement for the nearby Grand Hôtel Manolis when the latter apparently closed in the 1960s (see Chapter 2). Room rates at Hôtel de la Poste in 1970 ranged from $3.66 for a single to $6.33 for a double.

I believe from his descriptions that the journalist Maslyn Williams stayed at Hôtel de la Poste when he visited the city in the late 1960s, although he does not actually name his lodgings in *The Land in Between: the Cambodian Dilemma.* He writes that the "small hotel at which I stayed is used mainly by Frenchmen who work on the upcountry rubber plantations, or are technical advisors attached to one or other of the several industrial and developmental projects in which the French Government is interested."

Nor does Williams name the hotel's adjoining restaurant or its owner, though Milton Osborne told me that Williams' description of the man clearly identifies him as La Taverne's Monsieur Mignon, who was still running the place in 1971 when Dr. Osborne last dined there. "There is a restaurant alongside the hotel," writes Williams. "The proprietor, who owns both, has red hair, yellow freckles, soft fat hands and a stomach that makes it difficult for him to incline when bowing to patrons. He wears a large signet ring, smokes thin cigars and leaves much front-of-the-house business to his Cambodian wife, whose figure, tightly wrapped in a black sarong, is also considerable."

Williams also remarked on Hôtel de la Poste/La Taverne's French clientele:

> These people are leftovers from the French exodus that followed upon independence ... They all seem pale,

tentative and unsettled. They wear the vague, abandoned air of bric-a-brac left behind in an empty house ...

The Frenchmen who use this modest hotel or frequent its restaurant congregate a little before lunchtime to take an apéritif either at the bar or at the outside tables set up on the footpath and separated from the street by a hedge of clipped shrubs. They buy mini-drinks or local cordials because imported liquor is expensive in Phnom Penh, whisky being $2 a nip, beer $1 a half bottle, and the other standard little drinks averaging $1 each.

Williams continued in the rather condescending tone still common today with many Anglo expats toward their French counterparts, of whom there were approximately 6,000 resident in the city in the 1960s: "They stick together like refugees, talk French with unending gestures and aggressive facial expressions, giving the impression that they are describing dreadful events instead of wondering whether to order fish or an omelette."

The block of Preah Ang Eng Street (St. 13) between streets 100 and 102 (Map 2, #43); La Taverne was located in the building with a pitched roof behind the tree in the center of the picture, between Artisans d'Angkor on the left and the three-story building which has taken the place of Hôtel de la Poste on the right.

The cuisine at La Taverne must have made putting up with the French regulars worthwhile: the food was so favored by Prince Sihanouk, as he reported in his 1981 memoirs *Souvenirs doux et amers*, that the prince called on La Taverne's M. Mignot [*sic*] whenever he needed special help to prepare gala meals for foreign dignitaries, notably Josip Broz Tito, President of Yugoslavia.

The historian David Chandler stayed at Hôtel de la Poste for three weeks in 1971. "The hotel was a replica of small hotels in France," Dr. Chandler wrote to me, "as nothing is in Phnom Penh anymore." He ate his three daily meals next door at La Taverne. One of the restaurant's waiters from those days survived the Khmer Rouge and in 1995 resurfaced as the mâitre d'hôtel at the French Embassy. When Dr. Chandler was invited by the ambassador to dine at the embassy, he and La Taverne's former waiter greeted each other with a warm embrace.

La Taverne was located on the plaza in front of the post office, in the middle of the block of Street 13 between streets 100 and 102. A "Seeing Hands Massage by Blind People" parlor, a private residence, and the Apple travel agency/souvenir shop now occupy the site, though present occupants of the buildings whom I queried were unaware of La Taverne's existence.

ON SISOWATH QUAY, ON the other side of the block from La Taverne, was Bar Jean, described by Dr. Osborne as a "quintessentially Gallic establishment, which seemed to have been transplanted, together with its customers, from Marseille." Jean was another of the *anciens de l'Indochine*, as the French who remained in the city following the close of the protectorate were affectionately known. Jean had once worked in Saigon but, put off by the regime of Ngo Dinh Diem and his brother Ngo Dinh Nhu, left for Phnom Penh in the mid-1950s. "He had a fearsome Vietnamese wife," Dr. Osborne told me over scallops and squid at a riverside restaurant a couple of years ago. "They had a shrewd ability to choose girls who could serve the bar's customers in a range of ways." Jean and his wife moved back to Vietnam in 1970 after the coup that ousted Prince Norodom Sihanouk.

Bar Jean was on this block of Sisowath Quay, in the
building just to the left of the large mango tree

Bar Jean was located on the block of Sisowath Quay between
streets 100 and 102 (Map 2, #42) in a building that the photograph
above suggests now houses California 2. The business was sold as we
went to press and, by the time you read this, it will be the Sundance
Riverside. Bert's Books, a secondhand bookshop and guesthouse,
occupied the site in the 1990s, the building having been resurrected from a massage parlor cum brothel by Bert Hoak, a bearded bear
of a man who had come to Phnom Penh as a monitor for the 1993
elections and stayed on. In 1997, Bert left for the US with his Cambodian wife and their child, frustrated and despairing at "the rapid
decline of Cambodia, socially, politically, and environmentally," to
use his words, culminating in the bloody fighting that year between
the forces of First Prime Minister Norodom Rannarith and those
of Second Prime Minister Hun Sen.

ANOTHER POPULAR WATERING HOLE was the seedy Zigzag Bar on
Rue Dekcho Damdin (St. 154) south of Norodom, where regulars
downed their midday apéritifs while snacking on smoked meat and
brochettes prepared by Albert Vandekherkove, "a lugubrious former
French legionnaire who regularly played their marching song," as

The Zigzag Bar may have been here, at #62 Street 154

Dr. Osborne remembers. This establishment is difficult to precisely locate, though it could well have been in one of the shops in the photograph above, between Norodom Boulevard and Street 19.

WE HAVE MORE LUCK with the Café de Paris, which my 1971 guidebook puts at #15 Street 114 (Map 3, #49). Now at that place is a pair of small shops, one selling car accessories, the other a factory outlet for clothes. Its present undistinguished appearance notwithstanding, the Corsican-owned Café de Paris was once considered to be Phnom Penh's finest French restaurant, where one could dine "at a price that would have shocked all but the wealthy in a Western city," according to Dr. Osborne. "We dined on local venison washed down by fine French wine, beneath cheap posters of Nôtre Dame and the Place de la Concorde," wrote Agence France Presse's Jon Swain, reporting from the city in Lon Nol days. Cyclo-girls congregated outside, waiting for well-fed customers ready for a post-prandial dalliance.

The Café de Paris' proprietor was Albert Spaccesi (or Spaccessi or Spacezi, depending on the source). Not known for his modesty,

Spaccesi proclaimed that Café de Paris was "the best restaurant in Southeast Asia." He had cooked for de Gaulle during the general's celebrated visit to Phnom Penh in 1966. Spaccesi lectured on French cuisine to the flight attendants of Royal Air Cambodge, to whom he claimed that for lunch he would eat nothing but an apple.

Milton Osborne returned to the restaurant the same year as de Gaulle visited: "Fine meals could still be eaten at the Café de Paris, where Monsieur Spaccesi, the corpulent Corsican owner, wore his Legion of Honour ribbon next to his trousers' flies as his derisory comment on the politics of metropolitan France." And when Jon Swain crossed the Café de Paris' threshold some five years later, "Albert Spaccessi, the fat Corsican proprietor, his loose trousers hitched up with braces under his nipples, greeted us with loud effusiveness and positively glowed with hospitality."

Spaccesi remained in Phnom Penh until it fell to the Khmer Rouge in April 1975. He was among those who sought sanctuary at the French Embassy, where, as François Bizot puts it in *The Gate*, "he kept moaning, stifling his sobs as he spoke about the fortune he had invested in his fine restaurant, 'where General de Gaulle and Prince Sihanouk used to come' and which was now lost. He had nothing left." Spaccesi was on the convoy of trucks that took the refugees to Thailand shortly thereafter.

Street 114 (Kramuon Sar St.), where the Café de Paris was once located, was not spared the terror of the Khmer Rouge's deadly, indiscriminate rocket and artillery bombardments in the months that preceded their takeover of the city. Here's how one witness, the war photographer Christine Spengler, described what she saw in 1974:

> The center of Phnom Penh, the city of a thousand bougainvillea, is nothing but an open cemetery where lie corpses streaked with red who gaze at the leaden sky with their still open eyes. Others, their bodies overturned, lie on the sleeping child they tried to shelter. A young man about fifteen years old rushes from a building in flames to tenderly

slip a pillow under the head of his sister, who lies at rest on the pavement, dead, across the street from the Café de Paris.

If you happen to be walking down Street 114, have a look at the magnificent mahogany trees which grace the islands that divide this street and parallel Street 110 (Ang Duong St.; see Map 3, #50). Two species of these tall trees grow the length of the streets from Monivong to Norodom boulevards, the African mahogany (*Khaya senegalensis*) and the Mexican mahogany (*Swietenia macrophylla*). The hard, reddish wood of the trees is highly prized in furniture making. In Khmer, the trees are called *kandeng damrei*, "elephant's bell," and *kroab bek*, "grenade," for the explosive sound made by their ripe fruit – brown, pear-shaped pods – when opening.

ONE OF THE BETTER restaurants was on the ground floor of the Chinese-owned, three-story Thai San Hotel, built in the 1950s at #75 Rue Paul Bert. It was "the sort of place an elite Cambodian would take expatriates for lunch," Dr. Osborne wrote to me. The Thai San's outdoor terrace was edged with dwarf palms, thus separating its clientele of expatriates and well-heeled Cambodians from the hoi-polloi in the streets beyond. On September 30, 1970, the popular Thai San was blasted by a terrorist bomb. Today, neither the Thai San's appellation nor its terrace survives, but there is still a restaurant and hotel, recently renovated and renamed Asia Tune, on the corner of streets 148 and 19.

ITS NAME NOTWITHSTANDING, LE Nouveau Tricotin, at #126 Street 130 (Map 3, #53), now the well-known Sharky Bar, was one the city's foremost Chinese restaurants, though it also specialized in other cuisines. Here is how it was in 1955, shortly after Cambodia's independence, according to C. D. Rowley: "At Le Tricotin there were four sections – for French, Chinese, Vietnamese, and Cambodian food respectively – in the form of a cross, with kitchen and offices in the center; and to add to the international flavour one could watch there the last of the *légionnaires* jazzing with Chinese, Cambodian,

Sharky Bar, upstairs on Street 130, was once
Le Nouveau Tricotin; open only at night.

and Vietnamese girls." Though today Sharky's is reputed for its
Mexican cuisine, the pleasurable hospitality offered by Cambodian
and Vietnamese ladies is still available.

MORE HAS BEEN WRITTEN about Madame Chum's than about
any of the above wining and dining enterprises. Of Cantonese and
Vietnamese descent, Madame Chum (pronounced "choom" and
sometimes written Choum, Chhum, Chung, or Shum) was Cambodia's opium queen, and her den was Phnom Penh's most famous. She
opened it in the 1930s after she had been abandoned by the French
lover by whom she had become pregnant, a man who worked for
the French merchant house Denis Frères. Later the mistress of a
president of Cambodia's national assembly, Madame Chum ran her
fumerie for over thirty years.

132

The writer Norman Lewis was introduced to Madame Chum's in 1950, when Cambodia was still a French protectorate:

> The salon was a great bamboo shack among the trees, its empty window-apertures glowing feebly with death-bed light. In these romantic surroundings the raffish élite of Phnom-Penh meet together at night over the sociable sucking of opium pipes . . .
>
> We were received by Madame herself, who possessed all the calm dignity of her social position . . . We were served highballs on the veranda while Madame showed us the latest portrait of her son, who was studying medicine in Paris, and of her daughter, an extremely beautiful girl of seventeen who was at college in Saigon. They were by different French fathers, she mentioned.

Customers included "corpulent officials, these chiefs-of-staff and under-secretaries," who like others went to Madame Chum's "first because it was the thing to do, and secondly because you met all kinds of business and other contacts there." Lewis watched the whole process of preparing the opium pipes, though he could not get himself to indulge in smoking one. "These preparatory rites were performed by a corps of uniformly ill-favoured young Cambodian ladies, whose looks Madame excused by saying that all the pretty ones had recently been abducted by some ex-bandits newly formed into a patriotic army."

The imposingly named French diplomat Pierre Mathivet de la Ville de Mirmont, who had been a personal secretary to King Sihanouk in the 1940s, visited Madame Chum's in the late 1950s when he was chargé d'affaires at France's embassy in Phnom Penh, as he reported in his unpublished memoirs.

> Madame Chum's was both an opium den and a brothel, all in a vast Cambodian style house built on pilings. The interior was partitioned into rooms by walls of woven bamboo slats, giving an intimate atmosphere suitable for the

escapades which took place there. In fact, everyone went to Mme. Chum's, even if it was just to unwind among friends enveloped by the sweetish scent of opium which permeated the place . . .

A visit to this picturesque establishment was part of the welcoming ritual which we reserved for high-ranking French politicians whom we were assigned to receive. Dinner at the High Commission was followed by dancing with taxi girls at an open air establishment, the girls tasked with keeping the guests' glasses always filled. Then, to discover the depravity of Asia, it was off to finish the night at Madame Chum's.

What was extraordinary *chez la Mère Chum* was the surprising blend of debauchery and an ambience which I can say was almost familial, permitting even the most sober of guests to come and relax without restraint in long discussions or in daydreaming among friends. As to the proprietress of this place, she was a figure well worth meeting. Since confidences were so frequently exchanged on the mats of her establishment, she had always been for the French authorities a valuable source of information.

Awaiting her daughter's return from France for the school holidays, Madame Chum once invited monks to her house to perform a purification ceremony. "It was a total failure," wrote Mathivet, "the good monks having imbibed too much to follow their vows of chastity with the ladies of the place." Monsieur Mathivet added that Madame Chum "refused to admit to her celebrated establishment Uncle Sam's citizens, whom she found too boisterous for the subdued atmosphere that reigned there."

Madame Chum seems to have put this aversion behind her, for twenty years later one of her guests was the war photographer Sean Flynn, son of Hollywood heartthrob Errol Flynn (on Sean Flynn, see also Chapter 1). Here's how the younger Flynn's friend Carl Anderson, photo editor for the Associated Press in Saigon in the late 1960s, explained the bonding brought on by smoking a number of pipes together at Madame Chum's establishment: "In many ways, the lamp [used for heating the opium] became part of our friendship – we shared the 'opium understanding' a mystique of incomparable relaxation, conversations and impressions, and friendships."

Another of Flynn's opium smoking buddies, the journalist Perry Dean Young described Madame Chum's in these words: "The place looked like an ordinary house on the edge of town, but once inside, you took off all your Western clothes, put on a sarong, and lay down on mats to smoke while young girls (or old crones) massaged your body." Little had changed since the visits of Norman Lewis and Pierre Mathivet.

At about the same time as Flynn and friends were indulging in Madame Chum's opium, Jon Swain reported that her French customers were resentful of other expatriates frequenting her establishment. To escape their glares and snide remarks, Swain began patronizing another den, this one run by Chantal, one of Madame Chum's former staff, located a block from today's Tuol Sleng Genocide Museum.

A Cambodian friend of mine had an uncle who in those days was a friend of Madame Chum. Rather different from the accounts by foreigners reported above, my friend's uncle told him that among Cambodians Madame Chum's establishment was known more as an upper-class bordello than an opium den. Madame Chum was in fact one of the biggest brothel keepers in Southeast Asia, the uncle reported, and her girls were versed in an admirable range of love-making techniques. Among other pleasures Madame Chum's offered, or so I was told, was fornication with ducks, which apparently was a pastime of the French military in Indochina days known as "Cholon duck" and involved, as I'm sure all will be interested to know, wedging a live duck's neck in a drawer thereby loosening certain of the fowl's apertures and allowing the bestiality to proceed. Each thrust by the duck's virile partner tightened the neck jammed in the drawer and in so doing caused its penetrated orifice to constrict rhythmically. Together with the additional pleasure of having the suffering duck's flapping feet tickle the client's genitals, the result was a most delicious climax (see box). My friend added that a foreign ambassador hosted a yearly party at Madame Chum's, a soirée well-attended by the higher echelons of the diplomatic corps, though I'm not suggesting that any of the guests partook in the delights of Cholon duck.

Canard de Cholon, named after the Chinese quarter of Saigon, apparently originated in the late 1940s when a French soldier was stabbed to death in a Saigon brothel by the prostitute with whom he was making love, a woman sympathetic to the Viet Minh. As a result of the murder, brothel owners, understandably concerned about losing their clientele, then gave soldiers eager to relieve their energies but wary of such a terminal outcome the option of a Cholon duck. The duck was presumably gagged during the process, more often than not did not survive, and was later served up on a bed of rice – lacquered, grilled, or curried.

Madame Chum's attractive daughter, incidentally, married a young Cambodian magistrate and their wedding ceremony was attended by several members of the royal family. Madame Chum herself fed, lodged, and educated many homeless children. When she died in 1970 at the age of 67, she was given a grand funeral to honor her for her services, both charitable and opiate. Jon Swain wrote her obituary for the French newspaper *Le Figaro*.

In 1970, the ethnologist François Bizot, author of *The Gate* (see Chapter 16), lived in a wooden house next door to Madame Chum's *fumerie*, in an area of traditional village houses. (There are allegations that Madame Chum's landlady was none other than Queen Kossamak, Prince Sihanouk's mother, though if she owned anything at all, it was more likely the land, not the building, and certainly not the business.) Bizot recently wrote to me that Mme. Chum's establishment was located on Street 310, south of

Independence Monument. The opium den was the third or fourth house on the north side of the street, he said, just to the west of Norodom Boulevard (Map 4, #83). Today, the old wooden buildings on that street have all gone except for the fourth one, the innocuous-looking house pictured below, one which fits Perry Dean Young's description of the place as "an ordinary house on the edge of town" much more than it does Norman Lewis' "a great bamboo shack," though it's quite possible that Mme. Chum's changed location between the days of Lewis and those of Young. The present residents of the house, who have been there since 1979, told me they were unaware of a "bar" having ever existed there, and they added they'd been told that a high ranking police officer had lived there before the Khmer Rouge emptied Phnom Penh of its people in April 1975. However, when I sent Bizot the photograph, he replied that although he could not be absolutely sure due to the great changes the neighborhood has seen over the last years, the house indeed seemed to be the place where in times gone by certain in the city's elite passed many an agreeable hour.

La fumerie de la Mère Chum was most likely here, at #7 Street 310

137

Sources

Christopher Pym, *Mistapim in Cambodia*, Travel Books,1960.

Milton Osborne, *Phnom Penh, a Cultural and Literary History*, Oxford, 2008.

Samyl Monipong Sisowath, *Voyage au royaume de la panthère longibande*, Connaissances et Savoir, 2008.

Neil Manton, *Strange Flowers on the Diplomatic Vine*, Manton, 2007.

Andrew F. Antippas interviewed by Charles Stuart Kennedy, July 19, 1994, *Foreign Affairs Oral History Project*, The Association for Diplomatic Studies and Training, 1998.

Sichan Siv, *Golden Bones*, Harper Collins, 2009.

Loup Durand, *The Angkor Massacre*, Morrow, 1983.

John Swain, *River of Time*, Vintage, 1995.

François Bizot, *The Gate*, Vintage, 2003.

Maslyn Williams, *The Land in Between: the Cambodian Dilemma*, Morrow, 1969.

Christine Spengler, *Une femme dans la guerre*, 1991, in Dominique Bérad, editor, *Des Français au Cambodge*, volume II, undated.

C. D. Rowley, *The Lotus and the Dynamo*, Angus & Robertson, 1960.

Norman Lewis, *A Dragon Apparent*, Eland, 1951.

Pierre Mathivet de la Ville de Mirmont, *Je me suis bien amusé*, unpublished manuscript.

Perry Deane Young, *Two of the Missing*, Press 53, 2000 [1975].

On Cholon duck: cdojoubert.canalblog.com/archives/2007/01/12/12467121.html (the blog is in French; scroll about one-third of the way down to a section entitled *Le Canard de Cholon*).

16. François Bizot's Gate

If you have not yet read François Bizot's *The Gate*, you should pick up an original copy at Monument Books (Map 3, #68), if not a bootlegged one from a second-hand bookstore or a disabled vendor along Sisowath Quay. The book first recounts Bizot's sufferings in a forest prison camp run by Duch (the alias of Kaing Guek Eav), including his conversations with the future head of the Khmer Rouge's infamous S-21 interrogation *cum* torture center, today the Tuol Sleng Museum of Genocide. Bizot was later released, and the second part of his story deals with the entry of the Khmer Rouge into Phnom Penh in April 1975 and the detention in the French Embassy compound (located at the northern end of Monivong Boulevard) of all foreigners, including the Khmer Rouge's fellow communists of the Soviet bloc and the ever neutral Swiss.

Those events of April 1975 have also been described by one resident priest and two journalists who witnessed them, François Ponchaud in *Cambodia: Year Zero*, and Jon Swain in *River of Time* and Sidney Schanberg in *The Death and Life of Dith Pran* and in his more recently published *Beyond the Killing Fields*. Bizot's account is different from most others written about the Khmer Rouge and the fall of Phnom Penh (as is Father Ponchaud's) in that he was fluent in Khmer and as a consequence served as an interpreter in talks between French diplomats and the Khmer Rouge, notably concerning the Cambodians who had sought refuge in the embassy compound and who, after negotiations failed, were forced to leave it. As his friend John Le Carré put it in his introduction to Bizot's book, "Bizot, you see, was not an observer, not an analyst, not a silk-shirt expert in an air-conditioned office. He was a player."

Bizot's gate is the one that once protected the main entrance to the French Embassy (Map 2, #18). Following the Sirik Matak-Lon Nol coup against Prince Sihanouk, France had downgraded its diplomatic relations with Cambodia. There was now no ambassador, and the highest French representative was a consul, supported by a French staff of only seven. Here is how Bizot remembers the embassy's gate at the very beginning of Chapter One:

> From among my memories there comes up today the image of a gate. It appears before me and I recognize the pathetic hinge which was both a beginning and an end of my life. It is made of two swinging panels, which haunt my dreams, and wire mesh welded onto a tubular frame. It closed off the main entrance to the French Embassy when the Khmer Rouge entered Phnom Penh in April 1975.

On that April day, the seventeenth of the month, the gate opened to admit frightened foreigners and Cambodians seeking sanctuary. At first, virtually anyone who wanted to come in was admitted. But the embassy personnel were soon overwhelmed. One of the two French policemen responsible for the embassy's security, Georges Villevielle, would later remember it this way: "Very quickly, given the extensive size of the embassy, the low height of the surrounding wall, and the influx of refugees, we were completely inundated. I even recall seeing some Cambodians trying to lift over the wall, at some distance from the gate, a paralyzed man in his armchair."

Given the number of refugees – in all, about 1,600 had managed to enter the compound – the gate was then ordered shut and locked, turning away those imploring but without French or foreign papers. One of those refused entry was Prince Sisowath Monireth, once prime minister under his nephew King Sihanouk. Prince Monireth arrived at the gate wearing the Legion of Honor medal which France had bestowed on him. He was subsequently executed by the Khmer Rouge.

Manned by an embassy official named Migot, the gate continued to receive foreigners, but only foreigners, over the next days. Over one hundred Pakistanis; a livid Erich Stange, the East German diplomat who had recently arrived thinking to reopen his country's embassy ("They'll pay for this," he fumed); seven Soviet

Monsieur Migot mans the gate from the inside

diplomats, hands tied behind their backs, who had been ousted from their embassy by the Khmer Rouge after unsuccessfully trying to establish friendly relations with their fellow communists. (The Soviet Union had recognized the Lon Nol regime following the coup against Prince Sihanouk and had even renewed a financial accord with the new government; this rather surprising position was most likely due to the USSR's opposition to China, which supported the Khmer Rouge.)

Also passing through the gateway were Jean-Pierre Martini and his wife Danielle, French teachers and supporters of the Khmer Rouge, who arrived wearing black Khmer Rouge clothes. At the sight of them, Monsieur Migot at the gate "exploded with rage," witnessed Jon Swain. "He walked up to Jean-Pierre and slapped him hard on the face with a crack like a gunshot. 'Enlevez-moi ça,' he shouted. The pair were obliged to strip off their black pajamas on the spot and put on western clothes."

The gate later swung open on orders of the Khmer Rouge, not to receive but to expel all Cambodians inside. "The odd thing was that so few of them expressed surprise at being ejected," wrote Swain. "They were numbed and resigned, and bleakly stared ahead." All left the embassy for the highways which led from the city to the horror that awaited.

Among those forced to exit the embassy were Prince Sihanouk's third wife, Princess Manivane, together with their daughter Princess Norodom Sujata, her husband, and their children. They were murdered soon thereafter. (In all, five of Prince Sihanouk's children and fourteen of his grandchildren were exterminated by the Khmer Rouge.) The Khmer Rouge then ordered the embassy to hand over Prince Sisowath Sirik Matak, who along with Lon Nol had led the coup which ousted his cousin Prince Sihanouk five years before, and whom the embassy had sought to hide. "I am not afraid," Sirik Matak said at the gate. "I am ready to account for my actions." He was executed a few hours afterward.

The gate was opened ten days later and again the next week when the foreigners in the compound, about six hundred of them, were loaded onto two convoys of trucks and driven 420 kilometers to the Thai border. The embassy was now empty, the gate closed.

Through the years Pol Pot controlled Phnom Penh, the French Embassy suffered substantially, perhaps as much by neglect as by actual destruction. When the journalist Elizabeth Becker visited Phnom Penh in December 1978, during the last weeks of Khmer Rouge control of the city, she noted that the French Embassy was used as a dormitory, and when she passed by "black pajamas were hanging out to dry on the balconies and cadre were walking in the grounds."

After the Khmer Rouge were booted out of the city in January 1979, the embassy became a base for the Vietnamese army. Jon Swain returned to Phnom Penh in 1980 and reported that the embassy was "partly in ruins and stinking of human excrement, the walls were covered in soldiers' graffiti." It later became an orphanage for girls whose parents had died victims of Khmer Rouge rule.

The embassy was returned to its original function following the resurrection of diplomatic relations in 1992. The present French Embassy, completely rebuilt, is on the same site as the old one, even on the original foundations. The entrance gate is new, but the one of Bizot's title, or at least one half of it, still stands in the embassy compound, as he tells us:

François Bizot's gate as it stands today, in
the leafy grounds of the French Embassy

The south panel of the gate is preserved at the far end of the
grounds of the French Embassy . . . like a little altar erected
to the spirits of the dead. The several million dead. If you
hold your breath, you can still hear the heavy footsteps of
the exiles as they make their way along the old boulevard
with their bundles. The rust that has eaten into the panel
has not, in my eyes, affected its radiance. With time it has
taken on a surprising beauty. Like anything beautiful, or
accomplished, or enduring – anything finally worthwhile –
it has become simple, and the mesh has become regular:
like a line in a Matisse drawing. It expresses, in an instant, so
many things about the roots of life that you feel all at once
like crying, and dying, and living.

. . . The Khmer Rouge, some time after 1975, or perhaps
the orphan girls who took over the premises in 1980,
have treated it to a coat of green cellulose paint; now it is
chipped, but beneath it you can, here and there, make out
the original gray.

Down a dirt path at the far end of the embassy's four hectare compound, in one of the only bits of tropical forest in the city, this sad gate doesn't look like it could have kept anyone out, whether refuge seeker or thief. It was kept shut only by a simple bolt secured with a padlock. There is a hole in the mesh of the gate's upper right hand corner. One wonders whether it was made by the crowd trying to clamber in during those appalling days of April 1975.

The gate's distressing story is remembered on a grey marble plaque which lies on the ground in front of it. Sweep off the fallen leaves and you will read these incised lines, in French:

> From the 17th of April to the 26th of May 1975 this gate of the fence which enclosed the French Embassy in Cambodia opened then closed on unspeakable pain and on the death of millions of Khmer.

Bizot was an ethnologist and scholar of Buddhism working with the *École française d'Extrême-Orient*, at whose quarters on Monivong Boulevard he often stayed. The French protectorate era house was looted during Khmer Rouge times, and its valuable collection of books and documents on Cambodian archaeology, culture, and history were destroyed. The building still stands, and it is now the Heng Pich Guesthouse, on the corner of Monivong and Street 84 (Map 2, #22).

Bizot's negotiating partners were attached to the Khmer Rouge Military Security Committee, whose offices were in a building at #6 Monivong Boulevard (Map 2, #17), directly across the street from the French Embassy, a property which previously had been the South Korean Embassy and now is a branch of Mekong Bank.

THOUGH FOR SECURITY REASONS requests to tour the French Embassy's forested compound are rarely given (I was permitted entry once, hence the photos, but my second application was politely turned down), should you have the opportunity to visit Bizot's gate, look around among the tropical trees and the occasional

The former *École française d'Extrême-Orient*, now the Heng Pich Guesthouse

The former Khmer Rouge Military Security Committee offices

grazing deer for seven old tombstones. The French inscription on a bronze plaque in front of them informs:

> These tombstones are all that remain of the old French cemetery in Phnom Penh destroyed during the tragic years which Cambodia experienced.
> In Memoriam

The oldest and saddest tombstone belongs to Pierre Louis Marie Palasne de Champeaux, who died on February 5, 1889, at the age of

The infant's tombstone, dated 1889

145

just three months. His father Louis Eugène Palasne de Champeaux was acting *résident général* at Phnom Penh at the time of his son's death. Palasne de Champeaux *père* died in Marseille in August of that same year, shortly after his return to France, no doubt with a heavy heart.

Of the other deceased whose gravestones are in the embassy's forest, two were surveyors for the protectorate's department of posts and telegraph. The first, Pierre Biot, 1846–1891, had come to Indochina in 1868 as a naval infantry soldier and later became controller of the telegraphs in Phnom Penh. He was then asked by Auguste Pavie – the future leader of the Pavie Mission, a group of surveyors *cum* explorers who surveyed Laos in the 1880s and 1890s and by so doing claimed the whole of that country for France – to assist in constructing a telegraph line from Phnom Penh to Bangkok, a project that lasted from December 1881 to July 1883. Pavie wrote of Biot:

> He was gentle with the locals, a particularly useful approach in his job, and got along with them admirably . . . Bringing him, I was sure to have a devoted, courageous, and loyal colleague . . . For the accomplishment of the work we lived fourteen months together, in the forests and the great plains, enduring rain, marching through flooded terrain or on burning sand, sometimes gripped by fever. Biot, always in the same mood, transferred his drive to his local workers, lifting their morale when it weakened, by his example, his gaiety, and his pleasantries at their expense.

Biot for years kept a pet monkey also called Pierre, a ferocious animal that only he could approach. When Pavie passed through Phnom Penh in 1892 and didn't find Biot, Pavie "heard that Pierre, his monkey, which he approached to caress, had suddenly thrown himself on him and had half torn off one of his calves. Thinking that the animal had rabies, Biot had it killed immediately with a rifle shot, then he had the courage to walk to the doctor, had his terrible wound taken care of, and on returning went to sleep. Eleven days later, my poor companion, my simple courageous friend Biot was dead. Loved by all who knew him, he died after thirty years of service in Indochina in a modest position in which his merits had nevertheless been noticed. The news of his tragic end brought me great sadness."

Pierre Biot

The second surveyor with a salvaged gravestone was Joseph le Bidan, born in Lorient on February 26, 1877, died in Phnom Penh on August 5, 1927. Another gravestone remembers Jacques Goire, a sharpshooter with France's Far East Commandos, who died on October 26, 1946, a year after the French had regained control of Cambodia following World War II. The words on the remaining tombstones are virtually illegible.

Opened in the 1880s, the French cemetery was located between the northern end of today's Rue de France (St. 47) and Sisowath Quay, with Oknha Khleang Moeung (St. 70) bordering it on the north (Map 2, #15). The graveyard was called Providence Cemetery after the nearby church of the Sisters of Providence of Portieux, who came to Cambodia from France in 1881. Their church, incidentally, still stands, the only one in central Phnom Penh not demolished by the Khmer Rouge, though it is now divided up into numerous small apartments. Unlike the church, the cemetery was largely destroyed during the Pol Pot era, as the bronze plaque in the French Embassy implies, though following the ousting of the Khmer Rouge grave robbers eager for French jewelry and gold teeth were also responsible for the desecration. When French diplomats returned following that devastating time, only those seven tombstones remained. Presumably the bones of Pierre Louis Marie Palasne de Champeaux, Pierre Biot, Joseph le Bidan, and Jacques Goire, as well as those of many others lie somewhere beneath the ground of the Hun Sen-Bun Rany Wat Phnom High School, which now stands on the site.

The present French Embassy gate

Sources

François Bizot, *The Gate*, Knopf, 2003.

François Ponchaud, *Cambodia: Year Zero*, Holt, Rinehart and Winston, 1977.

Jon Swain, *River of Time*, Vintage, 1995.

Sidney Schanberg, *The Death and Life of Dith Pran*, Elisabeth Sifton-Penguin, 1980.

Sidney Schanberg, *Beyond the Killing Fields*, Potomac Books, 2010.

Roland Neveu, *The Fall of Phnom Penh*, Asia Horizon Books, 2009.

Elizabeth Becker, *When the War Was Over*, Public Affairs, 1998 (second edition).

Piotr Smolar, "Phnom Penh, 1975: nuits rouges sur l'ambassade," *Le Monde*, January 1, 2007.

Auguste Pavie, *Pavie Mission Exploration Work: Volume 1 of the Pavie Mission Indochina Papers (1879–1895)*, White Lotus Press, 1999; this is the first English translation of the original, which was published in 1901.

17. King Norodom's Head

On my first visit to the Royal Palace, I stopped in front of the Silver Pagoda to admire the equestrian statue of King Norodom (1834–1904), the sovereign himself splendidly fitted out in French general's attire (Map 3, #71). The king's steed had been colored white, and the royal pate was spotted with the odd pigeon dropping. When I opened my guidebook, however, I was surprised to read that the figure "is in fact a statue of Napoleon III with the head replaced with that of the Cambodian monarch."

A quick check of the history books revealed that Napoleon III (1808–1873), nephew of Napoleon Bonaparte, ruled France from 1848 to 1870 and was emperor for the last eighteen of those years. At the disastrous battle of Sedan in July 1870, he surrendered to the Germans along with 80,000 of his troops, thus ending the Franco-Prussian War. Three days later Napoleon III was overthrown and

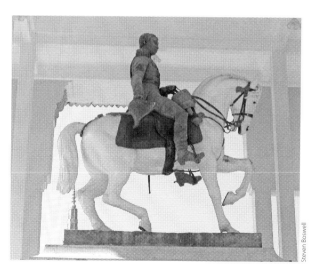

King Norodom I on the grounds of the Silver Pagoda

the French Third Republic was established. The deposed emperor then went into exile in England, where he died three years later.

I later came across other references to Napoleon III's acephalic body being used to support Norodom's cranium both in guidebooks and in more authoritative volumes. Here, for example, is Penny Edwards in *Cambodge: The Cultivation of a Nation, 1860–1945*: "A bronze statue of Norodom on horseback, in the trappings of a French general, graced the palace grounds: a gift from the French government, this former statue of Napoleon II [*sic*] had been decapitated and recapped with a bust of Norodom chiselled up from a portrait. This cosmetic surgery symbolized French visions of Norodom as a figurehead of the protectorate's body politic."

Charles Meyer, who in the 1950s and 1960s wrote speeches for Prince Sihanouk and directed the publication of the prince's periodicals and daily news bulletin, and who consequently had access to the prince, wrote about the statue in *Derrière le sourire khmer*: "This 'work of art,' originally a figure of Napoleon III in all his glory, had been offered to Cambodia by the French Republic, which did not know what to do with it anymore. The whole was not lacking in bearing, and for the slightest expense all that was needed to be done was to replace the bearded head of the emperor with that of his longtime royal protégé."

Joel Montague in his volume on Cambodian postcards reproduces one of King Norodom's statue standing amid abundant foliage, and he repeats what others have said, "A French equestrian statue of Napoleon III was shipped to Phnom Penh from France with the head of King Norodom placed on it replacing that of Napoleon III."

In his book on Phnom Penh, the historian Milton Osborne gives this account, though he doesn't specifically mention that the statue's body belonged to Napoleon III:

> In 1876, in what they regarded as a gesture of benevolence, the French even provided Norodom with a life-sized equestrian statue, in which he bestrode the horse dressed in a

general's uniform, and which now stands on the grounds of the Silver Pagoda. The best evidence is that the statue was a 'stock model', to which only Norodom's head had to be added to give it a 'personal' character. The background to the statue's origin became lost in the years that followed, so that it became prized possession for the modern royal family, particularly as Norodom Sihanouk promoted his ancestor in the 1950s and 1960s as a model of Cambodian nationalism.

Those who accept the story, however, do not seem to be familiar with Olivier de Bernon's short article "The Inscriptions of King Norodom's Equestrian Statue" in the January 1999 edition of the journal *Seksa Khmer*, though Meyer, admittedly, could not have read it as his book was written almost thirty years before de Bernon's article appeared. De Bernon, who in the 1990s was the representative in Cambodia of the prestigious *École française d'Extrême-Orient,* attributes the origin of the story of Norodom's statue to the colonial administrator and scholar Adhémard Leclère, who worked in Cambodia from 1886 to 1911, and who wrote in *Cambodge, fêtes civiles et religieuses,* published in 1916, "This equestrian statue is in fact a statue of Napoleon III on which a head of Norodom was attached."

The statue, as de Bernon points out, bears the names of both its sculptor and its manufacturer, as well as the year and place of its fabrication: "EUDE SCULP. 1875" on the left is followed by "J. RANVIER FABant Paris" on the right. Given that Napoleon III had died

The sculptor, Louis-Adolphe Eude
(1818–1889), and the date, 1875

The manufacturer (*fabricant*), J. Ranvier,
and the place of fabrication, Paris

in exile in 1873, it is highly improbable that statues of him were still being cast two years later. Thus, de Bernon dismisses the story of King Norodom's statue as a "tenacious" myth. The king's likeness, he says, was probably taken from a portrait, and dressing him in a French general's uniform was more likely a way to honor him, as well as to express his assimilation to the French metropole.

It is a bit surprising that a number of distinguished writers and historians seem to have ignored the sculptor, Louis-Adolphe Eude (1818–1889), and instead accepted the myth. No doubt the issue of King Norodom's head was simply too minor a matter to spend time on researching.

The question, then, is when and why the "tenacious" myth arose in the first place. Of the writers who contend that the head and body of King Norodom's statue are not one and the same, only Edwards gives a source, Eugène Lagrillière-Beauclerc in *Au Cambodge et Annam: Voyage Pittoresque*, published in 1900, sixteen years before Adhémard Leclère's volume. Perhaps Lagrillière-Beauclerc got his information directly from Leclère, who was mayor of Phnom Penh from 1899 to 1903. However, since the statue was inaugurated in 1876, it would seem strange that if the story of Napoleon's body and Norodom's head were true, it would not have been mentioned prior to Lagrillière-Beauclerc's 1900 account, much less Leclère's 1916 one.

In fact, King Norodom's statue was the topic of several official messages written in the 1870s and was mentioned in at least one book published in the 1880s, though none of them made reference to Napoleon III. On August 9, 1875, Representative of the Protectorate Jean Moura wrote to his superior, Governor of Cochinchina Jules Krantz, saying that upon his return from a trip to Saigon he observed that the masonry foundation of the statue was being built along the riverside. Moura, who had issues with Norodom, told the king that such a public site was contrary to custom and norms, and consequently he ordered that the statue be erected in the palace gardens, "where only the women would be admitted to contemplate His Majesty's countenance and favorable appearance on horesback." No mention of Napoleon III here, and if the statue was indeed erected in the palace grounds, it was moved to the riverside not long thereafter.

Three years later, on April 18, 1878, Moura wrote to Governor Louis Lafont in Saigon that he had tried his utmost to prevent the purchase of King Norodom's statue and its subsequent erection in a public place. Moreover, he had greatly ruffled the king's feathers by not attending the statue's inauguration ceremony. Again, no mention of Napoleon III. Finally, in another missive to Lafont, dated July 22 of that same year, Moura gave some background to the statue:

> A [European] merchant proposed to the King, three or four years ago, to have a bronze equestrian statue made for him. The order was placed, the statue arrived; it was made of zinc rather than bronze, but at first this was not noticed and a great festival was organized for its inauguration. Later, when it was time to pay, it was realized that the bill was excessively high, even without taking into account the fraud concerning the metal. To settle the issue, the merchant advised the King to have his subjects offer the statue to him. What was said was done: the contribution of princes was fixed at a certain amount, that of high mandarins at another, that of mid-level mandarins at another, and so on down to the poorest of the poor, who too had to put their sweat into this deceit. Thus, if memory serves me right, one hundred and fifty thousand francs was collected. One hundred thousand francs was paid for the object, though it was worth only twelve thousand, and fifty thousand francs thus remained as a bonus for the King.

Once more, no mention of Napoleon III. Moura's message does say that the order was placed "three or four years ago," which would be consistent with the date on the statue, 1875, two years after Napoleon's death in exile. Gregor Muller, who in *Colonial Cambodia's Bad Frenchmen* (2006) wrote in depth about French merchants in Cambodia in the early years of the protectorate, told me that the trader who cheated Norodom "may not have been a Frenchman but a German named Speidel, who had picked up a lot of orders from Norodom around 1875, to the chagrin of the French merchant houses in Phnom Penh. But one cannot be sure."

In *Ca et là: Cochinchine et Cambodge: l'âme Khmère – Ang-Kor* (1884), Paul Branda (a pseudonym for Rear Admiral Paul Réveillère: French military officers and civil servants often used a fictitious name in order to criticize without raising against themselves the ire of the powers that be) described King Norodom and his statue with a poisoned pen:

> The horse is handsome, Norodom, in general's garb, has the look of a disguised corpse. In front of the pedestal, two cast iron lions guard the statue, the massive bricks on which they lie have crumbled, and the two lions have fallen on their noses. This fake bronze, in a stagnant swamp, in the middle of miserable huts; it's always the same: the lighthouse without a lantern, the ruined steamships, one without a boiler the other without a propeller, the dirty gilding ... It is the Cambodian people who have become playthings in the hands of a spoiled and senile child. This statue – costing 90,000 francs – was supposedly offered to Norodom by his grateful subjects, but an official document set the minimum contribution according to the rank and the wealth of the donors, and the poorest could not offer less than one ligature [a string of coins] ... One could not exhaust the list of all the silly fantasies of this all-powerful despot who imagines himself as being great when he wastes the fruits of his people's labor on such foolishness.

Considering Branda's rancorous attitude toward the king, and given the fact that he knew about the alleged funding of the statue, he would presumably have written that the equestrian figure had originally been one of Napoleon III were the story indeed true.

So if the statue was cast for King Norodom, from where did the idea come that it was once one of the Emperor of France? Olivier de Bernon, as noted, believed it was from Adhémard Leclère in his 1916 book. However, in an entry from one of his notebooks dated August 2, 1886, describing the Royal Palace, Leclère wrote, "The statue of Norodom stands on the riverside, in front of the palace, in a small square where grow wild weeds." No indication here that the statue once carried Napoleon III's head.

The earliest reference to the statue recycling story that I know of is the one mentioned by Penny Edwards, Eugéne Lagrillière-Beauclerc in *Au Cambodge et Annam: Voyage Pittoresque*, published in 1900, though in the book he does not give the origin of his allegation. Moreover, Lagrillière-Beauclerc may not be the most reliable source. He was sent to Southeast Asia on a "study mission" by France's minister of colonies. After completing his assignment, he wrote *A travers l'Indochine* ("Across Indochina"), also published in 1900. A reviewer wrote in a 1901 issue of the scholarly *Bulletin de l'École française d'Extrême-Orient* that Lagrillière-Beauclerc could have written the book without ever having left his Paris office, for in it "one would look in vain for original views or new information," and "personal observation plays an imperceptible role." Was it necessary, the reviewer continued, to mention that in Indochina one can find dogs, horses, and chickens? As to the "zebras" which Lagrillière-Beauclerc noted, the reviewer remarked that one can only hope this was the typesetter's mistake, and that Lagrillière-Beauclerc's original word was "zebu," or humped ox.

If Lagrillière-Beauclerc did not hear the story of King Norodom's statue from Adhémard Leclère, then perhaps he picked it up from Paul Doumer, the governor-general of Indochina at that time, who was in Phnom Penh in 1897. Here is Doumer on the statue in *L'Indochine française: Souvenirs*, published in 1905:

> A French merchant resident in Cambodia persuaded the king that in order to assure his glorious renown he had to have in Phnom Penh a statue of him, a monumental

equestrian statue, one worthy of such a powerful monarch. Armed with a written order, at an inevitably high price, and several photographs of the august model to be reproduced, he departed for France. This was about 1872. Our merchant found at a foundry an equestrian statue of Napoleon III which had been completed at the time the war broke out and left in a storeroom. It could be purchased at a reasonable price, the price of the metal alone. However, as Napoleon did not at all resemble Norodom, the head of the statue was sawed off; a head which could pass for that of a Cambodian was fashioned following the photographs, then cast and welded onto the body of the ex-emperor of France. A few months later, the statue arrived in Phnom Penh; it was found to be magnificent and was raised in front of the royal palace, by the majestic river. The enormous horse and the body of Napoleon III, surmounted with the borrower's head . . . will announce to future ages the glory of Norodom.

Paul Doumer (1857–1932) was the governor-general of Indochina from 1897 to 1902 (he was president of France from 1931 to May 6, 1932, when he was fatally shot in Paris by a Russian émigré anarchist). Doumer may well have seen King Norodom's statue and heard its story from local Frenchmen – as could have Lagrillière-Beauclerc – when he visited Phnom Penh in 1897, twenty years after the erection of the statue, time enough for a myth to develop. Notice that Doumer does not mention the date on the statue, 1875, the year of its casting, which is Olivier de Bernon's main point for rejecting the story since it is two years after the disgraced Napoleon III's death.

In fact, this minor mystery could have been solved long ago had any of the above writers other than Olivier de Bernon paid attention to the sculptor, Eude, whose name is clearly etched on the statue, and researched his works. Had any of them, or at least the later ones, turned to page 310 of volume two of Stanislas Lami's *Dictionary of the Sculptors of the French school in the 19th century*

(1916), which has a comprehensive listing of the works of Louis-Adolphe Eude, they would have read that among the sculptor's accomplishments was: "Norodom I, king of Cambodia. Equestrian statue in zinc. This statue was exhibited in 1875 on the Champs-Élysées, subsequently erected on the great square of Phnom Penh, capital of Cambodia." No other equestrian statue is included in the inventory of Eude's works, though among them is listed a marble *bust* of Napoleon III, ordered in 1870 by the government of France for its legation in Brussels but placed in a state warehouse following the ousting of the emperor. Another scholarly volume, by Ulrich Thieme and Felix Becker, published in 1915, a year before Lami's dictionary, also attributes to Jean Louis Adolphe Eude a zinc statue of King Norodom I of Cambodia, 1875. There is no reason to believe that Lami and Thieme-Becker were mistaken in listing King Norodom's statue among Eude's works. Both volumes state that the statue was cast in zinc, not bronze, which is consistent with Moura's report to Lafont.

In the end, this episode serves to illustrate how actual occurrences can be disregarded or distorted, thereby leading to the concoction of myths, which are then taken as fact. As to when the myth of King Norodom's head arose, it was clearly sometime before Lagrillière-Beauclerc's visit to Phnom Penh in the late 1890s, and as to why, one can only speculate that it was to belittle the Cambodian monarch, whom French administrators often condescendingly dismissed as a *roitelet*, a "kinglet," or petty king.

Moreover, the story of Napoleon's body and Norodom's head is not the only myth concerning the statue. There is the contention that the statue was a gift from the French government. This fabrication is at least as egregious as whether the statue was a recycled one or not. If the statue had been a gift of France, one would think that this would be reflected in the archival records. Instead, we learn from the words of Representative Moura, France's highest official in Phnom Penh at the time, and from those of Governor-General Doumer that the statue was not an offering of France but of the people of Cambodia, though perhaps not a very willing one. Moura, moreover, tried to prevent the purchase of the statue. Sometime thereafter, however, France was given credit for generously bequeathing the statue to Cambodia, a mistake repeated by later writers, including Meyer and Edwards. Indeed, this myth too is a tenacious one.

Also worth noting is that Doumer in his memoirs wrote that the "Iron House" in the Royal Palace, allegedly King Norodom's favorite building, was purchased by the Cambodian monarch; Doumer did not say it was a gift of France, as is widely believed today. Then there is the frequently repeated contention that the French "persuaded" King Norodom to move his capital from Udong to Phnom Penh. No documents support this assertion. In fact, the 1866 move was Norodom's own initiative (see the Pierre-Lucien Lamat source listed below).

Olivier de Bernon also mentions an inscription in French on the north side of the statue's base, words which those who claim the statue was a gift of France seem to ignore. The inscription reads: "TO NORODOM I KING OF CAMBODIA, HIS GRATEFUL MANDARINS AND PEOPLE, 1860." This would seem to confirm that Norodom's "grateful mandarins and people" contributed to the purchasing and erection of the statue, whether willingly or not. However, there is obviously a mistake in the dating, as de Bernon points out. The year 1860 was when Norodom acceded to the throne, though in fact he wasn't officially crowned until 1864. As the French did not arrive in Cambodia until 1863, it is unlikely that in 1860 King Norodom or his subjects were writing inscriptions in French. Besides, as we have seen, the statue was not cast until 1875 and was inaugurated in 1876.

A NORODOM 1er ROI du CAMBODGE
SES MANDARINS ET SON PEUPLE RECONNAISSANTS
1860

Steven Boswell

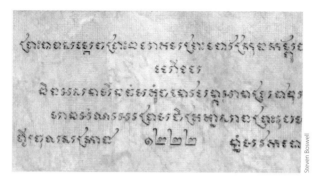

The inscription in a rather singular Khmer script

Another inscription, this one in a unique, rather fanciful Khmer script, is on the south side of the base. Unlike the first one, it declares that His Majesty King Norodom as well as his mandarins of all ranks and all his subjects had, as one heart, the joy of erecting this statue in the year 1222, the Year of the Monkey (1860). This would indicate that King Norodom had a hand in erecting the statue and that consequently it was not just a gift of his "grateful mandarins and people." De Bernon surmises that the inscription may have been copied from one originally attached to another memorial, doubtless one offered by Norodom and his subjects to his father, King Ang Duong, who died in 1860. In addition to having understandable difficulty carving the words in Khmer script, the French engraver responsible for the two inscriptions simply blundered when chiseling the year 1860 on the French dedication, most likely based on erroneous information he had received from Cambodia, an error not corrected once the statue was erected on the banks of the river. Quite the *faux pas*.

I recently took a photograph of a map dated 1886 belonging to the Royal Palace which shows King Norodom's statue as being located on the riverside – as Moura and Leclère indicated – just off today's Sisowath Quay, a bit south of where the Chaktomuk Conference Hall now stands. The statue wasn't installed in the Silver Pagoda's compound until the end of 1902, when Norodom himself opened this new pagoda. When King Norodom died of cancer in 1904,

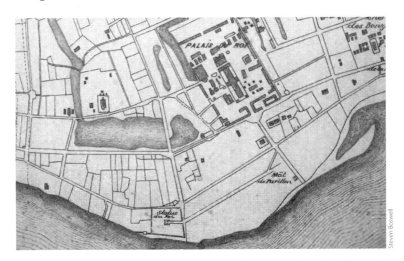

Steven Boswell

1886 map showing the location of King Norodom's statue (labeled *Statue du Roi*), near the riverbank at the bottom of the map, east of the Royal Palace

his ashes were placed in the white stupa just to the north of his statue. Some of King Norodom's ashes may also have been put in the base of his equestrian statue. Doing so, according to tradition, would give the statue a protective function, security for the royal family and for the kingdom. (Some of the king's ashes are also kept in a gold urn in the Pavilion of the August Bones, a small chapel off the Throne Hall in the Royal Palace, beside urns with ashes of King Ang Duong, King Sisowath, King Monivong, King Suramarit, and King Sihanouk.)

This is one reason why later on, according to Charles Meyer, the statue became the object of an official cult by members of the royal family, notably King Sihanouk: "his [King Norodom's] great-grandson Norodom Sihanouk made of him a sort of tutelary deity of the kingdom, residing in a bronze equestrian statue installed in the precincts of the pagoda of the royal palace during preceding reigns ... In front of the statue, princes, ministers, members of parliament, mandarins, and high government officials in formal dress were compelled to prostrate themselves and request the intervention of King Norodom to end flooding or drought, and to swear an oath of loyalty to the throne." Even the royal ballet corps participated in the ceremonies. King Sihanouk revered his ancestor, and he gained inspiration from him. During his 1953 crusade for Cambodia's independence from France, he often visited the statue in order to draw from his royal forebear the strength to pursue his struggle. On November 9 of that year, King Sihanouk added the Mondop canopy which still today protects the statue. He inaugurated the canopy in an elaborate ceremony based on traditional rites, thereby thanking King Norodom for his tutelary powers which had helped Sihanouk regain independence for his people.

King Norodom, cast 1875   King Norodom, circa 1863

Let me conclude by mentioning that while the face of the statue is a suitable likeness of King Norodom, the body of the rider on horseback is long and svelte, clearly not a truthful rendition of the physique of the king, who was a short man, just over 1.5 meters tall, or barely five feet. This could be nothing more than a bit of artistic license, permissible in such cases. But there is no artistic license in portraying the king mounted on that fine steed. Paul Le Faucheur, a leading French merchant who lived in Phnom Penh from 1864 to 1874 and who had excellent relations with the king,

161

reported in *Lettre sur le Cambodge* (1872) that "Norodom is a first-rate horseman and loves hunting; he is a skilled marksman, an able swimmer."

Sources

John Colet and Joshua Eliot, *Cambodia Handbook*, Footprint Handbooks, 2000.

Penny Edwards, *Cambodge: The Cultivation of a Nation, 1860–1945*, Hawaii, 2007.

Charles Meyer, *Derrière le sourire khmer*, Plon, 1971.

Joel Montague, *Picture Postcards of Cambodia: 1900–1950*, White Lotus, 2010.

Milton Osborne, *Phnom Penh, a Cultural and Literary History*, Signet, 2008.

Olivier de Bernon, "Les inscriptions de la statue équestre du Roi Norodom 1er," in *Seksa Khmer*, January 1999.

Eugéne Lagrillière-Beauclerc, *Au Cambodge et Annam: Voyage Pittoresque*, Charles Tallandier, 1900.

Paul Doumer, *L'Indochine française: Souvenirs*, Vuibert et Nony, 1905.

Paul Branda (pseudonym for Admiral Réveillère), *Ca et là: Cochinchine et Cambodge: L'âme khmère – Ang-kor*, Fischbacher, 1892.

Stanislas Lami, *Dictionnaire des Sculpteurs de l'école Française au 19e siècle*, Champion, 1916.

Ulrich Thieme and Felix Becker, *Allgemeines Lexikon der bildenden Kunstler, von der Antike bis zur Gegenwart*, E.A. Seemann, 1915.

Pierre-Lucien Lamant, "La Création d'une capitale par le pouvoir coloniale à Phnom Penh," in *Péninsule indochinoise. Études urbaines*, L'Harmattan, 1991.

François Bizot, "La Consécration des statues et le culte de la mort," in *Recherches nouvelles sur le Cambodge*, École française d'Extrême-Orient, 1994.

My thanks to Greg Muller for providing me with the following Moura and Leclère documentation, among others:

Representative Jean Moura to Governor of Cochinchina, 9 August 1875 (Centre des archives d'Outre-mer, Aix-en-Provence, GGI 13333); 18 April 1878 (CAOM, GGI 11829); 22 July 1878 (CAOM, GGI 11829).

Adhémard Leclère Collection, ms No.696, *Voyage au Cambodge 1886–87.* 20 notebooks. Ms paper XiXe. (Journal June 1886 – February 1888; October 1889). Incomplete. Alençon Library: "Anciens fonds" manuscripts.

18. The Streets of Phnom Penh

Both Phnom Penh residents and many visitors know that four of the city's main thoroughfares are named after recent Cambodian kings: Norodom (reigned 1860–1904), Sisowath (r. 1904–1927), Monivong (r. 1927–1941), and Sihanouk (r. 1941–1955 and 1993–2004). Almost all city streets have a number as well as a name, but most streets other than the main boulevards are in fact more commonly referred to by their number. The often-neglected names, however, offer glimpses of the kingdom's past, both historical and legendary. Many city streets are named after royals or members of the elite, while others are tagged after countries, cities, and even a few foreigners, though the names of the newest streets in the city's outskirts show a distinct lack of imagination on the part of city planners. What follows is a look at the names of some of Phnom Penh's streets, roughly following chronological order of the appellations. Note, however, that of the city's approximately 160 named streets, we only look at some eighty here.

Only one street, Viyadhapura (its corresponding number is Street 120), celebrates Funan and Chenla times during the first millennium. It is named after the city widely considered to have been the Funanese capital and for which at least three possible sites have been proposed. However, this belief may well be erroneous: the theory that Viyadhapura ("City of the Hunter") was the capital of Funan is based on Angkor era inscriptions, while the one pre-Angkor inscription that mentions Viyadhapura refers to it as a region or a minor city, probably in what today is Kompong Cham province, not as the capital city of Funan, which if one existed at all was more likely at Angkor Borei in Takeo province. Moreover, it is probable that Funan was not a unified kingdom with a capital city but rather a loose association of regional principalities and chiefdoms. There may be another reason the street bears this name: Viyadhapura was most likely the homeland of Jayavarman II, a local chief in Kompong Cham who moved his capital to the vicinity of Angkor at the beginning of the 9th century and is often referred to as the first of the Angkorian kings. Whatever the case, Viyadhapura Street runs southeast from Russian Federation Boulevard across Monivong Boulevard to the northwest corner of the Central Market.

Surprisingly, the Angkor era is barely remembered in the city's street names. Angkor itself gets the six blocks of Street 5, parallel to Sisowath Quay and the river. At the time, Angkor, which means "the city," was known as Yashodharapura, the name given to the city by Yashovarman (r. 889–915). There is also Preah Vihear Street (St. 82), named for the 12th century temple which has been such a bone of contention between Cambodia and Thailand. The great Jayavarman VII, builder of Angkor Thom with its Bayon, has to settle for two blocks of Street 172, between Street 63 and Norodom Boulevard. There is no street for the aforementioned Jayavarman II, nor for Suryavarman II, builder of Angkor Wat.

Before leaving the Angkor era, however, Baksei Cham Krong Street (St. 94) deserves mention. Legend has it that in the 11th century, the hero of that name was still in his mother's womb when his father, the king, died. The king's successor, Ponhea Krek, fearing possible contenders to the throne, ordered the killing of all male children of the royal family. The future Baksei Cham Krong's mother was disemboweled, but the infant managed to avoid the sword thrusts, crawled out of her womb, and was saved by a large bird of prey. Baksei Cham Krong (which means "bird providing shade") was raised by an elderly couple on Phnom Baset, a hill about fifteen kilometers northwest of Phnom Penh, and he eventually became king himself following the death of the cruel Ponhea Krek.

The first road name from the time which followed Angkor's grandest days is Trasak Paem Street. The Cambodian Royal Chronicles include myth and legend in addition to history (the historian Michael Vickery warns that the chronicles before the mid-16th century were often written to please the ruling monarch and are consequently of limited reliability), as can be seen in the above story of Baksei Cham Krong and in another about a man known as Trasak Paem, or "sweet cucumber," a tale that may well reflect troubled times and the collapse of the royal family. Trasak Paem was an aged gardener reputed for the sweet flavor of his cucumbers. So succulent were Trasak Paem's vegetables that the king reserved the entire cucumber harvest for himself. To protect his favorite treat, the king gave his gardener a royal lance, Preah Lompeng Chey, "August Victory Spear," and told him to stand guard at night and use the weapon against anyone who might try to steal a cucumber. One night when the king was hungry for his favorite food, he decided to test the alertness of his gardener *cum* watchman. He snuck into the garden, where the ever-vigilant Trasak Paem, thinking the intruder a thief, speared the king dead. The nobility of the realm gathered and they decided that the king's death was due to his karma. They then chose the loyal Trasak Paem to lead the kingdom. He ruled under the royal name of Nippean Bat, and, according to the chronicles, he was the first monarch of the present dynasty. All of this was supposed to have happened around 1360. You might spare a thought for the gardener and his sweet cucumbers every time you go along busy Street 63, Trasak Paem Street. The Victory Spear, incidentally, together with the sacred sword Preah Khan Reach, which was forged in the year 624 of the Buddhist era (c. 70 AD) by Vishnu and Shiva on orders of Indra and was to be given to the first Khmer king to ensure the prosperity of the country, became the sacred protectors of the realm. Both the lance and the sword disappeared from the Royal Palace following the overthrowing of Norodom Sihanouk in 1970.

Also from the 14th century, Grandmother Penh, for whom our city is named (see Chapter 13), has a grand venue, Street 92 from Wat Phnom's hill to Monivong Boulevard, passing the Sunway Hotel, Ministry of Finance, National Library, and Hôtel Le Royal. Other than Lady Penh and Queen Kossamak, mother of King Sihanouk, the only other street that I know of which is named for a

Street names are always written first in Khmer;
this is one of the few streets without a number

woman is Street 84, Neary Klahan, which translates as "courageous woman." Who this heroine was, I have yet to uncover, or perhaps the reference is to the female gender in general.

King Ponhea Yat, who brought the country's capital to Phnom Penh in the 1430s or 1440s and who allegedly was Trasak Paem's great-great-grandson, has a street of his own, the short but significant one running from the main entrance of the Royal Palace to the river. In the early days of the French protectorate, this brief street was known as *Rue de l'Éléphant Blanc*, Street of the White Elephant, in honor of the rare albino elephants that "were always given to the King and treated with great veneration, even eating sugar cane and cakes on silver platters as the Khmer believed them to be close to the incarnation of the Buddha," according to the historian John Tully in *France on the Mekong*. Today, King Sihamoni takes Ponhea Yat's street every year during the Water Festival when he leaves the palace for his riverside pavilion to watch the boat races.

Chey Chetha Street (St. 118) is named after the second king of that name, who reigned from 1619 to 1627. Chey Chetha II moved the capital to Udong in 1620, defeated the Siamese three years later, and continued the work of his father in unifying the country after a period of both internal and external troubles. He also married the daughter of Lord Sai Vuong, who ruled central Vietnam from his palace near present day Hué, a joining which would lead to a long period of Vietnamese involvement in Cambodia.

Lively Street 13 rather strangely belongs to Ang Eng (r. 1779–1796), as this king's reign is remembered more for troubles with Siam and Vietnam than for Cambodian accomplishment. He was only seven years old when he was crowned with Siamese consent. He spent the years 1783–1794 in Bangkok and had little power when he was finally permitted to return to Cambodia. In fact, despite his protestations, Ang Eng in 1795 had to acquiesce to Siam's annexation of Cambodia's western provinces, notably Battambang and Siem Reap, though he agreed to this seizure only for the lifetime of the then-reigning Siamese king. Ang Eng died the following year under unexplained circumstances, but it would be over a century before Siam was forced to return those lands. Some regard Ang Eng as the founder of Cambodia's current dynasty, and it is perhaps for this, rather than for his futile opposition to Siam's seizure of those provinces, that he is remembered today with a street of his own.

Ang Eng notwithstanding, the man generally considered as the father of the present dynasty is his grandson King Ang Duong (r. 1847–1860), who has his name on Street 110 (for more on this king, see Chapter 21). The subsequent monarchs of this dynasty include Norodom (St. 41) and Sisowath (St. 1), from whom come the two branches of the royal family, as well as Sisowath Monivong (St. 93), and Norodom Sihanouk (St. 274). The latter's father, Norodom Suramarit (r. 1955–1960), who succeeded his son as king when Sihanouk abdicated in 1954 in order to play a more political role, "to rule rather than reign," also has a street in his honor (St. 268), which runs east-west from Sothearos Boulevard to Pasteur Street (St. 51) and parallels a stretch of Sihanouk Boulevard. Street 106, which adjoins the grassy esplanade from Monivong Boulevard to the river, remembers Queen Sisowath Kossamak, Suramarit's wife and Sihanouk's mother, and for many years the head of the Royal Ballet. Lon Nol expelled the queen from the Royal Palace in 1973 but later, following intervention by Prime Minister Zhou En-lai and President Richard Nixon, allowed her to leave Phnom Penh and join her exiled son Prince Sihanouk in China. Queen Kossamak died in Beijing on April 27, 1975, ten days after the Khmer Rouge entered Phnom Penh.

You may be curious about Sothearos, who has that significant avenue named after him. Actually, "Sothearos" is a mistake in transliteration of the street's real name, "Sutharot," which is how it appeared on city maps of the 1960s. The error is presumably due to the fact that, rather inexplicably, no official, standardized rules exist for transcribing Khmer into the Latin alphabet. Norodom Sutharot (1872–1945), never a king himself, was the son of King Norodom, the father of King Suramarit, and the grandfather of King Sihanouk. Incidentally, Sutharot named his grandson, deriving the flattering moniker from the Sanskrit word for lion, *siha*. Had the succession to the crown followed primogeniture, as it often did, Sutharot might have succeeded his father. However, the Royal Council of the Throne, presently composed of nine members who represent the country's political and religious elites, chooses the next king from all the male descendants of Norodom's father, King Ang Duong, though in fact only a few are seriously considered. It should be noted that in practice, for the hundred years previous to Ang Duong, the Thai or Vietnamese greatly influenced the selection of Cambodia's monarchs, and later it was the French. Indeed, the French had long picked Sisowath to succeed his brother, and when King Norodom died, a pliant Royal Council, whose meetings were in fact presided over by the French *résident supérieur*, bowed to France's wishes.

When King Sisowath expired in 1927 at the age of eighty-seven, the Norodom branch of the royal family supported Sutharot as successor, while the Sisowath branch favored the deceased king's son, Sisowath Monivong, and indeed in his will Sisowath had named Monivong as his heir. French reports of the time refer to Sutharot as "intelligent and amiable, with a great deal of personal prestige and connections with powerful individuals in the French community," and ten years previously he was France's favorite to succeed Sisowath. However, Pierre Pasquier, who the next year would become governor-general of Indochina, viewed Sutharot as being pro-Siamese, and the prince was thus barred from contention. Monivong, who was the first Cambodian or Asian general in the French army, acceded to the throne. Finally, after King Monivong's death, according to King Sihanouk himself, the French offered the throne to Sihanouk's grandfather Sutharot but retracted it following intrigues raised in the name of Sutharot's brother Prince Norodom Phanauvong, but without the latter's knowledge. You can read all about it in the July 26, 1958, issue of *Réalités Cambodgiennes*. Prince Phanauvong, who early in the twentieth century opened Cambodia's first printing house, *Kambuja vorakas*, and was prime minister in the Cambodian Council of Ministers, but who was considered by Pasquier as too "greedy" to succeed King Monivong to the throne, has his own street, a stretch of Street 240 between Monivong and Norodom boulevards.

Among other streets named after royals, we have Monireth Boulevard (St. 217, which begins at the complicated intersection around Thorani's statue and runs way out through Stung Meanchey). Prince Sisowath Monireth (1909–1975), who had been a lieutenant in the French Foreign Legion and had fought in the Second World War, was the son and expected successor of King Monivong and the uncle of the future King Sihanouk. But Prince Monireth had independent tendencies and the Vichy French then in control of Cambodia had substantial reservations about installing a king whose political views might run contrary to their own (eventually, the Vichy French exiled Monireth to Vietnam and then placed him under house arrest in Kompot). The eighteen-year-old Sihanouk would certainly prove more malleable, or so they thought, and they harbored no doubts about his loyalty to France.

It is often claimed that, as Sihanouk was a great-grandson of King Norodom on his father's side and a great-grandson of King Sisowath on his mother's, his accession to the throne might dampen the rivalry between the two branches of the royal family. Prince Monireth dismissed this reasoning, saying that he himself was a Sisowath and his mother was the daughter of King Norodom. Following World War II and the return of the French, Prince Monireth was briefly

King Sihanouk's prime minister at a time when Cambodia was given a limited form of autonomy; he continued to be a conservative influence following independence in 1953. After the death in 1960 of Sihanouk's father King Suramarit, who had become monarch following Sihanouk's abdication in 1955, Sihanouk could have arranged for Monireth to accede to the throne. However, perhaps fearing a rival for authority, or perhaps because he was sensitive about his own legitimacy since as a youth he had been chosen as king by the disgraced Vichy regime over the much more experienced Monireth, Sihanouk instead named his mother Queen Kossamak, "Supreme Guardian of the Throne." Cambodia thus became a kingdom without a king. As to Prince Monireth, he was executed by the Khmer Rouge in April 1975 after having been refused sanctuary at the French Embassy (see Chapter 16). Also killed by the Khmer Rouge were Prince Monireth's wife ("assassinated on the streets of Phnom Penh because she took too long to pack her bags," as Sihanouk wrote in his memoirs), his children, and his grandchildren.

Continuing with royals, Street 19 bears the name of Ang Yukanthor (1860–1934), son of King Norodom. In Norodom's later years, Yukanthor became the monarch's favorite to succeed him, but this prince raised French ire because of a letter he allegedly sent to the newspaper *Le Figaro* and a memorandum he wrote to the French prime minister while he was on an official visit to France in 1900. The letter criticized France's role in Cambodia while the memorandum went further, accusing French colonial administrators of corruption, among other of his father's complaints. Although the letter may have been written by the French journalist Jean Hess, a friend of both Yukanthor and Norodom, the furious French forced Norodom to denounce his son and demand his return to Cambodia. Yukanthor, however, fled to Belgium. He then spent years in exile in Singapore and Bangkok, where he died in 1934, all the while carefully watched by the French whom he so despised.

The northern two blocks of Street 51, next to the Sunway Hotel and the US Embassy, are named after Sisowath Sophanovong (1886–1955), who among other high positions was minister of war from

1938 to 1942. Upset at not being considered for the throne follow-ing the death of his older brother King Monivong, he displayed "puerile" anger, according to Admiral Decoux, the governor-general of French Indochina.

Ang Hassakan Street (the part of St. 144 from St. 13 to the river-side) honors another of King Norodom's sons, Prince Hassakan, who was the maternal grandfather of King Sihanouk's mother, Queen Kossamak. When Sihanouk was a child, his parents en-trusted him to the care of *Chau Khun* (Lady) Pat, Hassakan's wife and Sihanouk's great-grandmother.

Lastly among royals, Street 84, or at least the stretch of it which runs between Rue de France (St. 47) and Sisowath Quay, recognizes Sisowath Yuthevong, holder of a doctorate in mathematics from Montpellier University in France, leader of the Democratic Party, and prime minister following his party's victory in the 1946 elections. Yuthevong, an honest and dedicated patriot, favored true democracy and advocated immediate independence from France, but to the great chagrin of many, he died in December 1947 from an attack of malaria and persistent tuberculosis at the age of just 33 and after only six months in office.

Some twenty streets are named after *oknha*, a non-hereditary title traditionally attributed to high government officials and provincial governors. Today, however, there are several hundred *oknha*, which has become more of an honorific business title honoring those who have made financial contributions to society or who, if street rumors are to be believed, have purchased the title for about $100,000. Consequently, the title is often translated as "tycoon" and, although even in past times *oknha* were expected to offer gifts to the king, it is rather less prestigious than it was during the days of those *oknha* who have streets named for them. One such street honors the national hero *Oknha* Kleang Moeung (St. 70), who in 1482 gave his life while trying to regain the throne for his king from the popular usurper Sdach Kan. Faced by an enemy force of greatly superior size, Kleang Moeung and his wife *Chum Teav* Khan Kheav committed suicide by throwing themselves on wooden stakes planted in a deep pit and then recruited an army of ghost soldiers from the underworld which put Sdach Kan's troops to rout. Later, when a Siamese army invaded Pursat, the Cambodian soldiers prayed to Kleang Moeung. His spirit came and helped the troops force the Siamese to retreat.

Short Street 98, which runs along the south side of Électricité du Cambodge and the north side of the post office and ends at the river, is named for *Oknha* Santhor Mok (1846–1908), a poet, chronicler, and palace official. In 1884, in order to tighten French grasp on Cambodia, Charles Thomson, the governor of Cochinchina, backed by troops and three gunboats, burst into King Norodom's private quarters in the Royal Palace in the middle of the night and ordered the king to sign a new treaty giving France significantly greater control over the country's affairs. Santhor Mok tried to block Thomson's entry to the royal bedchamber but was booted out of the way. Santhor Mok later wrote a poem about that event which begins, "Oh Frenchman, you miserable robber, you dared lift your foot and kick the secretary to the king."

Street 72, which begins at National Road 5 and leads to Chruoy Changvar Circle with its knotted gun memorial, is also Col de Monteiro Street. Col (written "Kol" on street signs) de Monteiro (1839–1908) was a descendant of one of the Portuguese traders and sailors who first came to Cambodia in the 16th century. One of his forebears had been court physician to King Ang Chan (r. 1806–1835). Col learned French and English in Singapore, having been sent there by King Ang Duong, for whom he then became interpreter. Col was one of the "new mandarins" in the court of King Norodom. He held numerous high positions and served as a middleman between the king and both European traders and local merchants. Col also collaborated with the French (as did a number of high officials, most of whom had attained their positions by making substantial "donations" to the throne) and because of these dealings, King Norodom, who had serious problems with the French, came to view Col with suspicion. Nonetheless, by the time of Col's death, he had amassed a fortune, several properties, eight wives, and fifteen concubines.

Another of the Francophile new mandarins is remembered in trendy *Oknha* Chhun Street, better known as Street 240, or at least that part of the street between Norodom Boulevard and Sisowath Quay. Alexis Louis Chhun (1851–1920), Catholic and with distant Portuguese ancestors, picked up French as a child from the French officers his father worked for in Kompong Luong, when the capital was still at nearby Udong. By the time he was 12, Alexis Chhun was serving the French as their interpreter, a position he kept through the early years of the protectorate. With the money and connections he made, he moved into property development, construction, and trade. He built a row of shophouses along the Grand' Rue, today's Sisowath Quay. He bought vast properties on the Chruoy Changvar peninsula, which he later sold to the French for a neat turnover. He gained the hugely profitable opium concession. Chhun then moved into government and became head of the treasury and minister of justice. Unlike many high officials, he remained faithful to King Norodom rather than siding with the French. When he died in 1920, he was one of the richest men in Cambodia. Alexis Chhun, like Col de Monteiro, exemplified the success achievable by balancing relations between the protectorate and the crown.

I believe *Oknha* Oum Street (St. 80), is named for the Oum (1821–1902) who was prime minister in the 1890s under King Norodom. In his later years, however, Norodom considered Oum, who was appointed minister of war in 1868 and participated alongside the French during the uprising of 1885–86, as being more loyal to the French than to the crown. Norodom's son Prince Yukanthor denounced Oum not only for siding with the French but for corruption and abuse of power. In 1898 Oum, then 77 years old, was accused by a young dancer of having confined and raped her. Since the dancer was Chinese and not Cambodian, Oum was to be judged by a French tribunal, much to the embarrassment of the French government as the prime minister was such a faithful servant of the protectorate. The powers that be intervened. Paul Doumer, Indochina's governor-general, wrote to *Résident Supérieur* Alexandre Ducos in Phnom Penh that all steps should be taken to assure such a trial would not take place lest the Francophile prime minister be found culpable, something which would reflect unpleasantly on the government. Doumer then asked Ducos to intervene personally in order to resolve the matter, if possible in an amicable way. If indeed *Oknha* Oum Street was meant to honor this prime minister, one must assume that it was because of his sixty-five years of service to the crown, not for the shameful incident reported above.

Oknha Nou Kan Street (St. 105) is named for a writer whose works were a transition between traditional verse literature and prose literature. The son of a farmer, Nou Kan (1874–1947) received a conventional pagoda education. He worked as a secretary in a provincial administration and in 1891 became a secretary in the palace of King Norodom. Upon winning a literary competition, he was sent by the French protectorate to study law in Paris. Following his return, he held several positions in the government, including president of the Court of Appeal. He is remembered today for his literary accomplishments, notably for *Teav Ek*, his version of *Tum Teav*, commonly referred to as the Cambodian *Romeo and Juliet*.

Today, the ninety years of French rule are barely remembered in the city's street names and few new street signs begin with the word *Rue*, as the old ones did. The only streets to retain their French names from the time of the protectorate are Calmette (St. 53) and Pasteur (St. 51), two names we have already seen in Chapter 11. One can understand why the city's streets no longer bear the names of domineering colonial administrators such as Charles Thomson, Huyn de Vernéville, and François Baudoin, as they once did, and why French oppressiveness and the humiliation of being colonized need not be memorialized in street names. Nonetheless, given that without France's intervention in the 1860s Cambodia may well have been divvied up by its two potent neighbors, Siam and Vietnam, and that France expanded Cambodia's territory from about 100,000 square kilometers when they arrived in 1863 to 181,035 square kilometers when Cambodia obtained independence in 1953 (excluding the contentious Mekong delta region, known as Kampuchea Krom), perhaps a small road could honor someone less controversial such as George Groslier (1887–1945), founder and longtime curator of the National Museum and initiator of the Cambodian School of Arts, who was born in Cambodia and died in Phnom Penh in 1945 the day after his arrest, interrogation, and torture by the Japanese military, and who, in short, according to his biographer Kent Davis, "spent his life documenting, preserving and reviving the great Khmer civilization … [and] committed his life and work to Cambodia and her people." In fact, Groslier had a street, or at least one block of a street – the perfect block of the perfect street – for a while. This is the block of Street 13 that passes in front of the National Museum. King Sihanouk himself presided over *Rue Groslier*'s inaugural ceremony in October 1946 and, with a sword, sliced the ribbon stretched across the street after Penn Nouth, Phnom Penh's governor (who has his own street, as will be mentioned shortly), had given the dedication speech. Today, that block and all of Street 13 is named for Ang Eng, as mentioned above. Still, it was, and would again be, the perfect block to celebrate a colonial Frenchman worthy of such an honor. Incidentally, Groslier resided nearby in a house that still stands on the southeast corner of the intersection of Ang Yukanthor Street (St. 19) and Ang Makhak Vann Street (St. 178), on the grounds of the Royal University of Fine Arts.

Not surprisingly, there are no street memories of the Khmer Republic (Lon Nol) period. March 18 Avenue, named in honor of the day in 1970 when Lon Nol and Sirik Matak ousted Prince Sihanouk, is once more Norodom Boulevard, the grassy square in front of the Royal Palace is no longer *Place de la République*, and *Avenue de la Libération* is again Mao Tse Tung Boulevard (note that some in the Lon Nol government wanted that street renamed Richard Nixon Boulevard after the US president's April 30, 1970, invasion of Cambodia in support of the Lon Nol regime against North Vietnamese and Viet Cong forces in the country; wiser heads vetoed the change).

Nor do any streets renamed during the Democratic Kampuchea (Khmer Rouge) and subsequent People's Republic of Kampuchea

(PRK) eras retain those designations. In those days streets were named for communist icons such as Karl Marx, Vladimir Lenin, and Tou Samouth (one of the founders of the People's Revolutionary Party of Kampuchea), to go along with streets already paying nominal tribute to Mao Tse Tung and Joseph Broz Tito. Karl Marx Quay has reverted back to Sisowath Quay, Tou Samouth Boulevard is today Norodom Boulevard, and Lenin Boulevard is again Sothearos (Sutharot) Boulevard, though the fading house sign below – notice that it is written in French, not Khmer – was still *in situ* until July 2011:

There is one exception, however, and old-timers to the city might recall that, on the street parallel to Russian Confederation Boulevard between Monivong and Nehru boulevards, there was once a bronze memorial carrying a nameless mustachioed face molded in relief, with only the dates 1882–1949 giving a clue as to the hero's identity. Sadly, the statue disappeared with the completion of the prime minister's new offices, dubbed the Peace Palace. The man is Georgi Dimitrov, and although that boulevard still bears his name, it is with the anglicized spelling George rather than Georgi, much less Jok, the version of his name used on his street sign a few years ago. The boulevard is now labeled a street, and it has lost its previous number, 114. The son of Bulgarian peasants, Georgi Dimitrov was an active labor unionist, a member of the Bulgarian Parliament (1913–1923), a founder of the Bulgarian Communist Party (1919), a dedicated (some would also add ruthless) Stalinist, Secretary-General of the Comintern (1935–1943), and Prime Minister of Bulgaria (1946–1949). He died rather mysteriously on a health visit to the Soviet Union. Dimitrov never set foot anywhere near Cambodia, so one may wonder why a prominent Phnom Penh avenue was named after him. According to my Bulgarian contact in Phnom Penh, who first came here as a child in the 1980s, naming streets, parks, and the like after people still alive was against Bulgarian tradition and would bring bad luck. Thus, when the People's Republic of Kampuchea expressed interest in thanking Bulgaria for its assistance in those difficult days, Bulgaria proposed the long deceased Dimitrov rather than a then living leader such as party boss Todor Zhivkov. Bulgaria contributed significantly to the UNTAC forces, and more of its soldiers were killed than those of any other UNTAC country, which is perhaps why this street is the only one to retain a name given during PRK days. Incidentally, should you go along George Dimitrov Street and pass by the Peace Palace, have a look at the palm trees lining the street. These are date palms, first cultivated over 4,000 years ago in Arabia and North Africa for their succulent fruit. Alas,

Georgi Dimitrov's memorial is no longer in situ, but the date palms behind are

Phnom Penh's trees are sterile, depriving the city's population of a sweet and nourishing treat.

George Dimitrov is not the only unexpected street name. Another street has recently been christened after a figure from DK and PRK days. Keo Chenda Street is the second right off of National Road 6 after crossing the Cambodian-Japanese Friendship Bridge. The street leads to the Mekong River and in fact it is commonly known as Mekong River Street, but there are at least two street signs as well as several house signs bearing Keo Chenda's name. A veteran of the anti-French Issarak independence movement, Keo Chenda had been among the so-called "Khmer Viet Minh" (a term coined by the French in the early 1950s) or "Hanoi Khmer" who moved to North Vietnam following the 1954 Geneva Accords. There, he became a broadcaster for Radio Hanoi. He apparently returned briefly to Cambodia during the Pol Pot era and was one of the few Khmer Viet Minh to survive that time. Under the PRK, he served as mayor of Phnom Penh and also in the key national position of minister of propaganda, information, and culture. As minister, however, he did not get along well with his Vietnamese advisers. Moreover, he had an independent streak and began cutting deals without the approval of the Vietnamese or the Communist Party leadership. In 1982 he was removed from his ministerial position, while continuing on as mayor. Keo Chenda then began advancing the private sector in Phnom Penh and he successfully promoted commerce, notably the purchase and sale of rice, without Party approval. According to one source, he was getting "bored with communism." In any event, under his leadership the Phnom Penh city government exported more goods than did the ministry of commerce. Not surprisingly, Communist Party leaders viewed him as a threat and he was replaced as mayor of Phnom Penh in 1984. That to some he was regarded as flamboyant may not have helped his cause, nor that he was associated with the few remaining Khmer Viet Minh, most of whom had been purged from power by the mid-1980s. Keo Chenda then essentially disappeared from public view and he died in 1989. One of his deeds deserves special mention.

Presumably "Street," not "Saint"

When Vietnamese troops entered Phnom Penh in January 1979 and discovered S-21, the Khmer Rouge's infamous prison and torture center, they found three children and a baby. They had been there only a week and unlike their parents had somehow survived the final purgings. Keo Chenda adopted the oldest of them, nine-year-old Norng Champhal. Keo Chenda was resurrected in the mid-2000s, at least in a street name, though I can only guess at the reason for his apparent return to good graces. One would like to think it was because of his kindness toward little Norng Champhal, but I rather doubt it. Perhaps because of his economic policies, he had come to be recognized as a man ahead of his time.

In 1994, following the demise of PRK and the return of King Sihanouk, about one hundred street names reverted to those of the Sihanouk's *Sangkum Reastr Niyum* (Popular Socialist Community) period of the 1950s and 1960s, just as the national flag and national anthem of that period were resurrected, seemingly, in the words of historian David Chandler, "to erase certain aspects of Cambodian history which had occurred since [Sihanouk's] departure from the scene" in 1970. Some streets were once more named after royals and dignitaries of that time. The city again had boulevards dedicated to Charles de Gaulle (St. 217), whom King Sihanouk so admired and who visited the city in 1966, Jawaharlal Nehru (St. 215), one of the founders of the non-aligned movement, Josep Broz Tito (St. 214), who kept his communist nation free from Soviet domination, and Mao Tse Tung (St. 245), who gave the deposed Sihanouk shelter after his ousting in 1970, and now to Kim Il Sung (a stretch of St. 289), who did the same.

A number of streets are named for Sihanouk loyalists. Most of Street 289 is Penn Nouth Street, for Sihanouk's long-time and most trusted adviser, who was prime minister six times between 1948 and 1969, was with the prince at the time of his ousting in 1970, followed him into exile in China, served as prime minister of GRUNK (Cambodian Royal Government of National Union, the government in exile formed to oppose the Lon Nol regime) from 1970 to 1976, and was at least in name an adviser to the government of Democratic Kampuchea. *Oknha* Tep Phan Street (St. 182) is named for Sihanouk's foreign minister in the early 1950s and leader of Cambodia's delegation to the Geneva Peace Conference of 1954. Nhiek Tioulong is another old-time Sihanoukist general and politician with his own street (St. 466). Among his accomplishments, he led the Cambodian military delegation at the Geneva Conference and later was minister of defense, among other high positions. Nhiek Tioulong was also a great builder of roads around the country and he developed the town of Kirirom, which Prince Sihanouk later rebaptized Tioulongville in recognition of the general's work there. He also acted in Prince Sihanouk's films, including *Apsara*, in which he took the part of a womanizing bachelor general who falls for the principal dancer of the Royal Ballet, played by Sihanouk's daughter Buppha Devi. General Nhiek Tioulong was the father of Tioulong Saumura, investment banker, vice-governor of the National Bank of Cambodia in the 1990s, parliamentarian, and a leading force in the women's movement.

Streets named for countries include Poland Republic Boulevard (St. 163), Yugoslavia Street (St. 214, the same number as Josep Broz Tito Boulevard; the street is divided by traffic islands), and, since the demise of the USSR, Russian Confederation Boulevard (St. 110), which in 1965 was dubbed Union of Soviet Socialist Republics Boulevard and was the first street in the city to be named after a foreign country. Not all is eastern European, however, as the European Union has its street (St. 143), and then there is Rue de France (St. 47), which goes from the Wat Phnom circle to the roundabout with the knotted gun statue near the Chruoy Changvar bridge.

In honor of the country that helped liberate Cambodia from the Khmer Rouge we have Hanoi Street (St. 1019), though it is way to the northwest in a new part of town, as its four-digit number suggests. The Vietnamese might not be as happy with politically loaded names like Kampuchea Krom Boulevard (St. 128), which remembers the southern part of Vietnam that many Cambodians still claim as their land, Koh Tral Street (St. 65), the Cambodian name for Phu Quoc island in the Gulf of Thailand, now a part of Vietnam but closer to Cambodian shores than to Vietnamese, and Prey Nokor Street (St. 126), which recalls the once-Cambodian town that became Saigon and is now Ho Chi Minh City.

One of the most recently named streets is Christopher Howes Street (St. 96), which parallels Daun Penh Street and runs from Monivong Boulevard to Wat Phnom Circle, passing the National University of Management, Lycée Descartes, and the US Embassy. Howes, a British employee of the Mines Advisory Group (MAG), was clearing mines in Siem Reap province when he and his team of Cambodian deminers were captured by the Khmer Rouge on March 26, 1996. Howes was offered release in exchange for a ransom, but he refused to leave his men. They were later freed, but Howes and his interpreter, Houn Hourth, were killed in Anlong Veng several weeks later. King Sihanouk himself named the street in recognition of Howes' sacrifice.

The only streets bearing the name of someone still living are two which honor Cambodia's present prime minister, *Samdech* Hun Sen Circle and the new *Samdech Techo* Hun Sen Boulevard in Meanchey district, as well as Chea Sophara Street in outlying Sen Sok district, named after the former governor of Phnom Penh.

Some streets are good for our health: Cambodian Red Cross (St. 180) and the aforementioned Calmette (St. 53) and Pasteur (St. 51), and one for our purse: Canadia (St. 284), named after the eponymous bank.

There are four streets named after pagodas: Wat Langka (St. 55), Wat Koh (St. 81), Wat Chas, and Wat Thmey. Like all streets on the Chruoy Changvar peninsula, Wat Chas Street (Old Pagoda Street) and Wat Thmey Street (New Pagoda Street), have no numbers.

Wat Chas Street crosses the peninsula, passing by Wat Puthyaram, which is the old pagoda in question (Map 1, #11). To the south, Wat Thmey Street passes Wat Prochum Sakor (Map 1, #12), the "new pagoda," which dates to 1880 and in fact is older than the "old pagoda." In Wat Prochum Sakor's grounds is a venerable boddhi tree where monkeys gambol, reputedly a descendant of the tree under which the Buddha gained enlightenment (a common claim, I might add). The tree was planted in the Royal Palace by King Norodom and transplanted here in 1951. Wat Puthyaram also has an old boddhi tree, one even older than Wat Prochum Sakor's, thus the reason for the newer pagoda being called the old pagoda.

Also crossing Chruoy Changvar peninsula is Cham Street, named for the Islamized descendants of the kingdom of Champa who found refuge here beginning in the seventeenth century after their lands in south central Vietnam were absorbed by Vietnam. Indeed, three mosques are nearby. The street that begins at the city's water works on the banks of the Mekong, crosses the peninsula then makes a ninety-degree turn to the south and descends the Tonle Sap river almost to the peninsula's tip is called *Machine Teuk* Street, Water Machine Street. North of that sharp turn, the street along the river which later passes under the Cambodia-Japan Friendship Bridge is Tonle Sap Street, while the street that descends the east side of the peninsula is Mekong River Street, or, as we have seen, Keo Chenda Street.

The great majority of streets south of Sihanouk Boulevard and west of Monivong Boulevard have numbers but no names. This is changing in the newer parts of the city, where street names are again becoming the fashion, but whoever is presently responsible for designating them needs an injection of inspiration. The area around Sovanna shopping mall has streets named Gold, Silver, Platinum, Diamond, Topaz, Jade, Emerald, and Ruby. In the western suburbs we have Fortune, Pleasure, and Goody. And in the newly developed area behind the Japanese and Thai embassies you can stroll down A, B, C, and D streets. Let's hope for a little revelation when it comes to naming future streets of our growing city.

19. The Assassination of Commissioner de Raymond

On October 29, 1951, Commissioner Jean de Raymond, France's
highest civil servant in Cambodia, was
murdered by his Vietnamese houseboy, Pham Ngoc Lan, who repeatedly slashed, stabbed, and hammered de
Raymond in his bed during his afternoon nap. The killing took place in the
commissioner's official residence, the
Hôtel du Commissariat, across the street
from Wat Phnom. Some two hours later,
when Commissioner (a position equivalent to governor) de Raymond failed
to keep a scheduled appointment, his
secretary went to call him. Finding the

Commissioner
de Raymond

bedroom door locked from the inside, de Raymond's secretary
climbed through a window and found the commissioner lying on
his bed.

Hundreds of police and both French and Cambodian troops
then engaged in a massive manhunt, focusing on the Vietnamese
quarter in the northern part of the city. Pham Ngoc Lan, the
assassin, was never apprehended, but an accomplice, Le Van Ngot,
also a Vietnamese servant at the *Hôtel du Commissariat*, was arrested
that night and confessed details of the crime, fingering Pham Ngoc
Lan in the process.

The government of the Democratic Republic of Vietnam
(DRV, commonly referred to as North Vietnam) quickly took
credit for the assassination, congratulating its agents and declaring

Pham Ngoc Lan a national hero. Two weeks later, reports David Chandler in his *A History of Cambodia*, a "clandestine Communist broadcast" asserted:

> For the French, the death of Raymond means the loss of a precious collaborator. For the puppets, it means the loss of a generous master. For the Cambodian people, Raymond's death means the end of a great enemy. For Buddhism, his death means that a devil, who can no longer harm religion, has been killed.

Pham Ngoc Lan, to whom de Raymond referred affectionately as *le petit Tho* ("little Tho"), had been hired just one month prior to the assassination to replace another house servant who had asked to be reassigned to Saigon. The French authorities had yet to run a security check on Lan, just eighteen years old at the time, whose "shy manner and rare smile had won the confidence of the household," according to a *Time* magazine article of November 12, 1951, two weeks after the assassination.

Following the killing, an investigation by the French security services revealed that Lan had been a follower of the Viet Minh in Phnom Penh since February 1951 and had joined the Communist Party in September. The assassination had been ordered several weeks previously by the head of the Viet Minh in Phnom Penh. The plot also involved two Chinese, one of whom, Ngo Giang, was a Communist Party member, as well as Le Van Ngot, the previously mentioned Vietnamese servant on the *Hôtel du Commissariat* staff. After assassinating Commissioner de Raymond, Pham Ngoc Lan together with Ngo Giang stole a number of official documents and then made good their escape, eventually ending up in North Vietnam, where a radio broadcast announced that "the patriot who liquidated General de Raymond is now safe." Lan later allegedly said that he had not acted out of hatred as "*Monsieur* de Raymond had been a very good employer, but for the public good and for the resistance."

Pham Ngoc Lan and Ngo Giang were tried in absentia by a military tribunal in April 1952 and sentenced to death. Their

Vietnamese accomplice, Le Van Ngot, was condemned to ten years of hard labor. The other Chinese involved in the plot, an unemployed 17-year-old named Ta Trinh Quang, who was born in Phnom Penh and lived on Ang Duong Street, was arrested in June 1952 after being denounced by an informer who lived on the same street. Ta Trinh Quang had hired the Renault car in which the killers escaped, and during the assassination he had been standing watch outside the *Hôtel du Commissariat*. On July 2, according to an internal report, a handcuffed Ta Trinh Quang tried to commit suicide by jumping out of a dormer window on the third floor of the security services' headquarters in Phnom Penh. He succeeded only in breaking both ankles, which makes one wonder whether he was trying to escape rather than kill himself.

Just forty-four years old at the time of his killing, Jean Léon François Marie de Raymond had spent fourteen years in Indochina. A 1929 graduate of St. Cyr, France's premier military academy, he served in Vietnam for seven years in the 1930s, fought in the French army in World War II until the armistice, then returned to Indochina in 1945, where he first was commissioner in Laos and then, from February 25, 1949, commissioner in Cambodia. He was one of the most promising civil servants in the French colonial system. According to the journalist Yvonne Pagniez, who interviewed de Raymond shortly before his death, "he was refined in his intelligence, his manners, and his taste; he took pleasure in Cambodia's magnificent ancient civilization." He had a passion for Khmer, Cham, and Vietnamese art. He was fluent in Vietnamese and was learning Khmer. Moreover, unlike many colonial administrators, he was at ease with the common people and treated all with equality. He had such confidence in those he worked with that he had a tendency to neglect his personal security. Indeed, according to that *Time* magazine article, when he was asked why he kept a house full of Vietnamese servants, especially after the murder in Vietnam in July of that year of General Charles Chanson, France's high commissioner (governor general) in Indochina, Commissioner de Raymond replied, "I am so good to my servants that they cannot betray me." In the eyes of many, Jean de Raymond was a popular and effective commissioner and an able negotiator during times when Cambodia was seeking independence.

De Raymond had been scheduled to return to France in the summer of 1951, but had been requested to stay on in Cambodia for a few months by General Jean de Lattre de Tassigny, France's high commissioner in Indochina, as the general was leaving for the United States on a critical mission to seek Washington's diplomatic and military backing for France's war in Indochina. De Raymond's wife had already left for France in order to prepare for the commissioner's return. De Raymond was only the second major French official in Cambodia murdered for political reasons during the colonial period.*

King Sihanouk, with whom de Raymond had excellent relations, was saddened by his death. He recalled the commissioner's "courtesy and high sense of humanity," and he said de Raymond was "one of the rare Frenchmen who was always able to politely tell me the truth, thus avoiding many inconveniences." The king later said that "his name is intimately tied to the independence of my Kingdom, of which he is one of the French craftsmen."

Following a funeral service in Phnom Penh attended by King Sihanouk, de Raymond's body was repatriated to France. Some time later, a plaque was fixed to a wall near the front entrance of the *Hôtel du Commissariat* with an inscription in French: "To the memory of Governor Jean de Raymond, Commissioner of the Republic of France in Cambodia from March 1949 to October 1951. He died for France, October 29, 1951." The plaque has since disappeared. To honor the commissioner, the Cambodian government erected a memorial stupa in the surrounding gardens. Attached to the stupa was a bronze medallion embellished with the face of the commissioner and inscribed "Governor Jean de Raymond." The building presently houses the Council for the Development of Cambodia (CDC). The stupa (Map 2, #38) is still there, just inside the gate facing Wat Phnom, but the bronze medallion, like the plaque, has disappeared.

* The first was Félix Louis Bardez, *résident* of Kompong Chhnang province, who was killed in April 1925. See David Chandler, *Facing the Cambodian Past*, 1996.

The commissioner's stupa

Some time ago, someone smashed a hole into the middle part of the stupa where relics are kept, doubtless looking for something of value. When peace finally came to Cambodia in the 1990s, the stupas on and around Wat Phnom were renovated, all but this one, which is slowly crumbling. Like the assassination of Commissioner de Raymond, which gets at best a passing mention in today's history books, the stupa seems to be forgotten.

It has been claimed that Ho Chi Minh himself ordered domestic staff to assassinate French officials, including Commissioner de Raymond. Regarding this assertion, the historian Christopher Goscha wrote to me, "I have never seen or read any order coming directly from Ho Chi Minh along the lines described … That the Democratic Republic of Vietnam's security services were behind the assassination seems highly likely to me, and the official history claims the state's role and made its 'assassin' a hero, regardless of the exact circumstances leading Lan to kill de Raymond." Dr. Goscha added that de Raymond was also very close to Léon Pignon, the mastermind of French policy in Cambodia and Laos as well as Vietnam, and the commissioner was deeply involved in building the Associated States of Vietnam, Laos, and Cambodia to oppose the DRV. Ho Chi Minh, Dr. Goscha continued, would have been happy to know of the success of this political assassination, because that's what it was, but he doubted that Ho would have taken the time to issue orders to domestics to kill such authorities as the government had already approved such methods. "I'm sure he never issued any such order," Dr. Goscha concluded. "This was all lower level stuff run by Vietnemese cadres in Cambodia and South Vietnam as part of this violent terrorist war, and both sides had targeted the killing of the other side's political leaders since, well, the 1920s."

A horrific killing such as this is bound to produce stories based on supposition, rumors, and gossip, and indeed a number of allegations emerged following the assassination of Commissioner de Raymond, all of them unsubstantiated and in contradiction to the French security services' version. One claim is that de Raymond was done in by his Vietnamese mistress, who committed the crime on orders of the Viet Minh and subsequently escaped to Vietnam with a number of important documents. In fact, one member of the CDC staff told me that she too had heard the commissioner had been murdered by his Vietnamese lover, though she added that present employees "are members of a younger generation and therefore not very interested in the matter." Yet there is nothing to corroborate this version. Indeed, if it were true, the Viet Minh would presumably have raised the mistress/assassin to national hero status rather than Pham Ngoc Lan. Let me add that Dr. Chandler told me that when he was a US diplomat in Phnom Penh in the early 1960s it was common knowledge that Commissioner de Raymond had been killed by his houseboy.

Another view is that Pham Ngoc Lan, the houseboy, committed the murder not for political reasons but out of personal vengeance, though this claim too is made without corroboration. According to this version, the Viet Minh had no hand in the murder but were quick to take credit for it. This claim probably comes from the excessively violent nature of the crime, including the use of both a knife and a hammer, from which it would appear that the killer was not a professional assassin. However, Pham Ngoc Lan may well have been acting on orders of the Viet Minh without being an accomplished hit man (after all, he was only eighteen), which could explain the inexpert manner of killing. Moreover, we have Lan's own words concerning his employer, quoted above. And if by chance it were a crime of vengeance, why wouldn't the French security services have reported it as such rather than let the Viet Minh take credit for it? It seems unlikely that the security services would go to such lengths as to falsify numerous internal documents in order to conceal such a motive for the killing.

Dr. Henri Locard, a distinguished historian and longtime resident of Phnom Penh, told me that he was visiting the site of the former *Hôtel du Commissariat* in February 2013 when "I spotted a middle aged couple who were looking around with great curiosity and I approached them. This is when the man told me it was the first time he had been to Cambodia and was visiting the crime scene where his father had been assassinated. He was most upset, not just by the painful memory of the crime, but by the fact that the reputation of his father, who had been a martyr of the Republic, had been sullied by ill-intentioned scholars" as well as by contributors to the Internet. The middle aged man was indeed Commissioner de Raymond's son Jean-François, a recently retired academic and diplomat. Jean-François de Raymond, who was just a boy at the time of his father's death, added that he was working on a biography of his father that would disprove the slanderous claims and the unfounded and unworthy insinuations which contradicted the official version of his father's killing, a version which he entirely accepted. Indeed, much of the official version which I have given above, as well as King Sihanouk's reaction to the commissioner's killing, comes from Jean-François de Raymond's article *Mise au point* (clarification) which he wrote in response to those "unsupported and shameful aspersions" cast on his father, and from personal communication I have had with Jean-François de Raymond.

In his *Mise au point*, Jean-François de Raymond says that "the identity of the terrorists, the interrogations of those who were arrested by the police, the Viet Minh messages intercepted and the documents seized by the French security services are kept in the [French] National Archives." He has consulted these documents, among them a copy of the July 5, 1952, report from France's head of security services in Phnom Penh to the director of security services in Saigon updating the investigation of Commissioner de Raymond's assassination, including the arrest of Ta Trinh Quang, a report he has shared with me. Jean-François de Raymond told me he is still working on his father's biography, a project he admits he should have completed by now.

I find no reason to dispute the official version, espoused by Jean-François de Raymond and supported by internal documents, as the opposing claims are uncorroborated. These assertions should therefore be regarded with a healthy degree of skepticism. Unless in the unlikely event new evidence comes up to the contrary, the assassination of Commissioner de Raymond should be considered case closed.

THE *HÔTEL DU COMMISSARIAT*, the building where Commissioner de Raymond was killed, is also mentioned in Chapter 1 of this book, *Anchors Aweigh*. There, as in most places, it is referred to as the *Résidence Supérieure*, which it indeed was until 1946 when the French protectorate ended and Cambodia gained ambiguous autonomous status within the French Union. France's *résident supérieur* now became its *commissaire*, and the *Résidence Supérieure* was redubbed the *Hôtel du Commissariat*. Built in the 1930s, the building became a government guesthouse following independence in 1953. During Khmer Rouge days it was referred to as House No. 1. It was here that on January 5, 1979, Pol Pot received Sihanouk in the main reception room. The Khmer Rouge leader surprised the prince by welcoming him with a traditional *sompeah*,

Hôtel du Commissariat, south wing

the gesture of palms pressed together in front of the face, a greeting which he had banned some years earlier. Pol Pot then seated the prince to his right in one of two armchairs reserved for the highest "friendly" foreign guests. As Sihanouk wrote in *Prisonnier des Khmers Rouges,* "Impeccably dressed waiters served us tea, cakes, and a delicious fresh fruit juice of Pursat oranges, those very sweet green oranges, which in the time of the monarchy was the delight of my guests. Deprived of such a pleasure for such a long time, I drank ten glasses during our meeting, which lasted four hours!" Pol Pot told Sihanouk that the Vietnamese invasion which had begun a week previously was in fact a Khmer Rouge trap to suck in and then eliminate the invading forces, something which would be accomplished in two or three months. Nonetheless, the Khmer Rouge leader asked the prince to argue Cambodia's case before the United Nations, which Sihanouk agreed to do. Two days later, the Vietnamese ousted the Khmer Rouge from Phnom Penh, less than twenty-four hours after Pol Pot and Sihanouk had fled the city, the latter on the last plane to leave Pochentong Airport.

In 1992–1993, the *Hôtel du Commissariat* was the headquarters of the United Nations Transitional Authority in Cambodia (UNTAC). As noted, the Council for the Development of Cambodia now occupies the building. In the picture above, the bedroom in which Jean de Raymond was assassinated was behind the fourth window from the left of the upper floor. The building is best visited on weekends, when photography is permitted.

Sources

Jean-François de Raymond, "Mise au point," *Études Coloniales*, November 2012.
Jean-Michel Rocard, "Histoire officielle, histoire secrète," *Études Coloniales*, January 2009.
Chicago Daily Tribune, October 31, 1951.
The St. Petersburg Times, October 31, 1951.
"Little Tho," *Time*, November 12, 1951.
David Chandler, *The Tragedy of Cambodian History*, Yale, 1991.
David Chandler, *A History of Cambodia*, Westview, 1996.
David Chandler, *Brother Number One*, Westview, 1999.
Yvonne Pagniez, *Français d'Indochine*, Flammarion, 1953.
Norodom Sihanouk, *Prisonnier des Khmers Rouges*, Hachette, 1986.

20. The US Embassy Was Here

When Cambodia achieved its independence from France on November 9, 1953, the United States already had a diplomatic presence in Phnom Penh. The US Legation officially opened on June 29, 1950, a year after the Franco-Cambodian Treaty had given a qualified form of independence to Cambodia as an associate state within the French Union. The legation (it was elevated to embassy status in 1952) worked out of Le Royal Hotel until office space was found in a Franco-Khmer style residence in the Daun Penh area of the city, on the corner of Preah Sisowath Yutevong (St. 84) and Oknha Hing Peng (St. 61, see Map 2, #24). The US Information Service (USIS) also had its offices here. If you happen to be touring the area, however, you will not find the former embassy, pictured below, as it was bulldozed into history a number of years ago.

Clearly, this site was not large enough to suit the needs of a growing embassy, and in 1954 a move was made to an apartment building farther downtown, just off Norodom Boulevard (Map 3,

US Embassy in the early 1950s

From 1954 to 1965, the US Embassy was
in this building, on the corner of Srok
Treang (St. 49) and Chan Nhat (St. 144)
streets, pictured here in early 2012.

#59). What the new embassy building gave up in character it made up for in space. Though weathered and soon to suffer the wrecking ball, this architecturally undistinguished construction outwardly appears about the same today as it did a half century ago.

Two buildings across the street from the embassy housed USIS and the US Agency for International Development (USAID), the latter involved in big-name projects such as the $33 million Khmer-American Friendship Highway (today National Road 4), which stretches 230 kilometers from Phnom Penh to Sihanoukville. Construction of the road suffered from Cold War rivalries of the time: anxious to complete the highway before the Soviet Union finished construction of their 500-bed Khmer-Soviet Friendship Hospital, the largest hospital in Southeast Asia, USAID contractors cut back on quality. They won the race (the highway was inaugurated in 1959, while the hospital had to wait until the following year), but the construction was so rushed and shoddy that substantial parts of the road were transformed into a pot-holed, barely drivable disaster after a single monsoon season. Had it been properly made, the significant repairs of the early 1960s (a 1961 USAID report mentions road repairs had to be made between kilometers 110 and 180) and the 1990s – the latter also US funded – would not have been necessary. Other US-financed projects were more successful, notably Vann Molyvann's elegant Chaktomuk Conference Hall on the banks of the Tonle Sap, which was inaugurated in 1961.

The new embassy also witnessed lows in US-Cambodian relations. Prince Sihanouk had long been suspicious of US policies in South Vietnam and he believed that conspiracies against him in the 1950s, notably the so-called Dap Chhuon affair, had been backed by the Americans. Though the US was Cambodia's largest foreign aid donor, in early 1964 Prince Sihanouk terminated all such assistance because of American acquiescence in numerous South Vietnamese incursions into Cambodia as well as clashes along the border which resulted in considerable loss of life, injuries, and destruction; alleged US support for the anti-Sihanouk Khmer Serei (Free Khmer), who blasted the government on broadcasts from stations in Vietnam and Thailand (the US denied any connection with the Khmer Serei); and the US' lack of support for Prince Sihanouk's proposed international conference to guarantee Cambodia's borders and neutrality. "[C]onditional, corruptive and humiliating," was how Prince Sihanouk described US aid. Sihanouk at that time also refused to accept the credentials of the proposed American ambassador, leaving the envoy to seethe in Phnom Penh before he returned to the US.

On March 11, 1964, "a large mob, most likely organized by the Ministry of Information on Sihanouk's instruction and led in part by the leftist former Minister of Information (and current Minister of Agriculture) Chau Seng, stormed the American embassy," writes Kenton Clymer in *Troubled Relations: the United States and Cambodia since 1870.*

> Demonstrators threw rocks and bricks at the embassy, broke windows, tore down and burned the American flag, broke into the embassy building itself, and wrecked the first floor. The mob, urged on by speakers, trumpets, drums, and a youth band playing stirring music, also stormed the United States Information Service library, wrecking the interior and burning books. They inflicted similar damage on the British embassy.

In fact, the British ambassador was at that time visiting the US Embassy, and the attack was announced by a brick hurled through a window which narrowly missed the envoy's head. The riot went on for several hours. Though there were no casualties, damage to the embassy was considerable, estimated at $160,000.

Prince Sihanouk had most likely ordered the ransackings; he had certainly consented to them. In any event, he quickly apologized for the attacks and agreed to pay the costs of the damage. Contributions were solicited, but apparently none of the collected monies were ever given to the American and British embassies. An outcome of the attacks was that by the end of the year the number of US personnel at the embassy had been cut back from three hundred to just twelve.

The attack on the embassy was repeated the following year on April 26. The spark was a *Newsweek* article by Bernard Krisher – today publisher of *The Cambodia Daily* – in which he reported that Queen Kossamak, Prince Sihanouk's mother, was said to be "money-mad and reportedly runs a number of concessions in town plus a string of bordellos at the edge of the city." In fact, she owned the land but not the buildings or businesses. *Lèse majesté* notwithstanding, the real reasons for the demonstration were the same as those that caused the previous year's protests: American involvement in Vietnam, South Vietnamese border violations, and the supposed US support for the Khmer Serei. The several

| The attack on the US embassy, March 11, 1964; Chau Seng is on the left with sunglasses and tie. | Same building, same camera angle, 48 years later, Srok Treang Street (St. 49) |

thousand demonstrators did not enter the embassy but broke its windows with rocks and smeared the outside walls with anti-US slogans. The police watched the riot for three hours before moving in and dispersing the crowd. This time the damage was only $4,878.06. The following week, Prince Sihanouk severed relations with the US.

Subsequent events, including an increasing North Vietnamese presence in the eastern part of the country and a financial crisis blamed in part on the rejection of US aid, caused Sihanouk to reconsider his renunciation of diplomatic ties. At the same time, the US sought to improve its relationship with Cambodia. Jacqueline Kennedy's 1967 visit helped pave the way for negotiations (see Chapter 5), though relations were not fully restored until June 1969, ironically under Richard Nixon, whom Prince Sihanouk had once called "a wicked man." Cambodia paid a price for normalization: Prince Sihanouk had to close his eyes to the secret and illegal US bombing of suspected North Vietnamese enclaves in the eastern part of Cambodia (though Prince Sihanouk never thought such bombing would involve air strikes by B-52s, whose bombardments subsequently wreaked massive death and destruction on the country), while the US finally agreed to respect Cambodia's borders.

The embassy reopened in August 1969 in a room of Le Royal Hotel (Map 2, #26). Lloyd M. (Mike) Rives, the chargé d'affaires, "sort of hung a flag out of the window," according to one diplomat's memory. The eight-man embassy soon moved into a villa that still stands at #81 Sothearos Boulevard, opposite the new Sofitel Phokeetra Phnom Penh Hotel (Map 4, #85). The house was actually Rives' residence, and for a time the chancery occupied the servants' quarters behind it, including a bathroom that served as the office of the embassy's three military specialists. When the chancery was relocated the next year, the villa on Sothearos Boulevard became the ambassador's residence.

In 1970 the embassy moved into more substantial quarters on the corner of Norodom and Sothearos (Map 4, #86). This is another building which in appearance has not changed much,

The 1969–70 US Embassy at #81
Sothearos Boulevard as it is today

though today it serves the needs of fishing (it houses the Fisheries Administration) rather than diplomacy.

While the new embassy was being renovated, a deafening explosion blew up part of its front wall, damaged four rooms, and shattered numerous windows. No one was injured. This was the first terrorist attack aimed at Americans. Though no culprit was caught, the blast was believed to have been caused by a communist agent who had smuggled the explosives into the compound. Embassy security, till then not the highest of priorities in relatively quiet Phnom Penh, was substantially ratcheted up.

Five years later, on April 12, 1975, the embassy was evacuated, five days before the Khmer Rouge entered Phnom Penh. (By that

US Embassy, 1970–75 (left), on the corner of Norodom and
Sothearos, today the Fisheries Administration (right)

198

time the building was almost entirely covered in wire mesh, the idea being that the metal netting would cause any enemy projectiles to explode before they could hit the building.) On that April morning, the embassy staff were driven to a barren field till then used by Cambodian children to hone their soccer skills and for the odd embassy pick-up softball game. The grounds were protected to the east by two large apartment buildings. Some 360 US Marines in full battle dress ringed the dusty field, which to them was known as Landing Zone Hotel. In progress was Operation Eagle Pull, during which twenty-four CH-53D Sea Stallion helicopters from the carrier USS *Okinawa* in the Gulf of Thailand landed to evacuate 82 Americans, 159 Cambodians, and 35 third country nationals.

During the operation, four or five Khmer Rouge mortar shells landed near the field, though none of the marines or evacuees were hurt. "But crowds of curious Cambodian children had gathered to watch the evacuation," wrote *New York Times* correspondent Sydney Schanberg, "and one teenaged boy was killed by shrapnel and another wounded in the back. An American corpsman rushed over to bandage his wound before departing on a helicopter, and the boy was removed to a local hospital."

Embassy evacuation from a besieged Phnom Penh on April 12, 1975; notice the the apartment buildings with the raised VVV-shaped roof.

The last to board the helicopters was Ambassador John Gunther Dean, grim-faced, carrying the embassy's Stars and Stripes. As he clambered on, Cambodian children watching the inglorious departure innocently waved and cried out "OK, bye-bye. OK, bye-bye." After thirty-five rotations to the *Okinawa*, the last choppers took off from LZ Hotel at 10:59. Not long thereafter, Khmer Rouge shells crashed directly onto the now empty field.

The two apartment buildings at the east end of the field were initially designed by the French architect Henri Chatel to house the personnel of the National Bank of Cambodia. Their VVV-shaped roof, raised above the flat main roof, not only provided protection from the tropical climate but also an airy, open place for relaxation. The VVV roof, incidentally, became a symbol of the New Khmer Architecture of the 1950s and '60s. During the Khmer Rouge era, Pol Pot used the buildings as his headquarters. In 1979, following the liberation of Phnom Penh from the Khmer Rouge, the government of the People's Republic of Kampuchea offered the two buildings to the Soviet Union, their main supporter at the time. After renovation, the structures served not only as the embassy's chancery but also as lodgings for its staff and their families. Today, however, few of the apartments seem inhabited, at least from casual

The same area today. The empty spaces between the VVV roofs have been filled in and the leafy grounds of the Russian Embassy occupy much of what had been Landing Zone Hotel

observation while walking along the unnamed and unnumbered street running east off of Sothearos Boulevard (Map 4, #84).

Following a lapse of eighteen years during which time the Khmer Rouge ravaged the country, the People's Republic of Kampuchea (the post-KR Cambodian government) renounced communism, and UNTAC's intervention allowed for elections, diplomatic relations between the US and Cambodia were reestablished in September 1993. The embassy was restored to full status in May of the following year. Unwilling or unable to reclaim its old structure, the embassy now moved into several private houses and modest businesses around streets 240 and 55 (Map 3, #67), the main building being the one below.

US Embassy, 1992–2006, at #27 Ang Phanauvong Street (St. 240), now a private residence.

Surrounded by other residences, the embassy was a "sitting duck," as one local newspaper announced following the 2002 Bali nightclub bombings. That may have been one reason that the US had purchased the International Youth Club, formerly the French era *Cercle Sportif*, built in 1929 on what is now Christopher Howes Street (St. 96, see Map 2, #29), where French colonials and later generations of Cambodians swam, played tennis and *boules*, and sipped afternoon *apéros*.

The purchase of this full block caused consternation among some Phnom Penh residents, fearful that a massive bunker-like construction surrounded by concrete would mar the beauty of the Wat Phnom area. "The US Government normally likes to put embassies in nice, historical districts … to reflect the dignity and stature of the [United States] and our respect for the country in which [the embassy] is located," Ambassador Kent Weidemann told *The Phnom Penh Post* when the embassy was still in the planning stage. And to assuage people's fears he added, "I guarantee you that in terms of the architecture of the building, traffic patterns, and security, the embassy would not downgrade the aesthetic environment around Wat Phnom."

Given the new embassy's considerable size, rumors galore floated from the city's expat barstools, one being that the US needed a legation of such proportions because it was going to blast a canal through the Kra Isthmus in Thailand thereby joining the Gulf of Thailand with the Andaman Sea and the Indian Ocean, and subsequently Sihanoukville and Phnom Penh would become major economic and military hubs.

As the *Cercle Sportif* was an alleged site of mass killings by the Khmer Rouge following their occupation of Phnom Penh, notably the execution of ranking Lonnolian (to use a Sihanoukist term) officials, including Lon Nol's brother Lon Non (who was allegedly put to death just to the right of the swimming pool in the picture below) and Prime Minister Long Boret, local embassy staff requested that monks be invited to banish from the grounds any wandering spirits. In the end, the $60 million state of the art embassy arose. This fifth US Embassy was the first built specifically for diplomatic purposes.

International Youth Club, formerly the *Cercle Sportif*, viewed from a helicopter in the mid-1990s. In addition to the Olympic size swimming pool, it included nine tennis courts, two squash courts, a jai alai (*pelotte basque*) court, *pétanque* lanes, an exercise gym, a restaurant, a bar, and at one point a nightclub.

Jean-Marc Khao

Present US Embassy opened in 2006 on
Christopher Howes Street (St. 96)

It was officially opened on January 17, 2006, its architecture much more pleasing than some had anticipated.

In the embassy compound is a concrete slab with a heart cut into it. The block originally came from embassy's previous site near the corner of streets 240 and 51. The bronze plaque on the base of the block reads, in part:

> The "Heart" of the Old Embassy
>
> Centrally located at the old embassy compound, this concrete and brick heart was rumored to have been a signpost for one of the two former brothels that constituted part of our labyrinthine complex of 14 buildings . . .

"In 2006 when we moved to our current location near Wat Phnom," said a former embassy staffer, "we brought the Embassy's 'heart' with us as a reminder of our history and to mark our deepening bilateral relationship with Cambodia."

I had intended to close this chapter with a photograph and a word not of one of the US embassies but of the present residence of the US ambassador at #96 Norodom Boulevard. However, after I snapped the shot, I was politely called over by a machinegun-toting police officer, who brought me to the embassy security personnel at the gate, who in turn walkie-talkied a higher up, presumably in the embassy itself. The upshot was that I was asked, again very courteously, to delete the

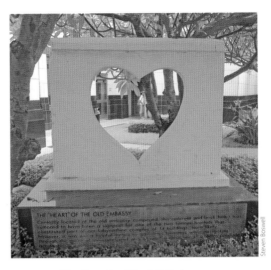

The "heart" of the US Embassy

photo. In any event, the residence does not lend itself to photography from the street outside – too much foliage.

Though we don't have the photo, we still have the word, which is from the Australian historian Milton Osborne. The present US ambassador's residence, he said, was the British Embassy in 1960 (whose consular section would be ransacked during the anti-US demonstrations of March 11, 1964; the building was rented from Lon Nol). Next to it at #94 was Australia's embassy, now demolished. At about that time, the branches of a tall leafy tree in the British Embassy compound overhung the Australian compound precisely where Dr. Osborne, then a young diplomat, parked his sports car, a Triumph TR2 painted British racing green. The tree, however, was the lair of an evil spirit. This would not do, the Cambodian staff told Osborne. The spirit might cause a branch to fall and wreck the car, or perhaps even whack the envoy's pate. Sensitive to local qualms, Dr. Osborne invited monks from Wat Botum to perform an exorcism ceremony, and from then on his flash car rested safely under its arboreal cover.

Sources

Kenton Clymer, *Troubled Relations: the United States and Cambodia since 1870*, Northern lllinois, 2007.

Wilfred P. Deac, *Road to the Killing Fields*, Texas A&M, 1997.

Leslie Fielding, *Before the Killing Fields*, Tauris, 2008.

Bernard Krisher, "Norodom Sihanouk," in *Sihanouk Reminisces: World Leaders I Have Known*, by Prince Norodom Sihanouk with Bernard Krisher, Duang Kamol, 1990.

Charles Meyer, *Derrière le sourire khmer*, Plon, 1971.

Andrew F. Antippas interviewed by Charles Stuart Kennedy, July 19, 1994, Foreign Affairs Oral History Project, The Association for Diplomatic Studies and Training, 1998.

Helen Grant Ross and Darryl Leon Collins, *Building Cambodia: 'New Khmer Architecture' 1953–1970*, Key, 2006.

Sydney Schanberg, *The Death and Life of Dith Pran*, Penguin, 1980.

Sydney Schanberg, *Beyond the Killing Fields*, Rosetta, 2010.

60 Years of Diplomatic Relations: United States-Cambodia 1950–2010, Public Affairs Section, US Embassy, Phnom Penh, 2010; three of the photographs in this chapter are from this publication.

The Phnom Penh Post, August 18–31, 2000.

21. The Gold of King Ang Duong

About half way up National Road 5 to Udong from the new Prek Kdam bridge over the Tonle Sap, you cannot miss at a bend in the road the equestrian statue of King Ang Duong, who ruled Cambodia from 1847 to 1860 (Map 1, #4).

The two steles at the site won't help much unless you not only read Khmer but are familiar with the formal language used with royalty. The first stele identifies the king by his royal titles and then

Statue of King Ang Duong (1796–1860),
father of Cambodia's royal dynasty

does the same with his parents and his son, King Norodom. The second stele describes the building of the statue.

When Ang Duong became king in 1848 at the age of 52, Cambodia was finally at peace, but it was in a perilous, exhausted state. Since the 16th century, intrigues and infighting in the royal family over succession (there were no rules for an orderly succession), at times resulting in assassination and civil war, had greatly weakened the country, allowing for intervention by neighboring Siam and Vietnam. Provinces had been lost, villages and pagodas looted and burned, and the ranks of both civil and military mandarins decimated. Thousands had perished. Poverty reigned and famine was common. Prior to ascending the throne, Ang Duong himself had for many years been effectively held hostage in Siam by that country's king in order to ensure the compliance of the Cambodian monarchy, a common practice in those times.

During the time of the French protectorate (1863–1953), the years of King Ang Duong's reign were rather wistfully considered by many Cambodians as something of a golden age because he had kept the country free of Siamese, Vietnamese, and French encroachments. In fact, though Vietnamese troops had withdrawn – with the notable exception of the Mekong River delta, claimed by Cambodia but occupied by Vietnam – and the kingdom was now at peace, Cambodia was only partly independent. The Siamese had powerful influence on the court (for example, all ministers had to be approved by the Siamese king) and still controlled the western provinces of Battambang, Sisophon, and Siem Reap, which they had forced Cambodia to cede in 1795. In spite of some obeisance to Siam and Vietnam, however, King Ang Duong acted independently within his country and his reign marked the first time in over one hundred years that Cambodia was at peace and under a unified government. As for the French, they had not yet set foot in the country, but in 1853, King Ang Duong, urged by a French missionary, Monsignor Jean-Claude Miche, had written to Emperor Napoleon III asking for French assistance in regaining Cambodian lands lost to the Vietnamese. The Cambodian king never received an answer.

Although King Ang Duong was constantly watched by the Siamese, he proved to be a popular and dynamic ruler, feeding the poor, pursuing brigands who roamed the countryside, reconstructing Udong's damaged pagodas from dismantled Vietnamese-built structures in Phnom Penh (including the fort they had named An Man, "pacified barbarians"), reorganizing the administration, creating an appellate court at which he himself regularly presided, popularizing the use of coinage in commercial exchanges, and building a port at Kompot together with a road linking it to the capital Udong, thereby freeing Cambodia from dependance on the Mekong River and hence Vietnam for international trade. He was also a pious Buddhist (he forbade his mandarins to hunt animals or drink alcohol), and with the Vietnamese gone he restored Theravada Buddhism as the state religion. In addition, King Ang Duong was a poet of note and the version of the *chbap srei* (a collection of moral poems dealing with proper behavior for women) that until recently was taught in schools was based on a text attributed to him. Although he ruled justly, the king was nonetheless a traditional monarch who kept all legislative and judicial powers in his own hands.

Charles-Émile Bouillevaux, a French missionary who lived in Cambodia when Ang Duong reigned, described the king as being small, very fat (and thus the new equestrian statue on Route 5 appears to bear little resemblance to the king, at least as concerns his physique), scarred by smallpox, and intelligent, but also childish. According to Bouillevaux, the king liked to repair watches and clocks, a skill he apparently developed in his youth when he was a virtual prisoner in Siam and by which he earned his living there. Bouillevaux also reported that the king shook hands with foreigners and spoke a little Latin. He liked to imitate Europeans and he collected European articles such as crystal glasses, decanters, and flasks.

The French naturalist and explorer Henri Mouhot had an audience with King Ang Duong in 1859. "He is about sixty years of age, short and stout. He wears his hair cut rather close, and his countenance is good-natured, mild, and intelligent."

Ang Duong ruled from Udong. He resided there in a wooden palace he built in 1854 and which was later known as Veang Chas, the Old Palace. The palace was turned into a pagoda – today appropriately called Wat Veang Chas – by Ang Duong's widow, Moneang Pen, who remained in Udong after her son King Norodom moved the capital to Phnom Penh in 1866.

In 1891 King Norodom erected a stupa on Udong's royal hill, Phnom Preah Reach Troap (Mountain of the Royal Domain), to hold the ashes of his father Ang Duong. The stupa still stands, but in 1903 King Ang Duong's remains – or at least a portion of them – along with those of his wife Moneang Pen were moved by King Norodom into a grand stupa in front of the newly constructed Wat Preah Keo, commonly known as the Silver Pagoda, in the compound of the Royal Palace in Phnom Penh. The transfer was celebrated with an elaborate ceremony that included dances, fireworks, feasting, and the pardoning of convicts.

Udong and many of its pagodas were substantially damaged during the turbulent 1970s. The great seated Buddha in the pagoda atop Udong's hill was smashed, though it has recently been rebuilt. As to Wat Veang Chas, during the Pol Pot years of trauma it was used both as a prison and a warehouse.

I FIRST VISITED WAT Veang Chas (Map 1, #2) on a solitary journey back in 2001. I spotted a number of old cast-iron cannons lined up

19th century cannons protecting King Ang Duong's treasure in front of the hall where monks now have their morning and midday meals; at left in 2001, and at right in 2011 after renovations

in front of a dirt mound atop which was an open-sided structure, its corrugated metal roof upheld by wooden columns. As I was examining the cannons, one inscribed with Chinese characters, an elderly monk approached for a chat. The monk told me that the building with the cannons stood on the site of the king's throne hall. He then led me around the sparsely visited pagoda grounds, explaining various points of interest in a mixture of French, English, and Khmer.

I seem to have gained the monk's trust, for when we reached the king's pond, he told me the following secret. "Few people know this," he said, "but in those times of tension and fear of Siamese or Vietnamese attack, King Ang Duong buried much of his treasure. He did so in two places he thought no invader would search. The first place was under the building with the old cannons in front. The second place was right here, below the bottom of this pond."

I returned to Wat Veang Chas several times over the ensuing years, most recently in 2011 when I was startled to see that the old building protected by the cannons had been completely rebuilt, thanks largely to a donation from Prime Minister Hun Sen and his wife Bun Rany. On those subsequent visits, however, I never again met my friend the old monk. I do not know his name, nor do I know

Pond that hides King Ang Duong's gold

what happened to him. Perhaps he died, and perhaps you and I, dear reader, are the only ones who know the whereabouts of the gold of King Ang Duong.

Cannon inscribed with Chinese characters

THE CHINESE CHARACTERS INSCRIBED on the aforementioned cannon indicate that the gun was cast in 1849 at Mengjia Ying, a military encampment north of Taipei. Perhaps it is one of the cannons mentioned by Charles Lemire when he visited Udong in 1864, shortly before King Norodom moved the capital to Phnom Penh: "... soldiers were rather awkwardly doing training drills with the cannons, rather small pieces mounted on crude gun carriages. They seemed to be more skillful at handling rifles and lances."

On my most recent visit, I noticed next to the main altar of a subordinate hall a statue of the Buddha standing with his right hand raised with its palm facing outward in the *Abhaya mudra*, the gesture of dispelling fear or giving protection. The statue was cast as a representation of King Ang Duong. Giving the Buddha the appearance of a particular Cambodian king might seem surprising, but this statue did not set a precedent. In 1798, the regent Pok repaired two stupas on Udong's royal hill for the ashes of the recently deceased King Ang Eng (1772–1797) and in the stupas he also placed two statues of the Buddha fashioned as effigies of the departed monarch. Also of note is that King Norodom ordered that following his cremation his solid gold funeral urn be melted down and cast as a statue of the Buddha Maitreya, the Buddha of the Future, believing that he would be reincarnated as Maitreya in the year 4457. The gold, diamond-encrusted statue, its hands also raised in the *Abhaya mudra*, stands in front of the main altar of Wat Preah Keo Morokat, the Silver Pagoda, inside the compound of the Royal Palace, though I do not know whether the statue was cast to resemble King Norodom.

211

Statue of the Buddha in the guise
of King Ang Duong

Sources

Charles-Émile Bouillevaux, *l'Annam et le Cambodge, voyages et notices historiques*, Palmé, 1874.

Khin Sok, *Le Cambodge entre le Siam et le Viêtnam (de 1775 à 1860)*, École française d'Extreme-Orient, 1991.

Henri Mouhot, *Travels in Siam, Cambodia, Laos, and Annam*, White Lotus, 2000; originally published in French in 1863.

Charles Lemire, *Cochinchine française et royaume du Cambodge*, Hachette, 1869.

Julio A. Jeldres and Somkid Chaijitvanit, *The Royal Palace of Phnom Penh*, Post, 1999.

22. Staff Sergeant Charles W. Turberville, and the Last US Dead of the Vietnam War

I n the US Embassy compound (Map 2, #29), partially obscured from the view of passersby walking along St. 96 by two rows of oil palms, the United States Embassy Mayaguez-Marine Corps Memorial carries the names of fourteen Marine, two Navy, and two Air Force servicemen who died during the so-called *Mayaguez* incident, the last combat of the Vietnam War. The eighteen

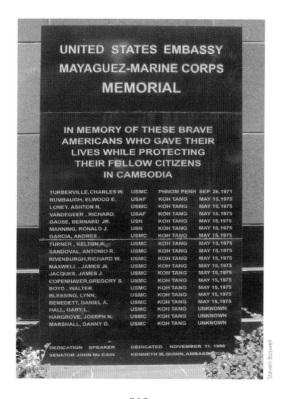

warriors are listed as having died on the island of Koh Tang off the coast of Cambodia, fifteen of them on May 15, 1975, the other three on dates "unknown." The inscription on the memorial reads: "In memory of those brave Americans who gave their lives while protecting their fellow citizens in Cambodia." It was unveiled on November 11, 1996, at a ceremony in which Senator John McCain gave the dedication speech.

I first came across the embassy's Mayaguez-Marine memorial in 2006 when it was in the garden of the US ambassador's residence on Norodom Boulevard. The first name on the memorial, however, is not one of those who died in the *Mayaguez* incident, but Charles W. Turberville, a US Marine who perished in Phnom Penh on September 26, 1971, almost four years before the fighting on Koh Tang. I asked

> TURBERVILLE, CHARLES W.   USMC   PHNOM PENH SEP 26, 1971

the then-ambassador who Turberville was and how he had died. To my surprise, the ambassador replied that he did not know.

Intrigued as to the marine's fate, I kept him in mind while I was preparing this book, and eventually I found out why his name is on that memorial. Staff Sergeant Turberville, 21 years old, from Finchburg, Alabama, was a member of the US Embassy's detachment of the Marine Security Guard Battalion. On that late September day of 1971, he and other American personnel were playing softball on a dusty field not far from the embassy. Two men suddenly rode up on a motorcycle and threw explosives onto the field, killing SSgt. Turberville as well as an American soldier working with MEDTC (Military Equipment Delivery Team, Cambodia) and a Cambodian child watching the game. Several other Cambodian spectators were injured, along with ten embassy staff, including four marines. The two terrorists fled on their motorbike. Thus, though SSgt. Turberville was not involved in the *Mayaguez* incident, he was a US Marine and that was reason enough to include his name on the embassy compound memorial.

Not so the other serviceman killed during that softball game. He was Master Sergeant John Henry Gregory, Jr., of St. Petersburg,

Florida, a quartermaster supply specialist with MEDTC. (MEDTC was responsible for discreetly administering the distribution of military assistance to Cambodia, though substantial quantities of these American arms and ammunition were sold directly to their North Vietnamese and Viet Cong enemies by corrupt Cambodian military officers.) MSgt. Gregory, a veteran of the Korean War and 41 years old, had been in Cambodia for barely a month at the time of his death. Since he was in the US Army rather than the marines, and since he was not involved in the *Mayaguez* incident, MSgt. Gregory's name does not appear on the memorial.

Four years after the killing of Sergeants Gregory and Turberville, the barren field where the softball game was being played would again enter the story of US involvement in Cambodia. On April 12, 1975, five days before the Khmer Rouge entered Phnom Penh, the US Embassy was evacuated. Known on that day as Landing Zone Hotel, the field was where US Marine helicopters landed to pick up the evacuees. The field now is in the compound of the Russian Embassy on Sothearos Boulevard (Map 4, #84; see Chapter 20).

Although MSgt. Gregory's name does not appear on the embassy's memorial, he is honored on the Vietnam Veterans Memorial in Washington DC His name can be found on panel 02W, line 26. SSgt. Turberville's name is also on that memorial, one line above Gregory's.

THE VIETNAM VETERANS MEMORIAL, the most visited of Washington DC's monuments, rarely fails to raise emotions among those who gaze upon the seventy-two black granite panels etched with the names of 58,195 servicemen and women who died in Indochina between 1959 and 1975. The inscription following the names of the dead reads: "Our nation honors the courage, sacrifice, and devotion to duty and country of its Vietnam veterans. This memorial was built with private contributions from the American people."

The names on the memorial are listed in chronological order by day of death and alphabetically within each day. The very last name on the memorial is Richard Vandegeer. Second Lieutenant Vandegeer, US Air Force, died on Koh Tang island on May 15, 1975, during the *Mayaguez* incident, along with fourteen other servicemen, who are also remembered on the memorial. Three marines, those who are listed on the memorial in the US Embassy in Phnom Penh as having died on Koh Tang but at a date "unknown," were unintentionally left behind on the island and were later killed. Their names too are among the last incised on the black stone of the Vietnam Veterans Memorial, on panel 01W.

On May 12, 1975, four weeks after the Khmer Rouge entered Phnom Penh and twelve days after Saigon fell to the North Vietnamese, the SS *Mayaguez*, an American container ship sailing to Thailand with a civilian crew of forty, was halted 120 kilometers off the Cambodian coast by two Khmer Rouge Swift boats, American-built war booty from the defeated Lon Nol regime. The *Mayaguez* was boarded by the Khmer Rouge, who then ordered it to be sailed to Koh Tang island, some fifty kilometers from the mainland, where it was anchored about one kilometer offshore. The ship's crew was then put on a captured Thai fishing boat and eventually set ashore on the island of Rong Sanloem, not far from Kompong Som. (This was the town's original name; it was called Sihanoukville in the 1950s and 1960s and was changed back to Kompong Som following Prince Sihanouk's ouster in 1970.)

President Gerald Ford and his top advisers, including Secretary of State Henry Kissinger, eager to show the world American resolve following their humiliating withdrawal from Vietnam and Cambodia, decided on a show of strength. "We haven't reached the point yet where American ships get captured by Cambodians," Kissinger said. "I know you damned well cannot let Cambodia capture a ship a hundred miles at sea and do nothing." The mission would therefore not only be to rescue the *Mayaguez* and its crew, but to punish the Khmer Rouge with bombing raids on the mainland, notably the harbor facilities at Kompong Som and the airfield and port at nearby Ream.

Tragedy was not long in coming. Five US Air Force crewmen and eighteen USAF security policemen died when their helicopter crashed in Thailand while on the way to liberate the *Mayaguez*. (It should be noted that the names of these air force dead are not included on the US Embassy's memorial, though they most definitely were part of the mission to liberate the *Mayaguez* and its crew; the airmen are listed on the Vietnam Veterans Memorial in Washington, just before those who died in the *Mayaguez* incident.)

Then, an American surveillance plane reported that it had seen Caucasians on a fishing boat off Koh Tang and a small group of people on the island itself. This report was later misconstrued into some of the *Mayaguez*'s crew being on the island. In fact, not one of the crew ever set foot on Koh Tang. This misinformation would result in the wrong island being attacked. In addition, although planes flying over the island met considerable shooting from the ground and the US military brass believed the island to be well defended – which in fact it was – this information was inexcusably not passed on to the troops who would invade the island. Rather, they were told that they would meet only light resistance, based on information from a Lon Nol naval officer who had escaped from Koh Tang fully a month before and had found refuge in Thailand. These intelligence and communication blunders led to the deaths of eighteen more Americans, not to mention numerous Cambodians.

The assault of Koh Tang began at sunrise on May 15 with two helicopters coming in from the west and two from the east, their troop bays loaded with marines. The first met heavy ground fire but managed to unload twenty marines before ditching at sea, about a kilometer off the island. A helicopter attacking from the east was also hit and fell into the water. Another chopper went down in the surf, but the marines managed to make it ashore. The fourth helicopter, badly shot up, headed back to Thailand with its consignment of marines still aboard. In all, fourteen Americans were killed by KR fire during this initial helicopter assault. Helicopters managed to pluck from the sea a number of the marines and crewmen who had not made it to the island. Other helicopters then were able to land over one hundred more marines, mostly on the west beach, where they met strong resistance.

At almost exactly the same time as the first helicopter attack on Koh Tang, the Khmer Rouge released the crew of the *Mayaguez*, putting them on the same captured Thai fishing trawler and sending them back toward their ship. An hour later, US Navy planes bombed the mainland, destroying Kompong Som's port, airport and what was left of its oil refinery, the country's only one, but which had been largely blown up by the North Vietnamese/Viet Cong in 1968 (a few years later much of the metal was looted by locals and sold as scrap to Thai dealers), as well as much of Ream's naval base. The release of the crew was thus not due to the attack on Koh Tang or to the naval bombing. However, US aircraft had been constantly flying over the island and the mainland since May 13, strafing Koh Tang and sinking at least three patrol boats, a show of force that may well have persuaded the Khmer Rouge to free the men of the *Mayaguez*.

Even after the White House was informed of a radio broadcast from Phnom Penh announcing the crew would be released, President Ford ordered the planned bombing of the mainland to be carried out. Shortly before, the *Mayaguez*, still at anchor off Koh Tang, had been boarded by marines from a US Navy destroyer escort. No one was found aboard. Two hours later, another US warship pulled alongside the Thai fishing trawler, and the *Mayaguez's* crew scrambled on board. Nonetheless, the American bombing of the mainland continued, punishment exacted by the White House.

Back on Koh Tang, a second wave of helicopters unloaded another one hundred marines, including a machinegun team consisting of Lance Corporal Joseph Hargrove, Private Gary Hall, and Private Danny Marshall. Some six hours later, with the *Mayaguez* and its crew safely in US hands, helicopters were ordered to extract the marines from the beaches of Koh Tang. Only one marine had died on the island itself that day, Lance Corporal Ashton N. Loney, though forty-three had been wounded. The evacuation was completed by 8:30 p.m., May 15. About three hours later, marine officers realized that they had left three men behind. Also abandoned on the beach was the body of LCpl. Loney; the helicopters had been too full to take him aboard.

In Washington, President Ford and his senior advisers celebrated. The media shouted their praise. Initially, the government reported only one serviceman killed. Not mentioned was that forty-one had died to save forty. Reports of the others who died in the waters off Koh Tang appeared over the next days; news of the deaths from the helicopter crash in Thailand was released only the following week. As to the three marines of the machinegun team, they were "presumed" to have died before the evacuation. The truth was withheld for another twenty years.

AS NOTED, THE US Embassy Mayaguez-Marine Corps Memorial lists fifteen of the servicemen as having perished on Koh Tang on May 15, 1975. Fourteen of those warriors died at sea in the initial helicopter assault. The remains of thirteen, all of whom had been on the same helicopter, were retrieved in underwater searches conducted by US and Cambodian specialists between 1991 and 2013 and returned to their next of kin. The thirteen were buried together at Arlington National Cemetery in Virginia on May 15, 2013, exactly thirty-eight years after they died. The body of the fourteenth, USAF Staff Sergeant Elwood E. Rumbaugh, who died while saving his co-pilot after their chopper was hit by enemy fire and crashed into the sea, has not been recovered. The remains of Corporal Loney too are still officially unaccounted for.

Three other marines, Joseph N. Hargrove, Gary L. Hall, and Danny G. Marshall, are also listed as having perished on Koh Tang, but for each the date of death is marked as "unknown." Due to miscommunication on the battlefield, the three leathernecks, who formed a machinegun team protecting the right flank of the American perimeter, were inadvertently left behind on the island following the extraction of the US troops. Ordered to hold their position "at all costs," the three had done just that, courageously repelling Khmer Rouge attacks. As the evacuation of the marines proceeded and the

LCpl. Ashton Loney   SSgt. Elwood Rumbaugh

perimeter closed, the three men pulled back to the beach, then again dug in. They had been told to wait for the sound of a whistle before retreating to the helicopters. The officer with the whistle, however, thinking that all his men were accounted for, boarded one of the first helicopters to leave the island for ships offshore. The whistle was never blown. The three remained behind.

Once it was known that the three were missing, a marine lieutenant volunteered to return to the island with his squad to look for them, but the decision was made not to risk further casualties unless the three men could be confirmed as still alive. Beginning at 6:30 the next morning, a US destroyer sailed round Koh Tang looking for signs of the three marines. When none was spotted, the three were presumed dead. At 10:00, after less than four hours circling the island, the destroyer abandoned the search.

Searches led by the US Department of Defense in the late 1990s and early 2000s found pieces of bone belonging to Caucasians both on Koh Tang and on the mainland near Sihanoukville, as Kompong Som once again was known. DNA tests could not be carried out, however, because the fragments were too small, and consequently the three marines remain listed as missing in action, presumed dead. Separate investigations by the writer Ralph Wetterhanh and by Cary Turner, a cousin of Lance Corporal Hargrove, including interviews with the Khmer Rouge commander on the island at the time of the *Mayaguez* debacle, provide plausible answers about the fate of the troopers.

LCpl. Joseph Hargrove PFC Gary Hall Private Danny Marshall

They conclude that LCpl. Joseph Hargrove, 24, was captured and executed by the Khmer Rouge on Koh Tang on May 16, the day after the marines were evacuated from the island. Wounded in the leg during fighting the day before, Hargrove shot and fatally injured a Khmer Rouge soldier. The man died shortly after Hargrove's apprehension, which might account for the marine's hasty execution.

Private First Class Gary Hall, 18, and Private Danny Marshall, also 18, were captured on the island several days later. The Khmer Rouge noticed that leftover food had disappeared from their camp. A search revealed large, booted footprints that could not have been made by the rubber sandals worn by the Khmer Rouge. An ambush was laid and the two marines were soon caught. On orders from Phnom Penh, they were taken to the mainland and chained in the monks' quarters of Ti Nean Pagoda on a hill above Sihanoukville, a place which then served as a Khmer Rouge prison. A few days later, the two were clubbed to death in the pagoda's main prayer hall, first Hall and then Marshall. Private Marshall was thus the last American to die in the Vietnam War. Gary Hall was buried in a shallow grave overlooking the sea and Danny Marshall's body was deposited in a rocky alcove along the beach.

Should you ask, the Department of Defense would most likely tell you that the above is pure speculation. Cary Turner believes that the Department of Defense wants to hush up the discomforting fact that three marines were abandoned and minimal attempts were made to rescue them or retrieve their bodies in the hours and days following the evacuation of Koh Tang. The Department of Defense remained silent about the missing three for so many years, and they still seem reluctant to talk about them. Why so? Perhaps because tradition requires US Marines never to leave their dead behind, let alone those who may still be alive.

As for Koh Tang, today the island has a small Cambodian military presence but is otherwise uninhabited. But perhaps not for long: a Russian-owned company called Monarch Investment purchased a 99-year lease to the island in 2008, with plans to build – according to their website – a botanical park, a zoo, an oceanarium, an airport, a yacht club, golf courses, "bungalows on water," private villas, seven hotels "in the style (architecture, cuisine, design) and named as famous European cities like Paris (Eiffel Tower), Rome (Coliseum), London (Big Ben), Moscow (Red Square), Venice, and others ... 300–500 hotel rooms, in the form of reduced copies of the world-famous ancient temple of Angkor Wat," and, not unexpectedly, a casino. Let's hope that nothing comes of this venture, as the bones of corporals Loney and Hargrove would more than likely prefer to rest a bit more peacefully.

HALL, GARY L.	USMC	KOH TANG	UNKNOWN
HARGROVE, JOSEPH N.	USMC	KOH TANG	UNKNOWN
MARSHALL, DANNY G.	USMC	KOH TANG	UNKNOWN

On the US Embassy's memorial, the names of the three who were left behind. The inscription is in error, however, as Gary L. Hall and Danny G. Marshall were not killed on Koh Tang but on the Cambodian mainland.

Sources

Photographs of the five fighting men shown in this chapter appear in various websites. I found them at www.mayaguezfallenheroes.com/Marines.htm and www.vvmf.org/Wall-of-Faces/, but I was unable to identify the copyright owners.

On SSgt. Turberville: Wilfred P. Deac, *Road to the Killing Fields: The Cambodian War of 1970–1975*, Texas A&M, 1997.

On the *Mayaguez* episode: Ralph Wetterhahn, *The Last Battle: The Mayaguez Incident and the End of the Vietnam War*, Da Capo, 2002.

On current plans for Koh Tang: www.kohtang.org/devproject.

23. Just beyond the Killing Fields

In Chapter 4 we had a look at Wat Unnalom's Angkorian tower, Phnom Penh's oldest structure. About fifteen kilometers from the city center, however, there is a more ancient place, one that goes back to prehistoric times. The circular earthwork site at Chœung Ek, not far beyond the infamous killing fields of the same name, is one of the oldest known human settlements in the area (Map 1, #6). It resembles the much better-studied circular earthworks near Memot in eastern Kompong Cham province, in the part of the country known as red soils, earth which is the result of the erosion of volcanic basalt. Some thirty of these earthworks have been identified in Cambodia and another fifteen in the highlands of Vietnam.

The Memot earthworks, often situated on a hill or plateau, are on average 250 meters in diameter, with a slightly oval exterior wall several meters high and fifteen meters wide offering protection against human enemies and wild animals. The wall is pierced by an entranceway, sometimes two. At most sites, a deep ditch follows the wall on its interior side. It seems the purpose of the ditch was not to store water but to hold the village's domesticated animals, much like a corral. Inside the wall is a raised settlement area, referred to as a platform. The dirt extracted from the digging of the ditch was used to build the exterior wall and the platform. It has been estimated that it would take 150 to 200 workers four to five months to build an average size earthwork. Local people today call the earthworks *banteay kou*, which translates as "fortress enclosed by a ditch," although it is actually the wall which encloses the ditch.

Radiocarbon dating shows that these fortified settlements date from between 2000 BC to the second or first centuries BC, a transition period from the Neolithic Age to the Iron Age. Who their inhabitants were is still a matter of conjecture, though it seems reasonable to believe they were proto-Khmer and spoke a language similar to present day Khmer. They appear to have dwelled in houses raised on piles, much as many people still do in rural areas. They lived off of fish and rice, and they raised pigs and water buffalo. Their artisans made stone implements including axes, chisels, and scrapers. They also made stone bracelets and anklets, objects of wealth that perhaps designated high status. Lithophones, cut stones used for making music, have also been found. A stone spindle whorl indicates that the inhabitants probably wove cloth. They produced decorated pottery. Glass beads at the site may have come from present-day Vietnam, though some speculate an Indian origin, which if true would indicate overseas trade.

Unlike the Memot earthworks, the one at Chœung Ek is not in the highland red soils region. It is difficult to make out from the ground, largely because erosion and agriculture have destroyed much of the wall, and it was most recently discerned through aerial photography in the early 1990s, though it was apparently noted by French researchers in the 1920s. Somewhat different from those

Phon Kaseka

The circular earthwork at Chœung Ek

at Memot, the Chœung Ek earthwork is an almost perfect circle, thus making the structure unique. It has a diameter of about 740 meters, much larger than the earthworks at Memot, and the circular peripheral wall, or what is left of it, is about thirty meters wide. Like the red soils sites, the Chœung Ek earthwork had a circular ditch running along the inside of the exterior wall.

The site seems to have been continuously occupied since prehistoric times. Two pottery kilns have been uncovered inside the wall, though they date to a much later period. Villagers have reported finding stone artifacts such as axe heads, but the site has only recently begun to be properly studied and its exact age has not yet been determined. Presently the interior area is divided into numerous small rice fields. The earthwork is in danger of further destruction from nature and village agriculture, and one must hope that government and society make its protection a priority.

In the surrounding area, but outside the earthwork, fifty-nine other kilns and many potsherds have been found, with radiocarbon dating assigning the pottery to the fifth to seventh centuries AD. Also uncovered and postdating the circular earthwork are two pre-Angkor era temple foundations, a lintel, columns, pedestals, a seventh century inscription, three ancient reservoirs, and some settlement mounds.

As stated above, the Chœung Ek circular earthwork is very difficult to make out from ground level. On our visit, my wife and I approached a group of youths in the nearby village, but they had never heard of *banteay kou*. Nevertheless, by following an aerial photo, I thought I had found my way inside the earthwork, though I was far from certain. Nobody was around to query for information. We approached a small mound with a tree growing from it, surrounded by rice fields. "This tree has not been cut down for paddy fields," thought my wife. "Perhaps there is a spirit, a *neak ta*, who can help us."

"Mr. Tree," she inquired of the plant, "can you help us find *banteay kou*?"

Immediately she heard a rustling noise in the undergrowth, a sound she knew well and one which she feared. A cobra well over a meter long slithered out from the mound just in front of our sandaled feet and disappeared into the remaining stubble of harvested rice.

My wife turned around and was surprised to find right behind us was a well-dressed man, who later told us he worked as an immigration officer at the airport. "You are at the right place," he informed us. "Archaeologists have excavated a number of mounds around here, including one just beyond that sugar palm over there. They found artifacts. But some raised areas were destroyed and ponds filled in to make rice fields, especially when the price of land went up a few years ago."

"See," my wife told me, "the tree helped us. It's a good thing we were respectful when we climbed that low mound. It's the same when you enter a forest: always ask the trees – or actually their spirits – for permission." My wife's belief is a common one in rural Cambodia, no doubt dating back to ancient beliefs in the power of nature.

If you happen to visit the site, you might not be able to make out any more of the earthwork than we could, but a ride of less than a kilometer south, down the road from the Chœung Ek killing fields offers a tranquil taste of rural Cambodia. Tread carefully, however, once you arrive.

Sources

Thuy Chanthourn, *Banteay Kou Memotian Circular Earthworks*, 2002.

David Chandler, *A History of Cambodia*, Westview, 1996.

Ministère de la Culture (France), *Phnom Penh, développement urbain et patrimonie*, APUR, 1997.

24. The Graves of Ponhea Leu

The next time you travel up National Road 5 from Phnom Penh to Udong, slow down when you are twenty-seven kilometers from the Royal Palace. Look carefully to your right and, close to the road, in front of an entryway marked Cambodian People's Party, behind which are two large rain trees (*Samanea saman*, also known as monkey pod tree), you will see three concrete graves, side by side on a single base. One might guess that these sepulchers belong to three members of the same family, but the graves are now anonymous, each one marked only by the cross cut into it (Map 1, #5).

These three graves are all that remain of the Catholic church of Ponhea Leu, whose history dates back to the 17th century, when Cambodia's capital was at nearby Udong. At that time, the Catholic community was about three kilometers south of Ponhea Leu, where today an Australian-funded bridge (notice the silhouette of a kangaroo at either end) carries National Road 5 over a small stream called the Prek Don Sdaeung. The Catholics of Ponhea Leu were descendants of Portuguese and Spanish traders and adventurers

The remaining three graves at Ponhea
Leu, just off National Road 5

227

who had come to Cambodia as far back as the 1550s. The people of Ponhea Leu were joined in the late 1630s by Japanese Catholics fleeing religious persecution of the xenophobic Tokugawa shogunate. (In 1852, Cambodian Catholics from Ponhea Leu pointed out descendants of these Japanese to the French priest Charles-Émile Bouillevaux, but their families had apostatized long before.)

Another group of Portuguese and Portuguese-Asians came to Ponhea Leu from the Celebes Islands after being expelled by the Dutch around 1650. Here is what Father François Ponchaud says about their arrival on the shores of the Tonle Sap in his *Cathedral of the Rice Paddy*:

> It is reported that the new arrivals presented themselves to the king with a buffalo skin and a picul of silver [the equivalent of 61.76 kilograms of the metal]. After the customary prosternations [*sic*], they asked the king, in exchange for the picul of silver, a piece of land near the palace, the size of [the] buffalo skin. The king took these foreigners for simple-minded people whose propositions did not even warrant royal attention. But upon their insistence, His Majesty reconsidered and approved their request. Returning to their home, these Portuguese halfbreeds set out to cut the buffalo skin into very thin strips, finer than delicate thread. With these strips put end to end, they measured along the river a tract of land which began at Ponhea Leu and ended near the royal residence ... All the Cambodians who lived in the measured space were obliged, therefore, in the name of the king to leave these places. 'The king had the good sense to attach these strangers to his service, reasoning that people of such shrewdness should be excellent support for his throne.'

So, then, goes the story, with all its implications of greater Portuguese – or Eurasian – acumen.

Back in those first days of the Catholic community in Ponhea Leu, a thatched hut raised on stilts must have served its religious needs, but the first recorded church was built in 1686 by two missionaries, Jean Genoud, a Swiss priest of the Society of Foreign Missions, headquartered in Paris, and Louis of the Mother of God, a Portuguese Franciscan. They also built a hospital, where Father Louis, a doctor and surgeon, healed the sick.

But these were bad times in Cambodia. The government had little control of the countryside, where bandits roamed and Vietnam made incursions into Cambodian lands. During a Vietnamese attack on Udong, the church and hospital at Ponhea Leu were burned to the ground, villagers were massacred, and the two missionaries were wounded and left for dead. Father Louis succumbed to his wounds, but Father Jean survived and was eventually sent to Burma.

Incidentally, in the town's name of Ponhea Leu, *Ponhea* is a royal title dating from the 15th to 17th centuries which was also given to the sons of court mandarins, and *Leu* is a Khmer deformation of Louis (or perhaps Luis). One theory is that, sometime in the 17th century, a Cambodian king gave the title to a Portuguese named Louis – though not the martyred Father Louis – and subsequently the town was named after him. Another contention is that *Leu/* Louis is a deformation of Ruiz, and the person in question is the Spanish soldier/adventurer Blas Ruiz de Hernan Gonzales, who came to Cambodia in 1593, fought for King Sattha, was captured by the Siamese when they sacked the capital Longvek, escaped, returned to Cambodia, was involved in an attack on the palace in 1596 during which the usurper King Ram I was killed, was elevated to a high position by a successor king, and was himself killed in Phnom Penh by resident Malay adversaries in 1599.

At the beginning of the 18th century, the Portuguese-Khmer Catholics were divided into two groups: the Soarez clan took their lead from the church in Lisbon and the smaller Diaz clan followed Rome. These ecclesiastical differences ensured that there was little love lost between the two bands, though the entire Catholic community could not have counted more than a few hundred. In 1713, a Japanese priest, Michel Donno, was sent to serve the Catholics of Ponhea Leu. Initially he sided with the Soarez clan, but his superiors in Rome ordered him to join the Diaz. Rendered furious by this switch of allegiance, a member of the Soarez group attacked Father Michel one night and sliced off a foot. The priest died from the loss of blood a few hours later.

To ease tensions, the Diaz clan then moved a couple of kilometers north to the village of Thonol and in 1734 the Soarez clan left Ponhea Leu for a site closer to Udong, the royal capital. Nonetheless, this minor religious war lasted until 1784, when a Siamese invasion resulted in the plunder and destruction of both Catholic villages.

In 1848, following a decade of Vietnamese rule over Cambodia, King Ang Duong gave permission to the French missionary Jean-Claude Miche, the Vatican's first apostolic vicar of Cambodia, to settle Portuguese-Khmer Catholics on the land where Thonol had been. Father Miche rebaptized the place Ponhea Leu, thus resuscitating the name of the original Catholic village. Soon thereafter, Vietnamese Catholics fleeing intolerance in their country arrived in Ponhea Leu, raising the population of the village by several hundred. It should be noted that, unlike their coreligionists in Vietnam and other countries in the region, Catholics in Cambodia were not persecuted, perhaps because converts were few and the crown consequently did not view the religion as a threat to Buddhism.

In August 1859, Monsignor Miche, who continued to preach at Ponhea Leu and who had very close relations with King Ang Duong, reported the following story regarding a bell of his church at Ponhea Leu in a letter to his superiors at the Society of Foreign Missions:

> While the king was on a sojourn at Compot, during the night a band of thieves stole one of my bells which hung in the vestibule of our Church at Ponhalu. In the morning, I examined the footprints left by the crooks, and I realized that they came from a hamlet located one league to the West of our town; I assigned a few Christians and even a

pagan whom I knew to investigate the suspected hamlet, telling them to be sure to visit the house of the foundry workers. My expectations were not wrong. A piece of my bell was found in a shack. I straight away set out for Udong with this proof, and I requested the second king [this was Prince Norodom] to have the guilty ones seized. Without delay, he set about rendering justice; he ordered three of his horsemen to bring in the thief. This one, realizing that he was done for (as in Cambodia theft in a church is punished by death), fled, and he sought refuge with the queen mother [most likely Mneang Ros, mother of King Ang Duong], imploring her help. Touched by his tears and sobs, she promised him aid and protection even before she knew what the matter was all about. Upon hearing of this, the young prince went to her to demand the extradition of the guilty one in order to judge him and punish him according to the law, but she chased him away saying it would be a dishonor for her if it could be said that an unfortunate had put himself under her protection to no avail. On my part, I urged her to conform to the laws of the kingdom, to punish the guilty man and to have my bell returned to me; otherwise, I would bring the affair to high places (she understood by this that I would take the matter to the tribunal of the king of Siam). As a result, she lowered her colors and sent one of her mandarins to implore me to have pity on her so that it could not be said that she did not keep her word; at the same time, she sent me six bars of silver to pay for the bell, together with a promise to chastise the delinquent. I left the matter at that and gave one of the bars to the spies who had uncovered the thief.

The story illustrates how one could escape justice by putting oneself under the protection of a high personality of the court. It also shows how Monsignor Miche was not above using a bit of blackmail – threatening to appeal to the powerful king of Siam, of whom the Cambodian king was a vassal – in order to reach his desired ends.

The descendants of those Spanish and Portuguese sailors and traders largely assimilated to Khmer culture, but many kept their Hispanic names and Catholic beliefs. They had served in the Cambodian military since the 16th century. Others in the Portuguese-Khmer Catholic community held positions in the kingdom's government. Some rose to high rank, such as Col de Monteiro, who started out as an interpreter with the French and then advanced to high positions in the court of King Norodom, while at the same time remaining close with the French. Today, a street still bears Col de Monteiro's name (it is also known as St. 72; see Chapter 18).

King Ang Duong died in 1860 and was succeeded by his oldest son, Ang Voddei, who took Norodom as his reign name. The succession, however, was disputed by Ang Duong's other sons, notably the third one, the popular Sivutha, who fearing arrest rose in revolt, as did a number of Muslims of Cham and Malayan ancestry. King Norodom soon fled to Siam, pursued by Sivutha. When the rebels reached Ponhea Leu, they looted and burned several buildings. This raised the ire of Monsignor Miche, who appealed to the French in Saigon. Father Miche presumably also hoped that French involvement would open the way to greater evangelization of Cambodians, something which till then had produced minimal results. The French, eager to establish a presence in Cambodia, responded by sending a gunboat off Cambodian shores, thus initiating France's involvement in the country. The French presence calmed the situation, and King Norodom, having in the meantime secured Siamese support, returned to his throne in Udong the following year. French influence over Cambodia was formalized in 1863 by the signing of a treaty of protection with Norodom.

When King Norodom transferred the royal capital from Udong to Phnom Penh in 1866, he invited the Catholics of Ponhea Leu to move to a place just north of the new capital, an area today called Russei Keo, not far from where three years previously he had given land to over 1,200 Vietnamese refugees. Most of the Catholics who remained at Ponhea Leu moved to the new site in 1867 after their church was burned by rebels who opposed concessions King Norodom had made to the recently arrived French.

This new site was then known as Hoaland, perhaps because the Dutch had a warehouse and trading post here from 1623 to 1682. Hoaland (also written as Hoalong) now became the center of Catholicism in the country, and in 1866 a church was built there called Preah Meada, Church of the Divine Mother (Map 2, #13). In 1897, Jean-Baptiste Bernard, a French priest from the Society of Foreign Missions, reconstructed the church, which retained its name.

With time the congregation became mostly Vietnamese, with a few Chinese and Cambodians. In fact, in 1970, of the estimated 61,000 Catholics in Cambodia, 56,500 were of Vietnamese origin and only 3,000 were Cambodians. Various reasons have been given for the lack of conversions among Cambodians, especially when compared to Vietnamese. In Father Miche's time, Catholic missionaries typically explained that the "natives are fanaticized by Buddhism and by nature apathetic." Another explanation, or at least a partial one, is that the preponderant role of Quan Âm in Mahayana Buddhism, the branch of Buddhism followed in Vietnam, facilitated Vietnamese conversion to Christianity. Quan

Preah Meada, Church of the Divine Mother, c.1899

Âm (her name in Vietnamese; in Chinese she is Guan Yin) is the Bodhisattva of Compassion. She is depicted as female, and the faithful who seek favors most often pray to her rather than to the Buddha himself, who left the world and its people when he achieved nirvana. Vietnamese receptive to conversion to Catholicism could thus relate to the Virgin Mary, and in fact Quan Âm may have come into contact with Mary on her passage from India to Vietnam (see Chapter 26). In the Theravada Buddhism practiced in Cambodia, there is no equivalent to Quan Âm.

In March 1970, while Prince Sihanouk was in France for reasons of health, Prince Sirik Matak and Prime Minister Lon Nol plotted his overthrow. Lon Nol had a visceral dislike of the Vietnamese, something he shared with more than a few Cambodians as a result of Vietnamese encroachments on Cambodian lands over more than three hundred years. Indeed, in the years following Cambodia's independence from France, the Vietnamese here were, in the words of the historian Milton Osborne, "an introverted community, apprehensive that the Cambodians' ethnic hostility towards them might boil over into anti-Vietnamese violence." To Lon Nol and many others, the ethnic Vietnamese in Cambodia were all potential subversives, supporters of the Viet Cong, North Vietnamese, and Khmer Rouge. In order to garner popular backing, Lon Nol appealed to these ancient prejudices and encouraged demonstrations against the Vietnamese, including those of the Hoaland parish, the pretext being the presence of 40,000 North Vietnamese and Viet Cong troops inside Cambodia's borders. Wild youths roamed Russei Keo and several nearby Vietnamese villages, looting and ransacking homes and churches. The ringleaders, according to Prince Sihanouk, were military personnel in civilian clothes. Those police who did not stand idly by joined the rampage and took their share of the booty. The Preah Meada church was saved thanks to a Catholic Cambodian army officer who stood between the demonstrators and the church itself. The pillage only ended when Queen Mother Kossamak demanded Lon Nol send in troops and stop the riots.

A few days later, on March 18, Lon Nol and Sirik Matak overthrew Prince Sihanouk. Lon Nol now unleashed his racial pogroms against the Vietnamese. Members of the Preah Meada church were interned near Pochentong airport. Much worse happened to the Vietnamese inhabitants of the Chruoy Changvar peninsula where many were massacred, as you can read about in Chapter 1 of this book. International pressure finally caused Lon Nol to ease up. Nonetheless, a substantial number of Cambodia's Vietnamese were confined in churches, including the Hoaland church, before being deported to South Vietnam. And while others left on their own – together with those deported they totaled about 100,000 – many remained. One consequence of the carnage was that when US and South Vietnamese forces illegally entered eastern Cambodia in April 1970, the Saigon troops took revenge on Cambodians by raping, looting, and burning, and their pilots essentially viewed the country as one large free-fire zone.

The last event that took place at the Preah Meada church was the ordination of Father Joseph Chhmar Salas as Bishop of Phnom Penh, the first Cambodian to hold the position. The ceremony was held on the evening of April 14, 1975, three days before the city fell to the Khmer Rouge. Father Salas, who was only 37 years old and had been spending a year at the Society of Foreign Missions in Paris, rushed back to Phnom Penh when called to do so. "I am leaving for Cambodia to die," he told his colleagues at the Foreign Missions. On April 17, Bishop Salas joined the thousands who were forced to evacuate Phnom Penh. Like so many of his compatriots, Bishop Salas perished from hunger and exhaustion brought on by the Khmer Rouge, sometime in 1977.

As to the remaining ethnic Vietnamese, many of whom were Catholic, the Khmer Rouge ridded themselves of them by transferring yet another 100,000 to Vietnam. They were thus spared the fate meted out to so many of their Cambodian neighbors and to about half of the 20,000 Vietnamese who remained – many of them spouses of Cambodians – who were eliminated by the Khmer Rouge.

Of Cambodia's seventy-three churches, the Khmer Rouge razed all but three (the church of the Sisters of Providence in Phnom Penh, the Carmelite church on Chruoy Changvar peninsula, and St. Michel Church in Sihanoukville; the chapel of the Catholic seminary in Russei Keo also survived), perhaps because they represented western colonialism, but probably more out of spite toward their enemies the Vietnamese, as most Catholics in the country were ethnic Vietnamese. The Preah Meada church at Hoaland was totally destroyed, and its cemetery was ploughed under as well.

Today on the church's site in Russei Keo, at #2118 National Road 5, just north of the Japanese Friendship Bridge, there is a local clinic, the Daun Penh Health Center. Of the church, all that remains is an artificial grotto, one wall still preserving a number of votive plaques with words etched in French or Vietnamese, gratitude for prayers answered. A statue of the Virgin Mary is in a glass case to one side of the grotto. A few bunches of flowers in front show that some still come to pay their respects, but the grotto itself seems to serve mainly as a sheltered parking space for motorbikes.

As for Ponhea Leu, when I asked a villager living nearby about those three lonely graves, she answered, yes, there used to be a

The grotto: all that remains of the Hoaland church

In the grotto, commemorative plaques written in French and Vietnamese

church on the raised area behind, not far from the river, but it was destroyed by the Khmer Rouge. The graves date from long ago, she told me, but she did not know who was buried there, nor why in their destruction the Khmer Rouge had left the three tombs untouched.

Sources

Much of the information in this chapter comes from François Ponchaud, *The Cathedral of the Rice Paddy*, Fayard, 1990.

The story of Father Miche's bell and the comments on it are from Khin Sok, *Le Cambodge entre le Siam at le Viêtnam*, École française d'Extrême-Orient, 1991.

Bernard Patary, "Jean-Claude Miche (1805–1873), missionaire catholique, témoin singulier et acteur ambivalent du fait colonial au Cambodge," in *Siksacakr*, #12–13, 2013

Charles Meyer, *Les Français en Indochine, 1860–1910*, Plon, 1985.

Milton Osborne, *Sihanouk, Prince of light, prince of darkness*, Hawaii, 1994.

Norodom Sihanouk and Wilfred Burchett, *My War with the C.I.A.*, Penguin, 1973.

25. Lest We Forget

Near the north end of the park stretching along the west side of Sothearos Avenue, not far from the Royal Palace and across the street from what used to be the National Assembly, stands a small stupa painted gold (Map 3, #72). Etched into the black marble panels on the base of the memorial are inscriptions in Khmer and English which tell of the heartbreak that occurred nearby and the names of the innocents who perished here on March 30, 1997.

On that March day, the Khmer Nation Party (KNP), led by Sam Rainsy, organized a small demonstration in the park across the street from the National Assembly. Sam Rainsy had been minister of finance in the first government following the UNTAC-organized elections of 1993 but had been forced to resign due to his attempts to do something about rampant government corruption. He subsequently formed the Khmer Nation Party, later renamed the Sam

Memorial stupa, with the buildings of the
prime minister's bodyguard unit behind

Rainsy Party and presently the Cambodia National Rescue Party, which in the 2013 elections may well have gotten a majority of seats in parliament if not for pre-election tampering with voter lists and other irregularities.

At the time of the gathering, Cambodia was in a state of high tension. Outbursts of fighting had broken out between the military wings of the two parties in the coalition government, First Prime Minister Ranariddh's Funcinpec and Second Prime Minister Hun Sen's Cambodian People's Party (CPP). Both parties viewed Sam Rainsy's KNP as a threat in the elections scheduled for July 1998.

The purpose of that Sunday demonstration was to demand an independent judiciary, an end to the corrupt judicial system. About two hundred supporters gathered in the park in front of the National Assembly, among them a number of children. Police presence was minimal. Unusually, however, there was a line of Hun Sen's personal bodyguards, heavily armed. Here's how Sam Rainsy described the tragedy that ensued in his book, *We Didn't Start the Fire: My Struggle for Democracy in Cambodia*:

> I stood on a chair and began to address the crowd. Sweat trickled into my eyes. I began to feel unwell. I could hear a voice telling me to stop speaking and get down. Get down from there, Rainsy, get down.
>
> I cut my planned speech short. Other speakers took my place. A woman with a baby and child told how her house had been confiscated by property speculators. She had been told that she could only get her house back by bribing a judge, but she had no money. She wept as she told her story.
>
> As we listened to the woman speak, there was a huge, sudden explosion. I was pushed to the ground. Instantly there was a second explosion, just as powerful. It felt like the ground was shaking with the impact. I heard someone shout that I was dead, but in fact I was covered with the blood of one of my bodyguards. I saw special unit troops in among the demonstrators seeking to verify if I had been

> killed. For a few moments Saumura [Sam Rainsy's wife]
> thought I had been. There was panic everywhere. I heard the
> dim thud of another grenade going off, and then another.

"The scene was unbelievable," said Ron Abney, the Cambodia country director of the International Republican Institute, a US government funded organization charged with promoting democracy worldwide, who was in attendance and was wounded in the thigh by grenade shrapnel. "People cut in half, kids with their faces blown off." Sixteen people were killed, including Sam Rainsy's bodyguard Han Muny, who died protecting him. About 120 were injured. In other words, most of those in attendance were either killed or wounded. Among them were garment workers, school children, motorbike taxi drivers, food vendors, and passersby.

As could be expected in such a confused situation, witnesses gave varying reports of what had occurred. Some said grenades had been thrown from a passing white car, others that the culprit was a man on a motorbike, and yet others that the perpetrators were two men on foot who then ran through the line of Hun Sen's elite bodyguards in the direction of Wat Botum.

The government's investigation put the blame on a man nick-named Brazil, who had been seen by witnesses running towards the bodyguards' lines just after the explosions. Brazil, whose real name was Kong Samreth, was a local tough who had spent time in the army and had worked as a bodyguard. Brazil was reportedly later detained by Funcinpec General Nhiek Bun Chay and allegedly confessed to throwing the grenades. He also admitted to trying to assassinate Sam Rainsy the previous month, when the opposition leader was to address striking garment workers outside their factory. Rainsy never showed up. During the fighting between Hun Sen's CPP and Ranariddh's Funcinpec in July 1997, Brazil was said to have escaped. He has not been seen since. In 2004, the spokesman for the ministry of interior told *The Cambodia Daily* that Brazil had died "accidentally by falling off a car," though today the ministry says they are still looking for him.

Because Ron Abney was a US citizen and the victim of a supposed terrorist plot, the FBI undertook its own investigation. However, the FBI agents were essentially stonewalled by the government's security authorities, including those in charge of investigating the attack. The FBI investigators were never allowed to interrogate Brazil, the prime suspect. Their main agent referred to the "sham of a Cambodian Investigative Commission."

In Bangkok in June 1998, two other suspects in the case, Chay Vee and Chom Bun Theun, admitted to the FBI that they had carried out the attack on orders from Hun Sen's bodyguard unit. They also said that they had seen Brazil's corpse at an army base near Pochentong airport. Five months later and now back in Cambodia, the pair recanted their confession, saying that a member of Sam Rainsy's party had offered to pay them $15,000 each to implicate Hun Sen's CPP in the attack. The pair has not been seen since. Sam Rainsy is convinced that Brazil and the two are dead, as was Ron Abney until his death in 2011.

The FBI ended its investigation inconclusively in 2005. Its report stated that although there was no conclusive proof the government had ordered the grenade attack, the possibility remained that its security forces were involved, based largely on witness reports that the line of bodyguards had parted to allow the suspected grenade throwers to escape and then stopped several demonstrators from pursuing them. Though the FBI's case remains open, it is essentially on ice.

The FBI report thus laid no definitive blame on anyone for the attack. Sam Rainsy repeatedly accused Hun Sen's government of the crime, an accusation which Hun Sen vociferously denied. Some high up in the CPP even accused Sam Rainsy of initiating the incident, saying that he had the most to gain from it. Indeed, one wonders who would have gained anything from the tragedy.

So matters stand today. The government has made little effort to find those responsible and bring them to justice. Though its investigation is supposedly still ongoing, few are holding their breath.

In March 2000, on the third anniversary of the attack, Sam Rainsy and his supporters tried to place a small memorial stupa beside the site of the killings. Shortly thereafter, the monument was thrown into a sewage ditch near the Tonle Sap river. It was retrieved the next day and placed back in the park. The following day the stupa was smashed to pieces. A new stupa was erected on the site on May 16, but that night it was pried up and tossed off the Japanese Friendship Bridge. Three more memorials were subsequently erected and all three were destroyed, including one containing some of the victims' ashes. Finally, after a request was made to King Sihanouk, the Phnom Penh municipality granted permission to build a small monument.

The stupa was commemorated on August 3, 2000. One of those black panels on the base of the simple, gold-painted stupa reads:

TO

the heroic demonstrators who lost their lives on 30 March, 1997

FOR THE CAUSE OF JUSTICE AND DEMOCRACY

The tragedy occurred 80 meters from this monument

on the sidewalk of the park across from the National Assembly

Also inscribed on the stupa's base are the names of twelve of the dead; four others remain anonymous. Here, then, are those martyrs, lest we forget: Chanty Pheakdey, high school girl, 13; Chea Nang, high school teacher, 28; Chet Duong Daravuth, medical student/ journalist, 29; Han Muny, bodyguard, 32; Nam Thy, motorbike taxi driver, 37; Ros Sir, high school boy, 13; Sam Sarin, bicycle repairer, 50; Sok Kheng, female student, 18; Yoeun Yon, high school boy, 17; Yos Siem, female garment worker, 36; Yung Soknov, female garment worker, 20; Yung Srey, female garment worker, 21; and others unknown.

ON SIHANOUK BOULEVARD CLOSE to its intersection with Pasteur Street (St. 51), at the tip of the triangular garden which stretches east to Independence Monument, is a rather unremarkable stone statue of another martyr, the union leader Chea Vichea (Map

Union leader Chea Vichea

4, #76). He stands addressing a mass of his supporters at a labor demonstration, his right arm outstretched, his left hand holding a microphone. Chea Vichea was gunned down on the morning of January 22, 2004, while reading *The Cambodia Daily* at one of the nearby newsstands on Pasteur Street, just behind Wat Lanka.

Chea Vichea, the leader of the Free Trade Union (FTU), the largest opposition union, was the most popular and most outspoken voice for workers in Cambodia. He worked untiringly for decent salaries and working conditions for workers, notably those in the garment industry. He was also a leading member of the opposition Sam Rainsy Party.

That January morning, two men riding a motorbike without a license plate pulled up at the newsstand, shot Chea Vichea dead, one bullet in the chest and one in the head, and sped away. Chea Vichea's supporters immediately labeled the killing a political

243

assassination meant to intimidate opposition activists and labor organizers. Facing an uproar, police shortly thereafter arrested two men, Born Samnang and Sok Sam Oeun.

If the authorities thought that would end matters, they couldn't have been more mistaken. Anticipating a whitewash, the case was taken up by national and international organizations including Amnesty International, Human Rights Watch, and the International Labor Organization. Va Sothy, the newspaper vendor who witnessed the shooting, said the two accused did not look at all like the men she saw shoot Chea Vichea. Fearing for her life, she fled to Thailand and was later given asylum in the US.

At the ensuing trial, one witness placed Sok Sam Oeun in another part of Phnom Penh at the time of the killing, while according to others Born Samnang – who had at first admitted to the killing but subsequently recanted, saying he had confessed under torture – was not even in Phnom Penh on that day. On March 19, the presiding Phnom Penh Municipal Court judge threw out the case against the defendants for lack of evidence. Shortly thereafter, the judge was dismissed from the court and transferred to distant Stung Treng province.

Then, in early June, the Court of Appeal overturned the banished judge's decision, though no new evidence had been presented. In August 2005, Born Samnang and Sok Sam Oeun were sentenced to twenty years in prison and ordered to pay $5,000 each to the family of Chea Vichea. The family refused the compensation, saying they did not believe the two were responsible. At the time of the killing, the Phnom Penh police chief, Heng Pov, was in charge of the case. When Heng Pov fell out of favor with the government and was accused of crimes including the murder of a judge, he fled to Malaysia, where he told the French newsmagazine *L'Express*, that he had been ordered to fabricate the case against Born Samnang and Sok Sam Oeun by National Police Commissioner Hok Lundy – who died in a helicopter crash in 2008 – and that the accused had nothing to do with the murder. Heng Pov was arrested in Malaysia, whisked back to Cambodia, and sentenced to 100 years in prison. He has made no further comments on the killing of Chea Vichea.

In 2007 King Father Sihanouk wrote to the parents of Born Samnang and Sok Sam Oeun that he believed their sons were innocent of the killing. Nonetheless, the Supreme Court in 2008 upheld the lower court's decision while at the same time sending it back to the Court of Appeal, though the two defendants were provisionally released on bail. Again, no new evidence was presented. The Court of Appeal in 2012 reconvicted the pair. It wasn't until September 2013 that they were freed, exonerated of the crime by the same Supreme Court that had found them guilty five years before. Born Samnang and Sok Sam Oeun had spent five years in jail for a crime nobody believed they had committed.

King Sihanouk once stated that the murder of Chea Vichea was "undeniably political." He asked the National Assembly to declare Chea Vichea a national hero. Chea Vichea's brother Chea Mony, who took over the leadership of the FTU, still maintains that the government is responsible for his brother's assassination, for the injustice committed against Born Samnang and Sok Sam Oeun, and for doing nothing to bring the real perpetrators to justice. As with the 1997 killings at the KNP demonstration, the Phnom Penh authorities say the murder of Chea Vichea is still under investigation. Indeed, an inter-ministerial committee was established in June 2015 to once more look into the assassination.

Requests to erect a statue of Chea Vichea were for many years denied by the government. Permission was finally given and the government even paid $5,000 of the $8,000 cost, the rest coming from workers' contributions. The two-meter tall statue was unveiled on May 3, 2013, before a large, emotional crowd. Chea Vichea's brother Chea Mony called the statue a symbol of "gratitude for his physical and mental sacrifice for workers across the country."

In 2014 Born Samnang was employed as a driver in Phnom Penh, while Sok Sam Oeun was working in construction in Siem Reap. That year, Sok Sam Oeun filed suit seeking damages from the Phnom Penh Municipal Court for wrongful imprisonment. Previously, the Supreme Court had refused such compensation, reasoning that the two had not suffered injury because of their period of incarceration.

Chea Vichea's wife, Chea Kimny, who was eight months pregnant at the time of her husband's murder, and her two daughters live in Finland, where they were granted asylum. She is still seeking justice.

Sources

Sam Rainsy, with David Whitehouse, *We Didn't Start the Fire: My Struggle for Democracy in Cambodia*, Washington, 2013.

Joel Brinkley, *Cambodia's Curse*, Public Affairs, 2011.

Rich Garella and Eric Pape, "A Tragedy of No Importance," *Mother Jones* magazine online, April 2005; find it on www.cambodiagrenade.info/main/.

Luke Reynolds, "Unsolved, But Not Forgotten," *The Cambodia Daily*, April 3 – 4, 2004.

Allister Hayman, "10 years after the grenade attack," *The Phnom Penh Post*, March 23 – April 5, 2007.

Theary C. Seng, article on p.10, *The Phnom Penh Post*, June 29 – July 12, 2007.

Special Supplement to *The Cambodia Daily*, October 2011.

Neou Vannarin, "Little Hope for Justice 16 Years after Grenade Attack," *The Cambodia Daily*, March 29, 2013.

Khy Sovuthy, "Jubilation as Pair Acquitted of Union Leader's Assassination," *The Cambodia Daily*, September 26, 2013.

26. Quan Âm, the Bodhisattva of Compassion

Most who come to Phnom Penh will have stopped at some of the city's pagodas, Wat Phnom and Wat Unnalom at least, and perhaps others, for instance Wat Botum and Wat Lanka. They may even have visited a temple or two of the Chinese community, such as the Teochew/Chauzhou temple near Kandal Market, the Hainanese temple on Street 63 not too far from the Central Market, or the Hokkien temple up Sisowath Quay opposite the old Phnom Penh port. But how many have entered a Vietnamese temple, or even know of one? Yet the Vietnamese represent a not insignificant minority in Phnom Penh and Cambodia and, though they have gotten little credit for this due to the long history of animosity between the two countries, they have played a noteworthy role in the kingdom's development.

Vietnamese started settling in Cambodian territory in 1617, when the future king Chey Chetha II wed Ngoc Van, daughter of the Vietnamese lord Sai Vuong, who ruled central Vietnam from near the present-day city of Hué. In return, King Soriyopor, Chey Chetha's father, sent the Vietnamese lord elephants that could be used in times of war. Ngoc Van (Ang Cheou, her Khmer name) was accompanied by "five hundred young men and five hundred young women," according to the Royal Chronicles, and their descendants along with later Vietnamese immigrants became involved in fishing, riverboat transportation, petty commerce, and artisanry.

In 1642 Chey Chetha II's son by another spouse took the throne in a violent coup, giving himself the name Ramadhipati I. He later married a Muslim woman whom he had spotted near Udong and converted to Islam. According to the historian Michael Vickery, his conversion was probably due less to romance than "to bring

Cambodia more closely into the international sea trade network in which Malays, Chams, and Indonesians were important." Another reason may have been that, having recently massacred a number of royals and their supporters during the coup, the new king was seeking political support from the Malay and Cham Muslim communities. Whatever the case, Ramadhipati's conversion was an unpopular move among his Buddhist subjects, as was the increasing influence of Muslims of Malay origin on the court. Consequently, Chey Chetha II's Vietnamese widow Ngoc Van and those royal nephews who had escaped the massacre and fled to Vietnam decided to seek Vietnamese intervention against their half-brother, King Ramadhipati I. Responding to this appeal, the Vietnamese lord sent troops to help remove Ramadhipati in 1658. Thus began a long period of Vietnamese military involvement in Cambodia.

The antagonism between the two peoples developed later in the 17th century, when disputes in Cambodia's royal family divided the country and allowed Vietnam to annex parts of southeast Cambodia, thus continuing the Vietnamese advance to the south and leaving many Cambodians under their rule. By the end of the 18th century, virtually all of what is now referred to as Kampuchea Krom (Lower Cambodia) was under Vietnamese control. The nadir in relations came in the first half of the 19th century, when on several occasions Vietnam occupied and oppressively ruled a substantial part of Cambodia. Thousands of Cambodians died when they were forced to dig the Vinh Té and Vinh An canals in the southeast part of the country. From 1835 to 1847, Vietnam ruled Cambodia through a puppet queen, Ang Mey. In addition to political and military control, Vietnam imposed extensive cultural change. Provinces and cities were given Vietnamese names. Cambodian mandarins were obliged to wear Vietnamese dress and follow Vietnamese customs. The people were compelled to abandon their Theravada Buddhism and adopt the Mahayana Buddhism of Vietnam. Pagodas were burned. Lands were appropriated. Many suffered and many died. The enmity felt by Cambodians toward their Vietnamese neighbors had never been so great.

At that time, the Vietnamese population of Phnom Penh was far from overwhelming. Increasing numbers came to the city with the French protectorate, whose policies further exacerbated relations between Cambodians and Vietnamese. French officialdom considered the Vietnamese to be hardworking and reliable, contrary to their stereotypical opinion of Cambodians. "Annamites," as the French called them (the term was derived from An Nam, or "pacified south," the disparaging name given to northern Vietnam by the Chinese when they controlled that country in the first millennium AD), were consequently favored by the French and chosen to fill low and mid-level positions in Cambodia's colonial administration. Vietnamese were also brought in as domestic servants and, in the northeastern part of the country, as rubber plantation workers. In addition, the principal seat of government of the artificial French creation called Indochina was in distant Hanoi, through which Cambodians had to go, much to their great resentment, in order to deal with Paris. In the words of the historian Henri Locard, the French regarded Cambodia as the backyard.

Many Vietnamese chose to remain in Cambodia following independence in 1953. Anti-Vietnamese emotions didn't explode until just before Lon Nol overthrew Prince Sihanouk in 1970 and subsequently unleashed his racist purges (see Chapter 24). Many of the Vietnamese who survived were expelled to Vietnam. Over 100,000 others were later driven out by the Khmer Rouge, who in their paranoia saw them as spies or CIA agents. Of the 20,000 or so who remained, mainly spouses and children of Cambodians, roughly half were murdered. The Khmer Rouge sometimes forced Cambodians to kill their Vietnamese spouses and even their mixed race children. Indeed, both of the former Khmer Rouge leaders who remain in the dock at the Khmer Rouge tribunal face, among other charges, allegations of genocide related to events such as these.

Many exiled Vietnamese returned to Cambodia following the ousting of the Khmer Rouge and the establishment of the Vietnamese-backed People's Republic of Kampuchea. Others came in the next years as expertise from doctors, teachers, technicians, and skilled workers was needed to fill the void created by the killings of the KR period, though many of these later arrivals returned to Vietnam when that country withdrew its troops and much of its assistance at the end of the 1980s. Also, one should not forget that an estimated 23,000 Vietnamese troops died and 55,000 were wounded while fighting for the PRK. (One prominent historian puts the figure at closer to 50,000 Vietnamese dead, almost as many as the number of US troops who died in the war in Vietnam.) Vietnamese were again brought in to help rebuild the city during and following the UNTAC period, and they continue to come to this day.

The number of ethnic Vietnamese presently living in Phnom Penh is hard to gauge, with estimates varying from 40,000 to almost ten times more. The actual number is most likely down from the roughly 200,000 Vietnamese in the city at the time of the 1970 Sirik Matak-Lon Nol coup against Prince Sihanouk and their ugly, xenophobic campaign against the Vietnamese. Many of these ethnic Vietnamese live in stateless limbo, denied Cambodian citizenship because the 1996 Law on Nationality and Immigration requires that a child born in Cambodia can acquire Cambodian citizenship only if both parents were born in Cambodia. Given that most of those who fled or were deported during the Lon Nol and Khmer Rouge years returned to Cambodia without documentation proving their birth, much less that of their parents, one wonders how they could obtain the Cambodian citizenship to which they should be entitled, unless the 1996 law is amended. Some of these families have been here for generations (except for the years of exodus during the Lon Nol and Khmer Rouge periods) and many have assimilated in varying degrees to Cambodian culture, while also retaining aspects that link them to their Vietnamese forebears.

I daresay, however, that few of the city's other residents know much about the Vietnamese and their customs. I doubt, for example, that many could tell you the location of a single Vietnamese pagoda, and indeed it took a number of inquiries before I could find those I have visited. Yet such pagodas are well worth a detour, as they are quite different from the Khmer pagodas.

THE RELIGION OF THE Vietnamese is often described as a combination of Confucianism, Taoism, and Buddhism, and the Vietnamese themselves have an expression for the faith: *Tam Giao,* or Three Religions. However, the buddhas, bodhisattvas, ancestors, deities, and other divine figures in Vietnamese conviction have not been combined or synthesized. Rather, they stand beside each other and, to the faithful, there is absolutely nothing contradictory about worshipping some or all of them.

Confucianism as a philosophical doctrine largely disappeared in Vietnam with the end of the mandarinate and the monarchy in the first half of the twentieth century, though many of its moral precepts remain, at least to some degree, notably those that urge harmony through correct relations such as those between children and father, wife and husband, and even citizen and government. Ancestor worship, perhaps the most important aspect of Vietnamese belief today, is sometimes associated with Confucius, though the practice long predated the sage.

Taoism in Vietnam is not the philosophical system once followed by Chinese literati, but rather a popular religious version involving mediums, exorcisms, and a multitude of divinities organized in hierarchical fashion under the Jade Emperor. In addition to the gods and goddesses who entered Vietnam from China, many indigenous Vietnamese deities are commonly included under the Taoist label.

As for Buddhism, the branch of that religion most widely observed not only in Vietnam but also in China, Japan, and Korea is Mahayana Buddhism, as opposed to the Theravada Buddhism of Cambodia, Thailand, Laos, Burma, and Sri Lanka. Theravada Buddhism is based on Pali sutras: discourses of the Buddha in the Pali language that his disciples memorized and passed on orally, and that only appeared in writing in the first century BC, almost four hundred years after the Buddha's death. Theravada Buddhism regards these sutras as the true record of what the Buddha taught. Mahayana, on the other hand, is based on new sutras that began to appear four hundred years after the Buddha's death, though they are also believed to be authentic words of the Buddha. According to Mahayana Buddhism, these sutras are secret teachings of the Buddha and were not intended for all his disciples at the time of his death. They were passed on only to a select few and were held until the appropriate time for their revelation. The differences between the two schools, therefore, lie to a large extent in what they say the Buddha taught, together with interpretations of his words.

In addition, while Theravada Buddhism focuses on the personal attainment of enlightenment, Mahayana believes in the assistance of bodhisattvas. Bodhisattvas are beings who could achieve enlightenment through their merits and virtues, thereby achieving buddhahood, and upon death they could reach nirvana. However, they have renounced entering this state in order to work for the welfare of others and help them achieve their own salvation. Because bodhisattvas help believers, they have become objects of worship, and requests are more often made to them than to the more distant Buddha. Bodhisattvas do not have such a significant place in Theravada Buddhism, much less the ideal place they hold in Mahayana.

In China many, many years ago, a king's wife gave birth to one daughter after another, until they had three. Though chagrined at being denied a male heir, the king resolved to find suitable husbands for his daughters and eventually pass on the kingdom to the most worthy of his sons-in-law. He accomplished this for his first two daughters, but the third, the most beautiful and virtuous of all, refused to marry. From an early age, she spent her time in prayer and meditation, and she avoided all the luxuries to which she was entitled, dressing herself in crude cotton cloth rather than fine silks. When she reached puberty, Princess Miao Shan, as she was called, decided to devote herself to the teachings of the Buddha and enter a convent. The king was at first furious at his daughter's intention to become a nun, but he soon relented, convinced that Miao Shan would tire of such a life and return to the palace before long. Miao Shan was thus permitted to enter White Swallow Convent, though her father the king had taken the precaution of ordering the abbess to assign the most tedious and arduous chores to his daughter. Miao Shan willingly undertook every task, all the while maintaining her resolve to remain in the convent and never marry. Now convinced of his daughter's determination to defy him, the king became so enraged that he condemned her to death, ordering that she be taken to the palace in chains and then decapitated. The executioner swung his great sword, but just as it touched Miao Shan's neck it shattered into countless pieces. Those in attendance had not yet gotten over their shock when an enormous tiger leaped forth from nowhere, grabbed Miao Shan in his powerful jaws, and bounded into the forest. The tiger was none other than the tutelary spirit of the land, ordered by the Jade Emperor to save the pious princess, and the animal transported her to a cavern in the limestone hills southwest of Hanoi where Chùa Huong Thích, or Perfume Pagoda, stands today. Here she was visited by the Buddha A Di Dà (Amitabha), who told her that she was the Bodhisattva Quan Âm and that henceforth her mission was to bring succor to all those who suffered. To assist her, she was given two acolytes: a lad named Kim Dông, Golden Boy, and Ngoc Nu, Jade Girl, the granddaughter of the ocean-dwelling King of Dragons.

Miao Shan emerged from her cave in the hills to perform many miracles. The most famous of these happened after her father, the king, fell gravely ill and no cure could be found. One day, a mysterious monk told the king he could be healed by drinking a potion made from the arm and eye of one who was "without anger," and that the only such person resided in that cavern in the mountains. The king sent a messenger to this most wondrous person, with orders to beseech her to comply with the request. When she heard of her father's illness, the compassionate Miao Shan immediately gouged out not one but both of her eyes and then cut off both arms. The monk made the potion and the king was instantly cured when he drank it. Awed by his miraculous recovery, the king and queen set out on a pilgrimage to express their gratitude to their most magnanimous and charitable benefactor. When they arrived at the cavern, the queen recognized her daughter, Princess Miao Shan, who now revealed to them that she was the Bodhisattva Quan Âm. Overcome with shame and remorse over their mistreatment of their daughter, the king and his wife devoted the rest of their lives to Buddhism and doing good works.

I realize that by recounting the legend of Miao Shan (there are numerous variations of this story, and there are further legends of Quan Âm in other manifestations) I risk inviting the reader to place Quan Âm in the realm of folk religion. Many Buddhists would explain her as the latent energy of compassion that exists in everyone's mind, and her images (as well as those of all buddhas and bodhisattvas) as representations of qualities within all beings, rather than as a legendary divinity carved into beautiful statues and invoked in fervent prayers for succor. However, in traditional Vietnamese Mahayana Buddhism, I believe that the popular form of Quan Âm, the beloved Quan Âm of legends and miracles and statues placed on altars, accounts for the celebrity of her cult, which is particularly widespread among women.

Of the bodhisattvas of Vietnamese Mahayana Buddhism, prayers are most frequently offered to the Bodhisattva Quan Âm. Quan Âm came to Vietnam from China, where she is known as Guan Yin, and before that from India through China's far west and Tibet. In India, Quan Âm was known as Avalokiteshvara (whom we met in Chapter 6 at the riverside shrine of Preah Ang Dongka), who is said to have emanated from the right eye of the Buddha Amitabha, the Buddha of the Past. Indeed, the name Quan Âm is the Vietnamese translation of Avalokiteshvara, Hearer of the Cries of the World.

While bodhisattvas have in theory transcended the male-female duality and are without gender, their representations are not. Avalokiteshvara was represented as a male figure in India. While journeying from India to China, the bodhisattva passed through lands where female deities were worshiped: in western China, Mary, mother of Jesus, and in Tibet, Tara, herself an emanation from the Buddha Amitabha. The bodhisattva became feminized in China. This may have been due to a perceived need among Chinese Buddhists for a female divinity to represent compassion

Quan Âm holding a flask with the nectar of compassion,
flanked by the pagoda guardians Hô Pháp and Tiêu Dién
at the entrance to the main hall of Chùa Kim Phuóc

and charity; indeed, Quan Âm is the only major feminine figure in the Mahayana Buddhist pantheon. Competition during the Tang dynasty (618–907) between male-dominated Buddhism (which, like male-dominated Confucianism, reflected the society from which it emerged) and Taoism, which at least in its popular form included many feminine deities, might also help to explain the emergence of a feminine Avalokiteshvara. The fact that Guan Yin in China and Quan Âm in Vietnam are still today the most beloved figures of Buddhism proves that their cult filled a significant need, the need for a personal, compassionate divinity.

By the 10th century, virtually all Chinese representations of Guan Yin were in her female aspect, and she entered Vietnam and, much later, continued on to Cambodia in this form. Today, Quan Âm is commonly represented in a flowing white robe (though at Thiên Phuóc Pagoda her robe is gilded) holding in one hand a vase filled with the nectar of compassion. Quan Âm blesses her followers with the heavenly ambrosia, thus relieving them of their woes. Every Vietnamese pagoda has a prominent altar dedicated to Quan Âm. Small statues of Quan Âm are placed on many family altars, gracing the home with the benevolence and protection of She Who Hears the Cries of the World.

In 1969 Phnom Penh reportedly had thirty-seven Vietnamese pagodas. Today, I know of only six, including one that is Sino-Vietnamese. The most centrally-located one is Chùa (the Vietnamese word for pagoda) Thiên Phuóc, at #64 Street 134 (Map 1, #9), near the intersection with Street 225. The walls of the pagoda's main hall are decorated with scenes of the Buddha's life, as they are in most of Cambodia's Theravada pagodas. Presiding over the main altar in the place of honor is Sakyamuni, the historical Buddha (Thích Ca Mâu Ni, in Vietnamese; except for the Buddha himself, I will use Vietnamese names for the buddhas, bodhisattvas, and other members of the Mahayana pantheon – though without all the diacritics – with their more commonly recognized Sanskrit versions in parentheses). This, however, is where the similarities between Vietnamese Mahayana and Cambodian Theravada pagodas end, and all of the following Mahayana figures are absent from Cambodian pagodas.

The exterior of this small pagoda shows a style resembling that of Chinese temples. Enter the main hall through the left-hand door and you will pass by the warrior deity Hô Pháp, the main protector of Vietnamese pagodas, his hand resting on his sword. Guarding the right-hand door is the fierce-faced Tiêu Diên, a representation of Quan Âm. Horned, fanged, and with a mouth that spews flames, Tiêu Diên's fierce countenance defeats evil with a simple glance. By throwing fear into ghosts and malignant spirits, Tiêu Diên not only protects the pagoda from them but is able to control and lead them toward salvation.

Two disciples dressed in monastic robes flank the Buddha himself on the main altar. On the left is Ca Diêp (Mahakasyapa), who presided over the Buddha's funeral and then assumed leadership of the Buddhist community, or *sangha*. On the right is A Nan (Ananda), the Buddha's cousin, who had a prodigious memory and could recall every word the Buddha had uttered during the twenty-five years he followed the master. A Nan was thus charged with compiling the sutras, those verses based on the Buddha's teachings which at the time were memorized and recited rather than written down. The middle level of the main altar is dedicated to the Tam

Thê, the Three Generations, all seated cross-legged on lotus blossoms: A Di Dà (Amitabha), the Buddha of the Past, Sakyamuni himself, the Buddha of the Present, and Di Lac (Maitreya), the Buddha of the Future. Two smaller figures are in front of the Tam Thê. On the right, the corpulent "Laughing Buddha" stands with his disheveled monk's robes open to the waist, allowing his corpulence to be admired. This jolly, pot-bellied representation is based on a 10th century Chinese monk, Budai, allegedly an incarnation of Di Lac. On the left, a small figure of Sakyamuni at the time of his birth points his right hand skyward and his left hand toward the earth. "In the Heavens and on Earth," he said at his birth, "only I am the Venerable One," adding that this life would be his last.

Doors on either side of the altar lead to the back hall. Enter the hall through the right-hand door and you will pass by another

Entrance to Chùa Thiên Phuóc

257

martial protector of pagodas: the stern, red-faced deified Chinese general Quan Công, hero of the Chinese classic *The Three Kingdoms*, holding a halberd. Next to the left-hand door, the bodhisattva Dia Tang (Kshitigarbha) stands wearing a monk's robe and Buddhist miter. In his right hand, he holds a beggar's staff that can open the gates of hell; the staff is ornamented at the top with metal rings whose jangling sounds chase away demons and also frighten off small animals lest they be trod on and killed. In his left hand, he holds a wish-granting jewel which has the power to cleanse the heart of all desire. Like all bodhisattvas, Dia Tang helps ordinary humans break the cycle of suffering and rebirth.

Much-loved Quan Âm stands on the main altar of the back hall holding a small vial of the nectar of compassion, the ring finger and thumb of her right hand touching each other in the preaching *mudra*, or gesture. Also on this altar is another representation of Quan Âm, eighteen-armed Chuân Dè (Cundi). One popular Chuân Dè story involves the eighteen La Hân (*arhat* or *arahant*). These early followers of the Buddha attained enlightenment and were about to enter nirvana. The eighteen wished to present themselves with heads freshly tonsured and, in pious haste, each wanted to be the first to enter. To avoid jealousies and allow the eighteen to reach nirvana at the same moment, Chuân Dè grew eighteen arms and shaved the monks' heads at one and the same time.

Facing Quan Âm on an altar in the rear of the hall is Dat Ma (Bodhidharma), an Indian Buddhist missionary who arrived in China in 526. In China, he introduced a doctrine of attaining perfection through meditation and concentration rather than through deeds and studying. His school of Buddhism is known in Vietnam as Thiên (Dhyana, or Zen, the Japanese name most commonly used in English). Dressed in brown monk's robes, his heavy beard meant to indicate his Indian ethnicity, he stands on a few leaves floating on water, an allusion to the episode in which, on reaching the Yellow River in China, he broke off some reeds from the bank and drifted across. Also here in the back hall are pictures of the pagoda's deceased former head monks. Notice too on the left-hand

Quan Âm, fronted by eighteen-armed
Chuân Dè, at Thiên Phuóc Pagoda

wall the paintings of the horrors of hell that sinners must suffer according to the wrongdoings they have committed.

Thiên Phuóc Pagoda, like the other Vietnamese pagodas, has other notable figures of the Mahayana Buddhist pantheon including the aforementioned Di Lac, the Buddha of the Future, who is actually a bodhisattva until he becomes a buddha and who is pictured in a wall painting with his disciples Phô Hiên (Samantabhadra) mounted on a snow-white elephant and Van Thù (Manjusri) seated on a fantastic blue lion. There are also a number of deities of Taoist origin such as the Holy Mothers, who are worshiped at several altars in the courtyard inside the entrance gate. Also, just inside the gate stands a small statue of Thân Tai, God of Wealth.

Finally, returning to Quan Âm's altar, you will notice a yellow box with red trim on which are two cylindrical vessels that hold 100 bamboo fortune telling sticks, called *xâm*. Should you wish to know something about your fate, shake the container until one of the divination sticks falls to the floor. Each stick has a number painted on it. Take the stick to the resident monk and he will tell you what your future will bring. Another divining method used here is known as *xin queo*. Pick up the two wooden crescents on the same yellow box as the *xâm*, pose a yes/no question to Quan Âm, and drop the crescents to the floor. The monk will tell you the answer to your query, depending on how the crescents land. Regardless of satisfaction or not, be sure to thank Quan Âm by leaving a small donation in the yellow box.

Sources

Much of the portion of this chapter which deals with Mahayana Buddhism and Quan Âm comes from my own unpublished opus, *Searching for Old Hué: The story of Viêt Nam's former capital as seen through its monuments and vestiges.*

Michael Vickery, *History of Cambodia: Summary of Lectures, 2001–2002.*

Mak Phœun, *Chroniques Royales du Cambodge (de 1594 à 1677),* École française d'Extrême-Orient, 1981.

Mak Phoeun, *Histoire du Cambodge,* École française d'Extrême-Orient, 1995.

Khin Sok, *Le Cambodge entre le Siam et le Viêtnam,* École française d'Extrême-Orient, 1991.

Stuart White, "Age an issue for KRT civil parties too," *The Phnom Penh Post,* March 21, 2013.

Jeff Mudrick, "Revisiting Cambodia's Laws on Nationality and Immigration," *The Cambodia Daily,* April 30, 2014.

Donald Lopez, *The Story of Buddhism,* HarperSanFrancisco, 2001.

Georges Dumoutier, "Les Cultes Annamites," *Revue Indo-Chinoise,* March 30, 1905.

Louis Bezacier, *L'Art Vietnamien,* Éditions de l'Union Française, 1954.

Martin Palmer, Jay Ramsay, and Man-Ho Kwok, *Kuan Yin,* Thorsons, 1995.

Jon Blofeld, *Bodhisattva of Compassion,* Shambala Dragon, 1988.

Louis Frédéric, *Buddhism,* Flammarion, 1995.

27. Ganesha, the God with the Elephant Head

In recent years, Phnom Penh has been graced with a number of new statues. We have already visited Grandmother Penh, for whom the city is named, at the foot of Wat Phnom, and the Venerable Chuon Nath (1883–1969), highly respected supreme patriarch of the Mahanikay sect of Theravada Buddhism, who is seated in the center of Hun Sen Circle. On National Assembly Street just south of this statue is a small memorial to Penn Nouth (1906–1985), the long-time Sihanouk adviser who among other accomplishments was prime minister seven times (Map 4, #80). And in the garden on Sisowath Quay across from the Cambodiana Hotel is Kram Ngoy (1864–1936), nationalist poet and balladeer, who is sculpted sitting cross-legged playing the *khsae muoy*, a traditional one-stringed instrument depicted in Khmer art at least since the seventh century.

One of the most recent sculptures, inaugurated in February 2012, is the statue of the Hindu god Ganesha, situated in a small garden at the triangular intersection of Monivong Boulevard, George Dimitrov Street, and Viyadhapura Street (St. 120, see Map 3, #48). The statue is a reminder of Cambodia's Angkorian grandeur. Like Angkor's statues, this one is unsigned, its sculptor

Penn Nouth's memorial   Kram Ngoy (Map 3, #74)

Ganesha

anonymous. Unlike many Angkorian statues, which were painted or gilded, our Ganesha remains the color of its stone.

Elephant-headed and corpulent (though rather less so than in many portrayals), our four-armed Ganesha, the son of Lord Shiva, stands upright, his loins wrapped in a *sampot* and his plaited hair held by a knotted headband decorated with floral motifs. Ganesha's trunk dips into a bowl, held in his left hand, filled with a sweet delicacy of which he was especially fond. Ganesha's right hand holds his broken right tusk, which is thus absent from his jaw. Of Ganesha's two upraised hands, one holds a disc while the other holds a conch. As both the disc and the conch are attributes of Vishnu, Ganesha here may well represent the joining of the two main sects of ancient Hindu worship, Shaivism and Vishnuism. Although a Hindu deity, Ganesha was later accepted into Cambodia's Buddhist pantheon.

Lord Ganesha has a singular story. The son of Shiva and Uma, he was born with a human head and a human body. Uma one day assigned her young son to guard her bathing place, insisting that he let no one enter. When Shiva returned after a long absence eager to see his wife, the obedient Ganesha refused to let him in, not recognizing his father. Shiva, furious, unsheathed his sword and sliced off Ganesha's head. The distraught Uma said she would have no relations with her husband until he brought their son back to life. Shiva then declared that Ganesha would be given the head of the next being that appeared. When an elephant passed by, Shiva lopped off its head and placed it on his son's body. Ganesha was thus restored to life and presumably Shiva was once again granted his conjugal visits.

This Hindu legend from India, where the cult of Ganesha originated, is familiar in Phnom Penh, but Cambodia also has its own tales of Ganesha, who is known here as Preah Pheakines. Most versions have been transmitted orally over generations and one of them, which I have taken from a French translation by Jean Ellul, goes like this:

There was once a man who went to the land of Roum to learn the magical sciences. He was accepted by a master magician there, but only on condition that when he finished his studies he would never leave Roum and return to his own country, on penalty of death. However, once the man had completed his studies, he escaped from Roum. When he arrived home, he took his son into the forest and began to teach him what he had learned. The magicians of Roum sent a magic sword to find the man and cut off his head. This was done, and the head was taken away while the body was left behind, thus making it impossible for the man to be reincarnated. The man's son, however, seeing a dead elephant nearby, sliced off its head and placed it on his father's neck. Thanks to the power of magic, the father came back to life and became Preah Pheakines, and he continued to teach his son the magic rites and formulas.

Other Cambodian versions of the Ganesha myth are longer and more elaborate, but all involve a man's journey to the land of Roum to study the science of magic, and there is always the condition of not leaving Roum and returning to the homeland. The student invariably escapes, with the magical formulas sometimes tattooed on his body (Ganesha is considered the founder of tattooing), sometimes memorized, and one time written down, swallowed, and regurgitated once safely home. Usually the student is a father who passes on the secrets to his son, sometimes a brother who transmits them to his sibling. In all versions, the man is decapitated by a sword or disc sent by the magicians of Roum, and the head is taken away. The son/brother then chops off an elephant's head and places it on the acephalic corpse, thereby reviving it and allowing the magic formulas to be further transmitted. These secrets deal with healing powers, invulnerability, and reincarnation or resurrection.

So go the legends of Ganesha, who has the strength of an elephant and the intelligence of a man. In a larger sense, according to the art historian Helen Ibbitson Jessup, "The syncretized god is the symbol of the unity of the small being, or man – the microcosm – with the great, the elephant – the macrocosm."

As to Ganesha's broken tusk, there are several accounts of how he lost it. One legend says that when Ganesha was transcribing the great Hindu epic *Mahabarata* as it was being dictated to him by the sage Vyasa, he realized that the task could not be done with an ordinary pen. Thus, he broke off his tusk and with it finished the writing. Another says the wound was from a fight he had with Parasurama, the sixth avatar of Lord Vishnu, who severed Ganesha's tusk when the latter tried to stop him from seeing the sleeping Shiva, whom Ganesha was guarding. Parasurama later asked for forgiveness. Finally, when Ganesha reached Cambodia – representations of the god in the country date to the seventh century – he was associated with fertility of the land, and his broken tusk represented a plough.

In Cambodia, Ganesha is traditionally associated with magic, tattooing, and certain medicinal rites. In addition, Ganesha is known as the god of prosperity, with accomplishment exemplified by his paunch. (Another explanation for his large belly is that in

Cambodian popular tradition intelligence is found there.) Prayers to him are often offered prior to the beginning of commercial ventures as he removes obstacles on the way to business success. In fact, one of Ganesha's Hindu names means "lord of obstacles" and he can set them up as well as tear them down. It is appropriate, therefore, that Ganesha's statue stands beside an avenue commonly known as "bank street."

Sources

Jean Ellul, "Le mythe de Ganesha," in *Seksa Khmer*, December, 1980. Ellul gives French translations of a number of Cambodian versions of the Ganesha legend, including the one given here.

Louise Allison Cort and Paul Jett, editors, *Gods of Angkor: Bronzes from the National Museum of Cambodia*, Washington, 2010.

Helen Ibbitson Jessup and Thierry Zephir, editors, *Sculpture of Angkor and Ancient Cambodia: Millennium of Glory*, Thames & Hudson, 1997.

Khun Samen, *The New Guide to the National Museum of Phnom Penh*, 2001.

28. The Furtive Kouprey

If you walk around Wat Phnom's hill to its west side, between the street and the Sunway Hotel you will see a statue of a powerful, humpbacked male bovine with imposing curved horns, its head bowed down, either grazing or preparing to charge (Map 2, #31). Evident too is the prominent dewlap, the fold of skin hanging from the animal's neck to below its knees. This singular creature is the kouprey (*Bos sauvelis*), one of the world's rarest mammals. Prince Norodom Sihanouk declared the kouprey Cambodia's national animal in 1963. Though the prince reportedly kept one in his garden as a child, he bestowed the honor on the kouprey due to the animal's elusiveness and mystery, certainly not because of the folk belief that the sighting of a kouprey is a bad omen that portends bloodshed in the country.

The kouprey, which means "forest bull" in Khmer, is known to Cambodians from legend and folk dance, but it is unlikely that

Statue of a male kouprey at Wat
Phnom circle, erected 2005

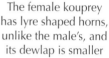

The female kouprey has lyre shaped horns, unlike the male's, and its dewlap is smaller

Young kouprey at the Vincennes zoo, 1937

Georges Brohanne

anyone in the country under the age of thirty or so has ever seen one. Though rumors float about from time to time, the last confirmed sightings date to the late 1980s. More recently, kouprey tracks have been seen and skulls have reportedly been on sale in village markets. Since 2004, the kouprey has been listed as "critically endangered" by the International Union for Conservation of Nature and Natural Resources (IUCN).

The only extant video pictures of the kouprey are grainy images taken in 1951 in the Choam Ksan and Koh Ker areas of Preah Vihear province (you can view the video on YouTube: youtube. com/watch?v=0FYwnjqHr6k). The last known still photograph was snapped in 1967.

The first recorded shooting of a kouprey by a European was by Dr. R. Sauvel of the Institute of Tropical Animal Husbandry and Veterinary Medicine in Paris. While working in Preah Vihear from 1921 to 1932, Sauvel observed herds of the animal on several occasions. In 1937, he was given a young kouprey, which he then sent to the Vincennes botanical garden in Paris. There, the kouprey was studied and given its species classification, *sauvelis*, in honor of Dr. Sauvel. The Vincennes kouprey died in 1940, shortly after the outbreak of World War II, probably of neglect.

In 1964 five kouprey were captured by an American biologist, Dr. Charles H. Wharton, whose team had made the video pictures mentioned above on an earlier expedition. Wharton's plans to initiate a breeding program of the kouprey failed, however, when two of his captured animals died and the other three escaped.

At its shoulders, a male kouprey grows to height of 1.65 to 1.80 meters, and it weighs 700 to 800 kilograms (I use the present tense in this description, perhaps too optimistically). It has a long tail with a bushy tip. Its color changes with age, from reddish brown to grey at about twelve years of age and eventually to black in older males. The bull's horns – longer than the female's – are often frayed from digging in the ground or butting against trees and stumps. The kouprey has well developed senses of hearing and smell. Never solitary, they live in herds of up to twenty led by a senior female who decides when to stop, when to walk, and when to flee from danger. The animal can live to a maximum age of twenty. Calves are born in December or January after a gestation period of eight to nine months. The kouprey is diurnal, grazing in grasslands on the edge of the forest during the day but seeking refuge in the woodlands during the hottest hours.

In the mid-2000s there was a hotly disputed contention that the kouprey itself was not a natural species at all but a relatively recent cross between another feral bovine, the banteng (*Bos banteng*) and a domesticated ox, the zebu (*Bos taurus indicus*). The study, based on the results of testing done of the DNA of banteng and zebu and of the remains of the Vincennes zoo kouprey, hypothesized that the hybrid kouprey's progeny later returned to the wild. Another study based on similar DNA testing, however, found that the kouprey was a separate species, members of which had mated with a banteng in the distant past, thus creating the Cambodian banteng. Then in 2007 the international scientific community learned of a 2004 description by two Thai scientists of a fossilized kouprey skull. That skull dates to sometime between the late Pleistocene and early Holocene periods, roughly 125,000 to 5,000 years ago. Though it seems surprising that their research couldn't have resulted in more precise dating, their description was proof enough that the kouprey was an original species and not a recent hybrid, and the controversy ended.

Although the kouprey may once have roamed over parts of Thailand, Laos, and Vietnam, if any survive today they are most likely in lightly forested areas of Oddar Meanchey, Preah Vihear, Ratanakkiri, or Mondulkiri; in the 1960s Prince Sihanouk designated in each of those provinces a nature preserve for the animal's protection. Sadly, the kouprey population has been decimated by habitat destruction (agriculture and logging), hunting/poaching (the meat was usually smoked or dried, the horns were believed to cure certain diseases), US bombing during the Vietnam War, and mines placed during the civil war with the Khmer Rouge. A Cambodian report presented at an international conference on the conservation of the kouprey in 1988 estimated there were 500 kouprey in 1950, 200 in 1964, and only 100 in 1970. A two week expedition by the Cambodian Kouprey Research Project to a remote area of Mondulkiri province in 1994 did not spot the kouprey but found footprints that fit the size and description given by Wharton. The researchers estimated that six to eight kouprey still lived in the survey area. Although optimists in the IUCN claim that up to 250 kouprey may still be alive, periodic searches since the early 1990s including the use of camera trappings have failed to detect even one. Given those failures, it is unlikely that any further scientific searches specifically for the kouprey will be funded.

Other wild bovines in Cambodia have survived in greater numbers, notably the banteng (*Bos banteng*), *tonsong* in Khmer, and the gaur (*Bos gaurus*), *khting* in Khmer. Both have less prominent horns and do not have a dewlap, or at most a rudimentary one. The banteng is smaller and slower than the kouprey, while the gaur is slightly larger. The banteng is also listed as endangered, with an estimated 2,700 to 5,700 living in the eastern highlands in 2011, a 90% drop since the 1960s, according to a World Wildlife Fund report. Their decline is attributed to illegal poaching and to the Cambodian government granting land concessions in protected

Banteng   Gaur

areas, often to foreign companies who clear vast areas for rubber plantations. As for the gaur, you can see several at the Phnom Thamao wildlife sanctuary *cum* zoo some forty-five kilometers from Phnom Penh, a few kilometers west off of National Road 2.

Though it is virtually impossible that the kouprey will once more reach the present numbers and range of the gaur or even the banteng, one may hope it will be spotted again. If so, it is imperative that conservationists be contacted immediately in order to assure the animal's protection. In the meantime, the kouprey survives in traditional dances, myths, some blurred images, a couple of postage stamps, the name of Cambodia's national rugby team, and that statue near Wat Phnom.

IF YOU ARE IN the vicinity of our Kouprey statue, walk a short distance to the south and between Wat Phnom and the US Embassy (Map 2, #32) you will come upon a small island of grass which holds a bronze image of another of Cambodia's critically endangered species, the Royal Terrapin, or *Batagar affinis*, which was believed to be extinct until several of the riverine turtles were found in 2001 along the Sre Ambel River in Koh Kong province. The reptile once lived in the mangrove forests of Koh Kong and the Tonle Sap lake but was poached to near extinction for its meat and eggs.

Also in the area, just to the north of the Kouprey statue, is Sanderson Park (Map 2, #30), named after the Australian general who commanded UNTAC forces. The park has a small memorial

Royal Terrapin, *Batagar affinis*, whose eggs
were once offered as a gift to the king

which once bore a bronze plaque inscribed with the names of forty-one UNTAC soldiers from eleven different countries who paid the ultimate price. The inscription on the plaque read, "They gave their lives in the service of peace, United Nations Transitional Authority in Cambodia, March 1992 – September 1993." Of these fallen warriors, eleven were Bulgarian, far more than any other nationality. Sadly, the plaque was stolen not long ago, though its base remains. Beyond the memorial is a statue of a dove, that popular symbol of peace, fashioned from the recycled metal of weapons of war.

Peace dove

271

Sources

"Le Kouprey, Novibos Sauvelis," report by the Cambodian delegation to a seminar on the protection of the kouprey and its ecological habitat, held in Hanoi, January 15–16, 1988; reprinted in *Seksa Khmer* #1, January 1999.

"Vet: Ten Head of Kouprey in Mondulkiri," *The Phnom Penh Post*, April 22, 1994.

"Search for the kouprey: trail runs cold for Cambodia's national animal," Charles McDermid and Cheang Sokha, *The Phnom Penh Post*, April 21–May 4, 2006.

"A Celebrity Among Ungulates May Soon Be Dismissed as a Poseur," Nark Derr, *The New York Times*, reprinted in *The Cambodia Daily*, September 18, 2006.

"Cambodia's National Animal is 'Real,' Study Says," Anne Casselman, *National Geographic News*, October 5, 2007.

"Kouprey, *Bos sauvelis*," cardamom.org/kouprey.html.

Rohan H.P. Holloway, "Natural History notes on the River Terrapin Batagur Baska (Gray, 1831) in Cambodia," University of Canberra, 2003.

"Endangered Turtle Is Returned After 30-Year Stay in Vietnam," Simon Lewis, *The Cambodia Daily*, October 8, 2012.

29. Lord Vessanda

In almost all of Cambodia's pagodas, the walls of the *vihara*, the main prayer hall, are decorated with brightly colored murals. More often than not, the lower register illustrates episodes of the Buddha's life, while the upper register depicts scenes from stories of the Buddha's previous ten lives, stories known as *jataka* tales, or reincarnation tales. The Buddha himself told these stories to his followers in order to exemplify each of ten moral points, the so-called ten perfections, which include virtuosity, self-denial, wisdom, energy, patience, truthfulness, determination, benevolence, equanimity, and generosity.

Each of the Buddha's incarnations is usually depicted in one mural. However, one particular *jataka* tale is often represented by a series of frames. This is the *Maha Jataka*, the Great Reincarnation, commonly referred to as the Vessanda *Jataka*, which illustrates the perfection of generosity. Lord Vessanda was the Buddha's last incarnation prior to his being reborn as Prince Siddhartha Gautama, who became the Buddha upon attaining enlightenment. In Cambodia, the narrative of Lord Vessanda is the most popular *jataka*, which accounts for its representation in several paintings on the walls of a pagoda's *vihara*.

Here we will tell Lord Vessanda's story as illustrated by the murals decorating Wat Phnom (Map 2, #36). Unusually, at Wat Phnom these murals are in two registers on the lower, main walls, while those depicting the historical Buddha's life are on the smaller upper walls, which are held up by the *vihara*'s columns. Vessanda's narrative begins with the panel on the far right of the upper register of the west wall, the wall behind the main altar.

As even the gods are subject to the laws of *samsara*, the beginningless cycle of death and rebirth, or transmigration of the soul, when Indra, King of the Gods, saw the time of passing was

273

Figure 1 – Indra pours water on Suppati's
hands to confirm his gift of ten wishes

approaching for Suppati, his main wife, he promised to grant her ten wishes if in her next life she would become the mother of Vessanda, who would be the penultimate incarnation of the future Buddha. Among Suppati's wishes were to marry Sanjaya, the king of Jetoda, to give birth to a child of great virtue, and to keep her name. This scene is depicted in Figure 1, which takes place in Indra's paradise and shows the god pouring water on the hands of Suppati in order to seal his promise of granting her the ten wishes. Indra is frequently depicted with a blue face, as he is here.

Suppati was subsequently reborn as the daughter of the ruler of a small kingdom in northern India. When she was 16, she was married to Sanjaya, the king of nearby Jetoda, as she had wished. Soon thereafter, Indra invited the future Buddha to become incarnated in Suppati's womb, and he was reborn as Prince Vessanda.

From a young age, Vessanda was renowned and much beloved for his generosity, bestowing upon the poor jewels and rich clothes. Never did he refuse a request and he was even willing to offer his own life, should such an appeal be made. When he reached adulthood, Vessanda married Medri, a princess from a neighboring country.

Sanjaya, Vessanda's father, then abdicated from the kingship of Jetoda, passing it on to his son. Vessanda and Medri soon had two children, a son, Jali, and a daughter, Krasna.

At Vessanda's birth, the gods had given him a sacred white elephant, one that assured abundant rainfall, plentiful harvests, and prosperity for his kingdom. One year, a neighboring land suffered a lengthy drought. Its ruler, well aware of Vessanda's generosity, sent eight Brahmin priests to ask for the rain-inducing white elephant. As with any request, Vessanda could not refuse, for he believed that generosity would help him attain enlightenment and he would then be able to lead others on the way to deliverance from their lives of suffering. Indeed, Vessanda had long wanted to give from the depths of his soul a most precious gift, and now such an occasion had presented itself.

The narrative continues on the upper register of the north wall. Figure 2 depicts the scene of Vessanda's generosity: he and a servant holding a parasol ride the sacred elephant as the visiting Brahmins genuflect and plead for their gift. Vessanda confirms his donation by pouring water from a conch shell into the hands of the kneeling Brahmins. (The Khmer writing in white paint at the bottom of almost every painting gives the name of the *kan*, or chapter, of the Vessanda *Jataka* in which the scene appears. In the colophon below each painting are the names of those who contributed funds for the reproduction of the painting, and by doing so gained merit for a future life.)

The people of Jetoda were incensed by Vessanda's act of relinquishing the elephant, on which their own prosperity depended. For this crime of generosity, they demanded that Sanjaya again become king and send his munificent son into exile. Sanjaya reluctantly agreed and, after giving away all their possessions, Vessanda and his family left the city on a magnificent chariot pulled by a splendid pair of horses, heading for the wild forest of Hemapan and on to Mount Kirivong in the Himalayas, where the deposed king intended to live a hermit's life of prayer and meditation. Hearing of this, four greedy Brahmins from the farthest reaches of the

Figure 2 – Vessanda gives away
the sacred white elephant

kingdom intercepted Vessanda and asked for his fabulous chariot, which he immediately offered to them. No sooner had they left than another Brahmin emerged and asked for and received the two fine steeds. Figure 3 illustrates this scene. In the background to the right, Vessanda and his family proceed through the forest on foot while the four Brahmins depart with their loot.

On the first day of their long journey, Vessanda and his family, walking barefoot through dangerous forests, reached the land of Matol, which was ruled by Vessanda's uncle. Some women of Matol, distressed at seeing the conditions of the prince and his family, ran to call their sovereign. Equally upset upon hearing the plight of his nephew, the king immediately rushed to meet Vessanda, crying and beating his

Figure 3 – Having been banished from his
city, Vessanda gives away his chariot

chest. Figure 4 shows the king, two of his wives, and an official kneeling
before Vessanda, who is now dressed in the simple white robes of an
ascetic. After Vessanda recounted all that had transpired, his uncle not
only offered him food and shelter, but also his throne. Vessanda politely
refused, asking only to spend the night and then be shown the way to
Mount Kirivong. The next day, the king accompanied Vessanda to the
edge of the Hemapan forest. After the family had departed, the king
ordered a hunter named Chetabut to prevent any others from seeking
to take advantage of Vessanda's kindness. After many twists and turns,

Figure 4 – The King of Matol, accompanied by
an official and two of his wives, greets Vessanda
and his family and offers him his kingdom

Vessanda and his family reached their destination, where the gods set up for them a simple hermitage.

The story of Lord Vessanda now moves on to its most popular phase, that involving the beggar Jujuk. One description of Jujuk has him with "black skin, a beaked nose, a skinny chest, stiff hair, a bloated stomach, a withered hip, thick long ear lobes like a leper's, legs curved like a parrot's, crossed eyes, a crooked neck, a long head, and a body covered in tumors like the fruit of a *krasamn* tree or a *sama* tree." Jujuk may have been a sight, but he was a very clever beggar and he often gained 100 *damli* of gold in a single day. Afraid that thieves might steal his beggings, Jujuk entrusted them to a friend for safekeeping. The friend and his wife, however, lost the money on bad investments and found themselves penniless. When Jujuk came to reclaim his money, the couple could give him nothing but their beautiful daughter Amethida, thinking that the old beggar would soon die and she would then return to them. For his part, Jujuk joyfully accepted his new bride and took her home to his beggar's hut.

Amethida proved to be the perfect wife. So respectful, soft-spoken, and hard-working was she that the men of the village often chastised their wives for not being as dutiful. The village women became jealous of Amethida and decided to teach her a lesson, perhaps even get rid of her. One day when Amethida was fetching water at the riverbank, the village women descended on her, tore off her clothes, and beat her ferociously. Poor Amethida returned to Jujuk in tears, pleading with him to hire a servant to fetch water so she would never again have to leave their hut and face the village women. Amethida's ordeal is seen in the two scenes of Figure 5.

Jujuk, who had fallen madly in love with his wife, immediately promised he would do as she asked. Parsimonious as he was, however, he decided that rather than spend some of his earnings on a servant, he would seek out Vessanda at his hermitage on Kirivong mountain, where, being well aware of Vessanda's generosity, he would ask him for his two children. Jujuk then set out on his trek, barefoot, with a bundle over his shoulder and a stick to lean on.

Figure 5 – Jujuk's wife Amethida is beaten
by the jealous village women, after which
she returns to her husband in tears

When he arrived in the wild forest of Hemapan, Jujuk came across Chetabut, the hunter who had been given the task of protecting Vessanda and his family from others who might seek to abuse his generosity and ask for what little he had left. Chetabut had his dogs chase Jujuk up a tree, but the beggar managed to persuade the hunter that he was carrying a message from Vessanda's father, King Sanjaya, appealing to Vessanda to return to Jetoda. Convinced, Chetabut called off his dogs and invited Jujuk to join him for a meal, during which he indicated the way to Vessanda. Figure 6 illustrates these two scenes. On the left, Chetabut armed with a crossbow watches as one of his dogs scares the beggar up a tree and tears his robe, while Jujuk, hanging from a branch, waves the pretended message at the hunter. Below, another dog sniffs at Jujuk's dropped bundle. On the right, the second scene shows the hunter and the beggar sharing a meal, with Chetabut pointing the way through the dangerous forest.

In spite of Chetabut's directions, Jujuk managed to get lost in the forest. However, he fortuitously came upon Achot, a venerable hermit. Jujuk told the ascetic the same lie, with equal success, and Achot pointed the way to Vessanda's retreat (Figure 7).

Figure 6 – Jujuk is chased up a tree by
Chetabut and his dogs, but the hunter then
shares a meal after the beggar explains
that he is the king's messenger

Jujuk arrived at Vessanda's hermitage while Medri was gathering
wild fruits and tubers in the forest. Vessanda received the beggar
warmly. When Jujuk asked for the gift of his children, Vessanda was
filled with joy and he immediately agreed to the request. Indeed,
how better could he prove his generosity and progress toward
enlightenment? Overhearing this exchange, however, Jali and Krasna
fled in terror and hid under the lotus plants in a nearby pond, as is
depicted in the left of Figure 8. When Vessanda found them, the

Figure 7 – The hermit Achot shows Jujuk
the way to Vessanda's ashram

Figure 8 – Vessanda's children Krasna and Jali
try to hide from Jujuk as he approaches their
hut, but in the end Vessanda gives them to the
beggar, ignoring the children's pleadings

children beseeched him not to give them to Jujuk, but Vessanda told them to be as obedient as they always had been, for by doing so they would help him attain enlightenment. The children tearfully returned with their father to the hermitage, where they were given to Jujuk. The beggar, furious at Jali and Krasna for their attempted escape, tightly bound the two frightened children with vines, and he then took the road home, using a whip to cruelly urge on his new servants.

Medri, meanwhile, was prevented from returning to the hermit-age by three forest divinities who feared that if she saw her children bound and whipped she would be so overcome with grief that she would fall dead on the spot. The three divinities took on the form of a lion, a tiger, and a leopard and barred Medri's way back to Vessanda until after nightfall, by which time Jujuk and the children were far away. This scene is illustrated in Figure 9, which is located on the east wall, above the door. Here, a terrified Medri drops her basket of wild fruit and the stick she used for knocking them from high branches, though the artist has replaced the lion with the mythical *rajasingha*, or lion-dog, and forgotten one of the wild beasts.

281

Figure 9 – The gods appear as fierce animals – a lion-dog and a tiger – to keep Medri from returning home

When Medri returned to the hermitage, she found Vessanda deep in meditation. She asked about their children, but he remained silent and motionless. Distraught, Medri searched high and low, and when she could not find them, she fell in a faint in front of her husband. Vessanda broke off his meditating to revive her, and he then told her how he had bestowed the gift of his children on Jujuk the beggar. Hearing this, Medri bowed to her husband saying that she wished this offering would enable him to attain enlightenment and, afterward, guide all beings to deliverance from suffering.

God Indra, however, was concerned that Vessanda might now give away even his wife, should he be so asked. Indra thus took on the appearance of an old blind and deaf Brahmin, approached Vessanda, and asked him to give him his wife Medri to comfort him in his last days. Needless to say, Vessanda readily consented and Medri willingly accepted. The old Brahmin was so impressed that he returned Medri to Vessanda and, again becoming Indra, promised the couple they would be reunited with their children

Figure 10 – Indra, transformed into a
Brahmin, asks Vessanda for his wife, Medri

and once more rule Jetoda. This part of the narrative is shown in
Figure 10, which is on the lower register of the north wall, below
figures 5 and 6. Here, Vessanda pours water on the Brahmin's hands
to seal the gift of Medri, who sits next to her husband.

Jujuk and the children, meanwhile, continued their perilous
journey. At night, Jujuk tightly lashed the children to a tree, while
he slept safely in his hammock in the upper branches. Two gods,
however, took the form of Vessanda and Medri and gently cradled
the sleeping children in their arms, protecting them from the
forest's ferocious beasts. The scene is shown in Figure 11, on the
lower register of the north wall, below Figure 7.

One day on the long trek home, the gods made Jujuk take the
wrong road. He and the children ended up in Jetoda, the city of King
Sanjaya, the children's grandfather. The divinities then guided Jujuk
to Sanjaya, who soon recognized his grandchildren and offered to
buy them from Jujuk for a considerable fortune. Embracing their
grandfather, the children explained how their father Vessanda had
granted the beggar his request in order to become a buddha and
free all beings from suffering. Sanjaya then realized he had made a
grave error in listening to the people and banishing his son.

Figure 11 – Two gods protect the sleeping
children while, in the branches above,
Jujuk slumbers in his hammock

Jujuk with his reward headed for the nearest eatery and so voraciously stuffed himself with fine food that his stomach burst; he died on the spot. Sanjaya sent messengers to all parts of his kingdom to find a relative of the dead beggar, but no one came forward to claim Jujuk's fortune.

King Sanjaya, his wife Suppati, and their two grandchildren then mounted royal elephants and set off for Kirivong with a large escort. The reunion with Vessanda and Medri was as joyful as one can imagine, as seen in Figure 12. This scene and the following one are located on the lower register of the opposite wall, the south wall, next to the east door.

Figure 12 – Vessanda and Medri are reunited
with his parents and their children

Sanjaya again offered the throne to Vessanda, who only accepted
with great reluctance, for by doing so he would be setting back his
quest for enlightenment. At the head of a grand procession, the
royal family then returned to Jetoda, where they were received by
cheering crowds. The scene is depicted in Figure 13, the last picture
in Wat Phnom's story of Lord Vessanda.

Figure 13 – Vessanda and his
family return to their city

Vessanda ruled benevolently for many years. When he died, he passed a thousand years in paradise before being reborn as Siddhartha Gautama, whom we know today as the Buddha.

Thus concludes the narrative of Lord Vessanda, who not only embodies the perfection of generosity but also, in the words of Vittorio Roveda and Sothon Yem, "exemplifies the renunciation of feelings, detachment from material goods and emotional family ties but, above all, the total renunciation of one's own life; sacrificing oneself for ideology."

Sources

My principal source is Gérard Groussin, *Histoire de Vessandâr, le jâtaka du roi généreux*, Kailash, 2005; Groussin based his account on the popular version of the Maha Jataka written by Gnok Thaem (1903–1975) in Khmer in 1966.

Another important source, one with many illustrations, is Vittorio Roveda and Sothon Yem, *Preah Bot: Buddhist painted scrolls in Cambodia*, River, 2010.

Chan Vitharong, *Wat Phnom, Guide to Art and Architecture*, Chan, 2013.

Ray Zepp, *A Field Guide to Cambodian Pagodas*, Bert's, 1997.

Penny Edwards, *Cambodge: The Cultivation of a Nation, 1860–1945*, Hawaii, 2007.

30. The Birthplace of King Norodom Sihanouk

On October 11, 2013, King Norodom Sihamoni and Queen Mother Norodom Monineath inaugurated the memorial statue of King Norodom Sihanouk, four days before the first anniversary of the king's death in China at the age of 89. Protected by a high pyramidal canopy, King Sihanouk stands 4.5 meters tall and calmly faces the sunrise.

The statue (Map 4, #78) rises in the garden just east of Independence Monument, a suitable site not just because King Sihanouk is revered as the father of Cambodia's independence but because at 7 p.m. on October 29, 1922, Sihanouk was born nearby (Map 4, #77), presently #39 Suramarit Avenue (the street is named after King Norodom Suramarit, Sihanouk's father), a place now occupied by the North Korean Embassy. The house there had been given to Sihanouk's mother, Princess Sisowath Kossamak, by her father, King Sisowath Monivong, of whom she was the favorite daughter. In 2008, Sihanouk told his biographer Jean-Marie Cambacérès that he was in fact not born in this house but in an adjacent traditional wooden house on pylons which belonged to his maternal great-grandmother, *Chau Khun* (Lady) Pat, the widow of Prince Hassakan, one of King Norodom's sons. After Sihanouk's birth, the placenta was buried under the boddhi tree which still stands in the park across the street.

At Sihanouk's birth, King Monivong's astrologer declared, "Norodom Sihanouk will one day be called upon to occupy the highest of positions in Cambodia. His life will be extraordinary. Throughout his entire career he will confront enemies bent on his ruin. But he will weather the most dangerous trials and situations and will conquer all of his enemies, without exception."

King Sihanouk's memorial, with his boddhi
tree below the palms; his childhood
home is just beyond the palms.

The newborn prince may not have spent much time in his
parents' house, however, as the royal astrologer added that the
prince would die at a young age if he continued to reside with his
parents. Consequently, although he was their only child, Sihanouk
was committed to the care of Lady Pat, in her nearby house. (Lady
Pat had also raised Sihanouk's mother, Princess Kossamak, whose
own mother had died at a young age.) Lady Pat, who by birth was
not a royal, was seventy-three years old when she took over the

288

upbringing of the future king but "was still strong and healthy," according to King Sihanouk himself. Following Lady Pat's death some eight years later, young Prince Sihanouk was entrusted to his paternal grandfather, Prince Norodom Sutharot, a "worthy man" but an "unfortunate pretender to the throne," according to Sihanouk, to whose residence he now moved. Nonetheless, he must have frequently visited his parents' home in the compound in which he was born.

Many years later, Sihanouk turned his family's residence on Suramarit Avenue into the Preah Norodom Sihanouk Museum. After Sirik Matak and Lon Nol overthrew Prince Sihanouk in 1970 and he was in exile in China, they sent a delegation to Queen Mother Kossamak to expel her from the Royal Palace. Here is how Sihanouk reported the encounter in *My War with the C.I.A.*:

> "If you don't leave the Royal Palace we will throw you out," they said. "You and your son side with the Vietnamese against your own people. Good! If you don't leave, we are going to pile up outside your villa the corpses of the Vietnamese dealt with by the people. You can watch the vultures pick the flesh off their bones. You sold the country to the Vietnamese so we'll bring their corpses and stack them up under your windows. There they'll rot and stink you out."
>
> . . . To the threats of the Lon Nol delegates, my mother replied: "No need to bring the corpses – evidence of your crimes. I shall leave the Royal Palace. Give me the house where my son was born and let me live there." It was the villa where she had lived with my father before I was chosen as King. I had later given it to the nation as a national museum. (Some Western journalists wrote that I created it for my own glory. It was not so. I placed in the museum the various documents relating to our independence struggle and the gifts I had received as King, later Head of State, from foreign governments. I regarded these as having been given to me

for the nation, which is why I displayed them for all to see.) The museum, in any case, had been dismantled as soon as I was overthrown, so it was agreed that my mother could have her old home back. What Lon Nol and Sirik Matak did with the documents and other valuable gifts, I do not know. Perhaps like other precious relics looted after the coup, they can now be bought in antique shops in Hong Kong and Singapore!

In the summer of 1970, the plundered museum was returned to Queen Kossamak, as she had requested. She was strictly guarded and was not allowed to correspond to anyone nor to receive visitors other that the royal family's doctor, Arnaud Riche, who was frisked upon arriving at the house and again when leaving.

In October 1970, seven months after Prince Sihanouk had been ousted by Lon Nol and Sirik Matak, the prince was burned in effigy at Wat Phnom. Here is how Sihanouk put it in his memoirs: "On 9 October . . . the day the 'Republic' was proclaimed, a gang of Lon Nol storm-troopers carried my effigy to be burned at the Phnom – the temple-crowned hill from which the capital takes its name. But before the burning ceremony, they paraded the effigy before my mother's villa, insulting me – and thus her – in the crudest, most revolting terms. They insulted not only us but all our forebears and two thousand years of Cambodian history – right in front of my mother's windows."

Queen Mother Kossamak remained in her villa on Suramarit Avenue until 1973 when, following pressure from Prime Minister Zhou En-lai and President Richard Nixon, the Lon Nol government allowed her to leave Phnom Penh and join her exiled son Sihanouk in China. Queen Kossamak died in Beijing on April 27, 1975, ten days after the Khmer Rouge entered Phnom Penh.

In 1991 Norodom Sihanouk gave his childhood home to the Democratic People's Republic of Korea for use as their embassy for a period of twenty years, rent free, a token of thanks to North Korea's leader Kim Il Sung for the friendship he had given to Sihanouk over many years, notably during the prince's years in exile. Sihanouk's

For a brief time, the DPRK Embassy housed Yoshimi Tanaka, a member of the Japanese Red Army terrorist group, who in 1970 was among the hijackers of a commercial airliner on a domestic flight from Tokyo to Fukuoka. The plane landed in Seoul, where 130 hostages were released, then flew on to Pyongyang, the North Korean capital. In 1996 Tanaka sought refuge in the North Korean Embassy on Suramarit Avenue while being pursued by Interpol on charges of counterfeiting US dollars. After several days, Tanaka left King Sihanouk's childhood home in an embassy vehicle and tried to flee to Vietnam. Following a two-day standoff at the Cambodia-Vietnam border, during which time he and three North Koreans remained in the car, Tanaka was deported to Thailand, where he faced those counterfeiting charges. Found not guilty, Tanaka was denied political asylum and, in 2000, was extradited to Japan. He died of liver cancer in 2007 while serving a twelve-year prison sentence for the airline hijacking.

2005 will mentioned that his childhood home should be preserved forever and again serve as a museum, though this time for pre-Angkorian and Angkorian relics. Though the twenty-year period has expired, the house on Suramarit avenue remains the North Korean Embassy (see box).

MILTON OSBORNE ENTITLED HIS biography of the king *Sihanouk: Prince of light, prince of darkness*. It is appropriate, I believe, in concluding this volume to emphasize the light, for this is how King Sihanouk is remembered by the great majority of his people. Indeed, tens of thousands lined the route of his funeral cortege from the airport to the Royal Palace, the procession passing on its way Sihanouk's birthplace on Suramarit Avenue and the boddhi tree across the street. Many more of the King Father's people came to kneel and pay their respects outside the palace prior to his cremation. King Sihanouk had passed the throne on to his son in 2004, and he largely spent his retirement out of the limelight. Yet many of those ordinary citizens lining that road from the airport and kneeling in front of the palace were young people, teenagers, who were not even alive during the great part of his rule. Reflecting the views of many, Hi Sreypich, 24, told *The Cambodia Daily*: "When I heard it [the news of King Sihanouk's death], my body seemed to stop working . . . He was the great King of all. He was like a father in our Cambodian family."

No doubt many would admit that King Sihanouk's rule had its weaknesses and imperfections, notably his association with the Khmer Rouge in the 1970s but also, during the 1960s, the unchecked, rampant corruption among the urban elite and the military, the deteriorating economic situation, and the repression of dissent. However, those youngsters and their elders came to pay homage to the man whom many would say deserves credit for bringing independence to their country, for his encouragement of architectural creativity, notably in Phnom Penh, for greatly expanding the till then largely neglected educational system, for preserving Cambodia's neutrality in the face of strong foreign pressure and keeping it out of the war in Vietnam for many years, for ensuring Cambodia's territorial integrity, for negotiating reconciliation leading to the Paris Peace Agreement of 1991, and for mediating among the country's political factions in order to maintain a modicum of peace and stability in his later years on the throne. Most of all, those multitudes of common citizens came to show their affection for "Papa King" and to reciprocate the deep love he had for his "grandchildren," as he liked to call his people, and for his country.

Sources

Jean-Marie Cambacérès, *Sihanouk, le roi insubmersible*, Le Cherche Midi, 2013.

Norodom Sihanouk, *Shadow Over Angkor*, Volume One of the *Memoirs of His Majesty King Norodom Sihanouk of Cambodia*, from the original transcript of *The Cup of Dregs*, edited, introduced and with new material by Julio A. Jeldres, Monument, 2005.

Julio A. Jeldres, *The Royal House of Cambodia*, Monument, 2003.

Norodom Sihanouk and Wilfred Burchett, *My War with the C.I.A.*, Penguin, 1973.

"A gift that keeps on giving," Poppy McPherson, *The Phnom Penh Post*, November 7, 2014.

Index

Anchor, LST, xii#8, ix, 1–6, 11
Ang Duong, xii#3, xii#4, 53, 159–60, 172, **206–12**, 230–32
Avalokiteshvara, 48–49, 254–55

Bar Jean, xiii#42, 127–128
Bibliothèque and Archives Nationales, xiii#27, 63, 84–85
Bizot, François, 136–48, 162
Boddhi Tree (guest house), xv#82, 118–21
Bodhisattva, v, 48, 234, 251–60
Buddhism, Mahayana (Vietnamese), 48, 248, **251–55**, 259
    Christian conversion, 233
    Quan Âm, Ch. 26 passim
Buddhism, Theravada (Cambodian), 25, 37, 48, 76, 234, 248, 251–252, 256, 261
    François Bizot, 144
    restored by King Ang Duong, 208

Café de Paris, xiv#49, 129–130
    Albert Spaccesi, 130
Canard de Cholon, 136
Catholic influence
    18th and 19th centuries, 229–33
    Hoaland church grotto, 236
    Khmer Rouge response, 58, 85, 236
    Ponhea Leu, xii#5, 227–37
Chœung Ek earthworks, xii#6, 223–26
Chuon Nath, 37
    statue, xv#79, 261
Council for the Development of Cambodia (CDC), xiii#39, 114, 186–187

Embassy, British, 195, 204
Embassy, French, xiii#18, 139–144, 147
    Albert Spaccesi, 130
    François Bizot, 139
    seven gravestones, 80
Embassy, North Korea, xv#77, 290–91

Embassy, United States, 193–205
    1950–52, xiii#26, 193
    1952–54, xiii#24, 193
    1954–65, xiv#59, 194
    1969, villa, xv#85, 197
    1970–75, xv#86, 197–201
    1992–2006, xiv#67, 201
    2006– , xiii#29, 201–4
    the 'heart', 203–4
    VVV roofs, 199–200
    Mayaguez incident, 213–22
    See also United States, relations with

Flynn, Sean, 9, 10
Fourcros, Jules, xiii#37, 61–66
French cemetery, xiii#15, 147

Ganesha, xiv#48, 261–65
Glatkowski, Alvin, 4–8, 11–12
Grand Hôtel Manolis, xiii#41, 15–16, 18–23, 78, 125
Grandmother Penh, 63, 109–110, 117, 165, 261
Groslier, George, xiv#64, 14, 23, 81, 175

Hôpital Calmette, xiii#21, 90
Hôtel du Commissariat, xiii#39, 190
Hôtel Guérin, xiv#56, 18
Hôtel Le Royal, xiii#26, 10, 22
    and Jacqueline Kennedy, 40–42, 46
    and U.S. Embassy, 193, 197

Institut Pasteur, xiii#23, 90

Kennedy, Jacqueline, 40–46, 197
Kentucky Fried Chicken, xiii#41, 13, 78
    See also Grand Hôtel Manolis
Khmer Rouge
    Clyde McKay and Alvin Glatowski, 9–10
    French evacuation, 139–142
    Military Security Committee, xiii#17, 144
    physical and human destruction, 38, 51, 63, 67, 81, 84–85, 89–90,

118–21, 130, 139–145, 147, 175, 179, 181, 190–91, 198–202, 211, 215–16, 218–221, 231, 234–37, 249–250, 269, 290, 292
and Prince Monireth, 140, 170
S-21, 118–21
See also Pol Pot
Killing fields at Chœung Ek, 118, 223
Kouprey, xiii#31, 266–70

La Taverne, xiii#43, 122–27
Le Monument aux Morts, xiii#16, xiv#64, 67, 71
Le Nouveau Tricotin, xiv#53, 131–32
Lon Nol, 3–7, 9, 11
    landlord to British embassy, 204
    main residence, xiii#14, 59–60
    posters, 76
    residence at Chamkar Mon palace, xv#87, 57
    and Sihanouk, 51, 289–90, 202
    anti-Vietnamese, 54, 234–235, 249–50
    Soviet support, 141
Lon Non ('Little Brother'), 54–60, 202
Lost provinces monument, 80

Madame Chum's opium den, *La fumerie de la Mère Chum*, xv#83, 132–37
Mahogany trees, xiv#50, 131
Malraux, André, 13–18
    the caper, 14–15
    at the Grand Hôtel Manolis, 15–16, 18–23
Malreaux, Clara, 13–18
    feigned suicide, 16
    lost inheritance, 13
Mayaguez incident, xiii#29, 213–22
McKay, Clyde, 4–9

National Archives, xiii#27, 63, 84–85
National Museum, xiv#64, 14, 67–68, 81, 175
Norodom (1834–1904), 149–62
    and Alexis Louis Chhun, 173
    Ang Doung's son, 207
    as Ang Voddei, 232
    and boddhi trees, xii#11, 30, 182

Buddha Maitreya, xiv#70, 211
    Statue in Silver Pagoda, 211
    moved capital to Phnom Penh, 49, 51, 158, 232
    Napoleon Pavilion, 79
    opium concession, 63
    and Oum, 173
    and Prince Chantaleka, 50–51
    Prince Sivutha's rebellion, 112
    regal justice, 231
    relations with France, 170, 172
    and Silver Pagoda, 209
    succession, 167–69

Pol Pot, 52–60, 209
    childhood home, xv#75, 53
    education, 53–55
    and Sihanouk, 60, 190–91
    refined language, 53
    in the Royal Palace, 53
    on secrecy, 115
    Saloth Chhay, brother, 56–57
    Saloth Suong, brother, 54–56
    statue of, 114–15
    and VVV buildings, 200

Ponhea Leu graves, xii#5, 227–37
Preah Ang Dongka, xiv#65, 47–51
Quan Âm, 252–55
    at Thiên Phuóc pagoda, xii#9, 256–60

Rainsy, Sam, 238–42
Ramsey, Douglas, 44
Raymond, Jean de, xiii#39, 183–92
Relics
    the Buddha's bone, 24–31
    CDC stupa, xiii#38, 186–87
    on Lady Penh's hill, 110
    at the railway station, xiv#47, 26–29
    on the royal hill at Udong, xii#3, 29, 36
    at the Royal Palace, 30
    at Wat Botum, xiv#73, 30–31
    at Wat Prang, xii#1, 35–36
    at Wat Srah Chak, xiii#25, 26
    at Wat Unnalom, xiv#57, 34–35
Résidence Supérieure, xiii#39, 8, 71, 190

S-21, xv#81, 118–21

Saloth Sar, *See* Pol Pot
Sihanouk (1922–2012)
    Apsara, 91, 180
    birthplace, xv#77, 287–290
    at Café de Paris, 130
    and Chea Vichea, 245
    and his family, 6, 56, 60, 95, 142, 167, 170–71, 287
    and Jacqueline Kennedy, 40–46
    and Jean de Raymond, 186
    and King Norodom, 151, 160–61
    and kouprey, 266–69
    and Pol Pot, 53, 190–91
    and La Taverne, 127
    and the Buddha's bone, 24, 29
    and the French, 54, 139, 168
    memorial, xv#78, 287
    overthrow of, 4–6, 51, 57
    and the United States, 124, 195–97
Sirik Matak
    execution, 55, 142
    house arrest, 58
    residences, xv#88, 57–59
    Sihanouk's overthrow, 4–6, 289–90
Stone, Dana, 9–10
Stupas, 110–11
    Ang Duong, xii#3, 209
    Chuon Nath, xiv#57, 37, 261
    near Council for the Development of Cambodia, xiii#38, 186–87
    Duong Sung, xiv#57, 38
    King Norodom, xiv#71, 160
    King Ponhea Yat, xiii#34, 61, 112–14
    at railway station, xiv#47, 26–29
    on the royal hill at Udong, xii#3, 29, 30
    Martyrs of March 30, 1997, xiv#72, 238–42
    Wat Phnom, xiii#34, 110
    Wat Prang, Udong, 36
    Wat Unnalom, xiv#57, 32–34

Techo Meas and *Techo* Yort, xiv#58, 96–108
Terrapin, *batagar affinis*, xiii#32, 270
Thiên Phuóc pagoda, xii#9, 256–60
Thorani, xii#10, 27, 72–77
Tuol Sleng Genocide Museum, xv#81, 118–21, 139

Turberville, Charles W., 214–15

Udong
    Ang Duong, 206–11; ~ equestrian statue, xii#4, 206–7; ~ stupa, xii#3, 209
    Buddha stupa on the royal hill, xii#3, 29–30
    Historic capital, 49, 101, 158, 166
    Ponhea Leu graves, xii#5, 227–32
    Wat Prang, xii#1, 35–36
    Wat Veang Chas, xii#2, 209–10
United Nations Transitional Authority in Cambodia (UNTAC), xiii#39, 177, 238, 270–71, 291
United States, Cambodian relations with
    Clyde Mckay and Alvin Glatkowski, 9
    disruption in relations, 195
    Jacqueline Kennedy's role in restoration, 41–42, 197
    Landing Zone Hotel, 199
    Mayaguez incident, 213–22
    See also Embassy, United States

Vessanda story and murals, xiii#36, 273–286
Vichea, Chea, xv#76, 242–46
Victory Hospital, xii#7
    and Alvin Glatkowski, 8
Vietnamese influence, Mahayana Buddhism imposed, 248
    Thiên Phuóc pagoda, xii#9, 256–260

Wat Phnom's hill, xiii#35, 8, 36, 64, 80, 109–17, 266
Wats
    Botum, xiv#73, 30, 36, 53, 204, 240
    Koh, 36
    Lanka, 36, 243
    Phnom, xiii#34, 61–66, 75, 110, 112–15, 202
    Phorta Pi Rangsei, xiii#19, 75
    Prang, xii#1, 35–36
    Preah Keo (Silver Pagoda) xiv #70, 25, 79, 149, 151, 159, 209, 211
    Prochum Sakor, (new pagoda) xii#12, 182
    Put Kosacha/Put Koussa, xiii#20, 36, 74
    Puthyaram (old pagoda) xii#11, 182
    Unnalom, xiv#57, 30, 32–38
    Veang Chas, 209–10